THE OFFICIAL RED BOOK®

CHECK LIST
◄ AND ►
RECORD BOOK

OF UNITED STATES AND CANADIAN COINS

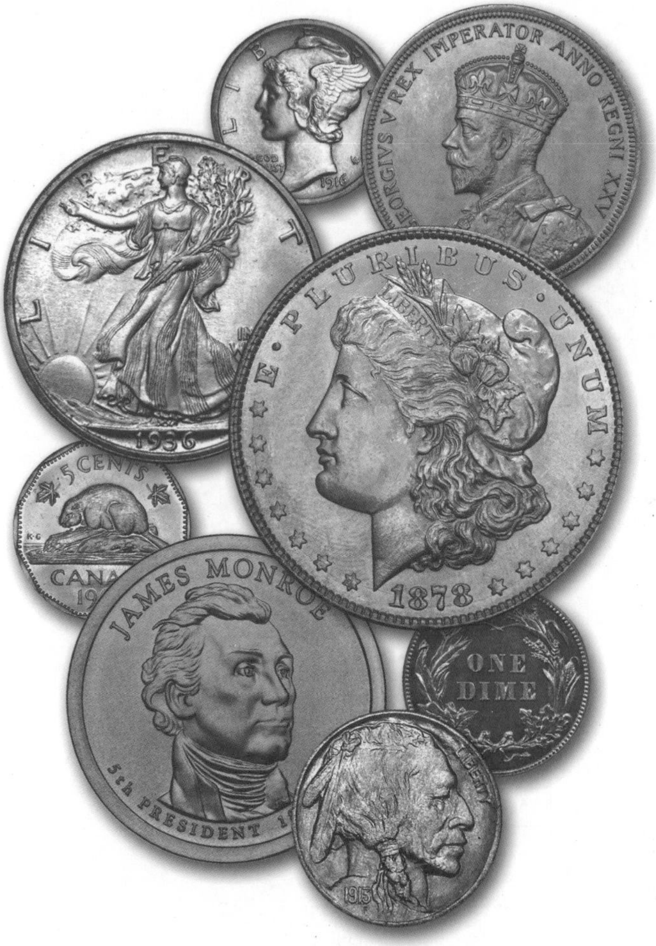

THE OFFICIAL RED BOOK®

CHECK LIST
—‹AND›—
RECORD BOOK
OF UNITED STATES AND CANADIAN COINS

THE OFFICIAL RED BOOK is a trademark of Whitman Publishing, LLC.
ISBN 0794836860

© 2012 Whitman Publishing, LLC
3101 Clairmont Road • Suite G • Atlanta GA 30329

Printed in China

Whitman Publishing, LLC
PUBLISHING SINCE 1934
www.whitman.com

Scan the QR code at left or visit us at www.whitman.com for a complete listing of numismatic reference books, supplies, and storage products.

Whitman®

HOW TO USE THIS BOOK

Use this book as a one-stop resource for keeping track of your United States or Canadian coin collection. It covers all popular modern U.S. coins from 1856 to date—from Flying Eagle cents to today's dollar coins, plus commemoratives (classic and modern), Proof sets and Uncirculated Mint sets, and more—as well as Canadian coins from 1870 to date. Popular minor varieties are included.

The images used throughout the Check List and Record Book are shown at actual size. Each listing gives the date and mintmark on the coin, as well as how many were minted (Proof mintages are in parentheses; italics indicate an estimated mintage). A series of columns in each chart represents the grades in which coins of that type and date range are commonly found. You can check off the grade for each coin in your collection and, in the Notes column, write down when and where you bought it, the price you paid, who sold it, and any other information you want to record.

Starting on page 250, you will find blank charts where you can add details about auction records, purchases of unusual varieties not listed elsewhere, and other details important to your collection.

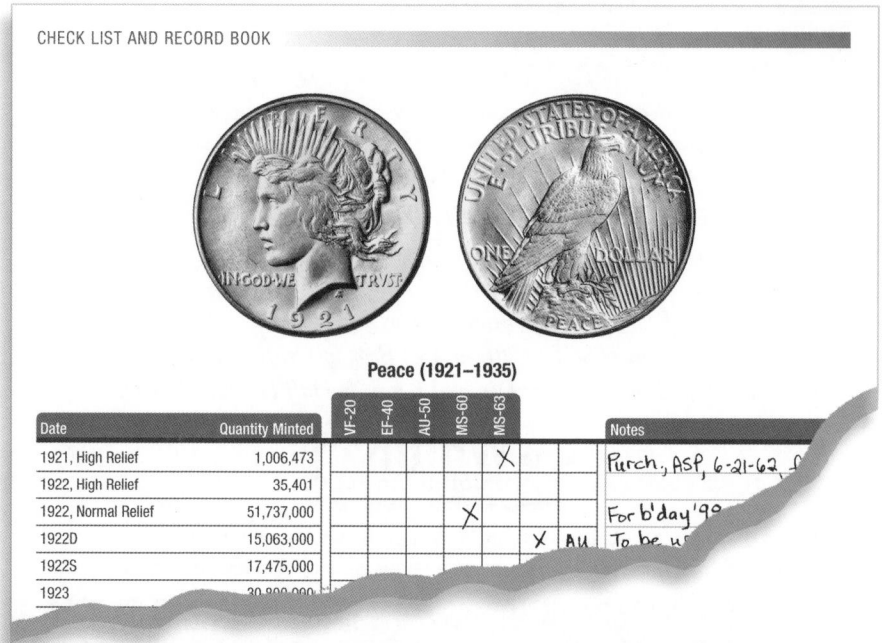

CHECK LIST AND RECORD BOOK

Peace (1921–1935)

Date	Quantity Minted	VF-20	EF-40	AU-50	MS-60	MS-63		Notes
1921, High Relief	1,006,473				X			Purch., ASP, 6-21-62,
1922, High Relief	35,401							
1922, Normal Relief	51,737,000			X				For b'day '99
1922D	15,063,000					X	AU	To be u
1922S	17,475,000							
1923	30,800,000							

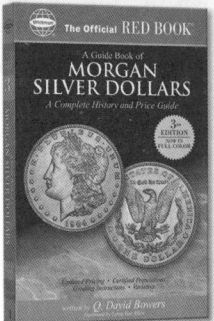

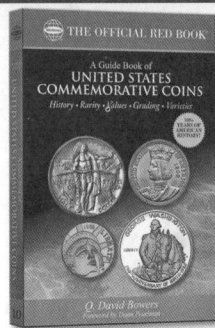

HALF CENTS

Liberty Cap, Head Facing Left (1793)

Date	Quantity Minted	G-4	VG-8	F-12	VF-20	EF-40	MS-60	Notes
1793	35,334							

Liberty Cap, Head Facing Right (1794–1797)

Date	Quantity Minted	G-4	VG-8	F-12	VF-20	EF-40	MS-60	Notes
1794, Normal Head	81,600							
1794, High-Relief Head								
1795, Lettered Edge, With Pole	139,690							
1795, Lettered Edge, Punctuated Date								
1795, Plain Edge, Punctuated Date								
1795, Plain Edge, No Pole								
1796, With Pole	1,390							
1796, No Pole								
1797, 1 Above 1, Plain Edge	127,840							
1797, Plain Edge, Low Head								
1797, Plain Edge								
1797, Lettered Edge								
1797, Gripped Edge								

Draped Bust (1800–1808)

Date	Quantity Minted	G-4	VG-8	F-12	VF-20	EF-40	MS-60	Notes
1800	202,908							

Date	Quantity Minted	G-4	VG-8	F-12	VF-20	EF-40	MS-60		Notes
1802, 2 Over 0, Reverse of 1800	20,266								
1802, 2 Over 0, 2nd Reverse									
1803	92,000								
1803, Widely Spaced 3									
1804, Plain 4, Stems to Wreath	1,055,312								
1804, Plain 4, Stemless Wreath									
1804, Crosslet 4, Stemless									
1804, Crosslet 4, Stems									
1804, "Spiked Chin"									
1805, Medium 5, Stemless	814,464								
1805, Small 5, Stems									
1805, Large 5, Stems									
1806, Small 6, Stems	356,000								
1806, Small 6, Stemless									
1806, Large 6, Stems									
1807	476,000								
1808, 8 Over 7	400,000								
1808, Normal Date									

Classic Head (1809–1836)

Date	Quantity Minted	G-4	VG-8	F-12	VF-20	EF-40	MS-60		Notes
1809, Small o Inside 0	1,154,572								
1809, Triple-Punched 9									
1809, Normal Date									
1810	215,000								
1811, Wide Date	63,140								
1811, Close Date									
1811, Reverse of 1802, Unofficial Restrike (extremely rare)									
1825	63,000								
1826	234,000								
1828, 13 Stars	606,000								
1828, 12 Stars									
1829	487,000								

Date	Quantity Minted	PF-40	PF-60	PF-63			Notes
1831, Original (beware of altered date)	2,200						

Date	Quantity Minted	PF-40	PF-60	PF-63					Notes
1831, Restrike, Large Berries (Reverse of 1836)									
1831, Restrike, Small Berries (Reverse of 1840–1857)									

Date	Quantity Minted	VG-8	F-12	VF-20	EF-40	MS-60	PF-63		Notes
1832	51,000								
1833	103,000								
1834	141,000								
1835	398,000								
1836, Original									
1836, Restrike (Reverse of 1840–1857)									
1837 Token (not a coin)									

 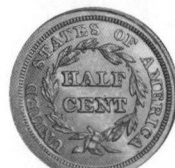

Braided Hair (1840–1857)

Date	Quantity Minted	PF-63	PF-65						Notes
1840, Original									
1840, Restrike									
1841, Original									
1841, Restrike									
1842, Original									
1842, Restrike									
1843, Original									
1843, Restrike									
1844, Original									
1844, Restrike									
1845, Original									
1845, Restrike									
1846, Original									
1846, Restrike									
1847, Original									
1847, Restrike									
1848, Original									
1848, Restrike									
1849, Original, Small Date									
1849, Restrike, Small Date									

Date	Quantity Minted	G-4	VG-8	F-12	VF-20	EF-40	MS-60	Notes
1849, Large Date	39,864							
1850	39,812							
1851	147,672							
1852, Original								
1852, Restrike								
1853	129,694							
1854	55,358							
1855	56,500							
1856	40,430							
1857	35,180							

LARGE CENTS

Flowing Hair, Chain Reverse (1793)

Date	Quantity Minted	G-4	VG-8	F-12	VF-20	EF-40	MS-60	Notes
1793, AMERI. in Legend	36,103							
1793, AMERICA								

Flowing Hair, Wreath Reverse (1793)

Date	Quantity Minted	G-4	VG-8	F-12	VF-20	EF-40	MS-60	Notes
1793, Vine/Bars Edge	63,353							
1793, Lettered Edge								
1793, Strawberry Leaf (4 known)								

Liberty Cap (1793–1796)

Date	Quantity Minted	G-4	VG-8	F-12	VF-20	EF-40	MS-60	Notes
1793, Liberty Cap	11,056							
1794, Head of 1793								
1794, Head of 1794								
1794, Head of 1795	918,521							
1794, Starred Reverse								
1794, No Fraction Bar								
1795, Lettered Edge	37,000							
1795, Plain Edge	501,500							
1795, Reeded Edge *(7 known)*								
1795, Jefferson Head *(not a regular Mint issue),* Plain Edge								
1795, Jefferson Head, Lettered Edge *(3 known)*								
1796, Liberty Cap	109,825							

Draped Bust (1796–1807)

Date	Quantity Minted	G-4	VG-8	F-12	VF-20	EF-40	MS-60	Notes
1796, Reverse of 1794								
1796, Reverse of 1795								
1796, Reverse of 1797	363,375							
1796, LIHERTY Error								
1796, Stemless Reverse *(3 known)*								
1797, Gripped Edge, 1796 Reverse								
1797, Plain Edge, 1796 Reverse	897,510							
1797, 1797 Reverse, Stems								
1797, 1797 Reverse, Stemless								
1798, 8 Over 7								
1798, Reverse of 1796								
1798, Style 1 Hair								
1798, Style 2 Hair	1,841,745							
1799, 9 Over 8								
1799, Normal Date								
1800, 1800 Over 1798, Style 1 Hair								
1800, 80 Over 79, Style 2 Hair	2,822,175							
1800, Normal Date								

Date	Quantity Minted	G-4	VG-8	F-12	VF-20	EF-40	MS-60		Notes
1801, Normal Reverse									
1801, 3 Errors: 1/000, One Stem, and IINITED	1,362,837								
1801, Fraction 1/000									
1801, 1/100 Over 1/000									
1802, Normal Reverse									
1802, Fraction 1/000	3,435,100								
1802, Stemless Wreath									
1803, Small Date, Small Fraction									
1803, Small Date, Large Fraction									
1803, Large Date, Small Fraction									
1803, Large Date, Large Fraction	3,131,691								
1803, 1/100 Over 1/000									
1803, Stemless Wreath									
1804	*96,500*								
1804, Unofficial Restrike of 1860 (*Uncirculated*)									
1805	941,116								
1806	348,000								
1807, Small 1807, 7 Over 6, Blunt 1									
1807, Large 1807, 7 Over 6, Pointed 1	829,221								
1807, Small Fraction									
1807, Large Fraction									
1807, "Comet" Variety									

Classic Head (1808–1814)

Date	Quantity Minted	G-4	VG-8	F-12	VF-20	EF-40	MS-60		Notes
1808	1,007,000								
1809	222,867								
1810, 10 Over 09	1,458,500								
1810, Normal Date									
1811, Last 1 Over 0	218,025								
1811, Normal Date									
1812, Small Date	1,075,500								
1812, Large Date									
1813	418,000								

Date	Quantity Minted	G-4	VG-8	F-12	VF-20	EF-40	MS-60	Notes
1814, Plain 4	357,830							
1814, Crosslet 4								

Liberty Head, Matron Head (1816–1835)

Date	Quantity Minted	G-4	VG-8	F-12	VF-20	EF-40	MS-60	Notes
1816	2,820,982							
1817, 13 Stars	3,948,400							
1817, 15 Stars								
1818	3,167,000							
1819, 9 Over 8	2,671,000							
1819, Large Date								
1819, Small Date								
1820, 20 Over 19	4,407,550							
1820, Large Date								
1820, Small Date								
1821	389,000							
1822	2,072,339							
1823, 3 Over 2	1,262,000							
1823; Normal Date								
1823, Unofficial Restrike, from broken obverse die								
1824, 4 Over 2								
1824, Normal Date								
1825	1,461,100							
1826, 6 Over 5	1,517,425							
1826, Normal Date								
1827	2,357,732							
1828, Large Narrow Date	2,260,624							
1828, Small Wide Date								
1829, Large Letters	1,414,500							
1829, Medium Letters								
1830, Large Letters	1,711,500							
1830, Medium Letters								
1831, Large Letters	3,359,260							
1831, Medium Letters								
1832, Large Letters	2,362,000							
1832, Medium Letters								

Date	Quantity Minted	G-4	VG-8	F-12	VF-20	EF-40	MS-60	Notes
1833	2,739,000							
1834, Large 8, Stars, and Reverse Letters								
1834, Large 8 and Stars, Medium Letters	1,855,100							
1834, Large 8, Small Stars, Medium Letters								
1834, Small 8, Large Stars, Medium Letters								
1835, Large 8 and Stars	3,878,400							
1835, Small 8 and Stars								
1835, Head of 1836								

Liberty Head, Matron Head Modified (1835–1839)

Date	Quantity Minted	G-4	VG-8	F-12	VF-20	EF-40	MS-60	Notes
1836	2,111,000							
1837, Plain Cord, Medium Letters	5,558,300							
1837, Plain Cord, Small Letters								
1837, Head of 1838								
1838	6,370,200							
1839, 1839 Over 1836, Plain Cords	3,128,661							
1839, Head of 1838, Beaded Cords								
1839, Silly Head								
1839, Booby Head								
1839								
1840, Large Date	2,462,700							
1840, Small Date								
1840, Small Date Over Large 18								
1841, Small Date	1,597,367							
1842, Small Date	2,383,390							
1842, Large Date								
1843, Petite, Small Letters	2,425,342							
1843, Petite, Large Letters								
1843, Mature, Large Letters								
1844, Normal Date	2,398,752							
1844, 44 Over 81								
1845	3,894,804							

Date	Quantity Minted	G-4	VG-8	F-12	VF-20	EF-40	MS-60	Notes
1846, Small Date								
1846, Medium Date	4,120,800							
1846, Tall Date								
1847								
1847, 7 Over "Small 7"	6,183,669							
1848	6,415,799							
1849	4,178,500							
1850	4,426,844							
1851, Normal Date								
1851, 51 Over 81	9,889,707							
1852	5,063,094							
1853	6,641,131							
1854	4,236,156							
1855, Upright 5's								
1855, Slanting 5's	1,574,829							
1855, Slanting 5's, Knob on Ear								
1856, Upright 5								
1856, Slanting 5	2,690,463							
1857, Large Date								
1857, Small Date	333,546							

SMALL CENTS

Flying Eagle (1856–1858)

Date		Quantity Minted	VG-8	F-12	VF-20	EF-40	MS-60	PF-63	Notes
1856		2,000							
1857	(100)	17,450,000							
1858, Large Letters	(100)								
1858, 8 Over 7		24,600,000							
1858, Small Letters	(200)								

Indian Head, Variety 1, Copper-Nickel, Laurel Wreath Reverse (1859)

Date		Quantity Minted	VG-8	F-12	VF-20	EF-40	MS-60	PF-63	Notes
1859	(800)	36,400,000							

Indian Head, Variety 2, Copper-Nickel, Oak Wreath With Shield (1860–1864)

Date		Quantity Minted	VG-8	F-12	VF-20	EF-40	MS-60	PF-63		Notes
1860	*(1,000)*	20,566,000								
1860, Pointed Bust										
1861	*(1,000)*	10,100,000								
1862	*(550)*	28,075,000								
1863	*(460)*	49,840,000								
1864	*(370)*	13,740,000								

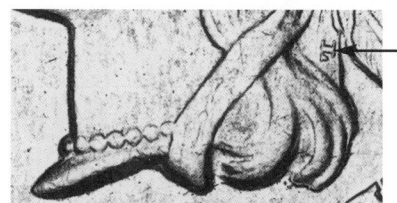

Indian Head, Variety 3, Bronze (1864–1909)

Date		Quantity Minted	VG-8	F-12	VF-20	EF-40	MS-60	PF-63		Notes
1864, No L	*(150+)*	39,233,714								
1864, With L	*(20+)*									
1865	*(500+)*	35,429,286								
1866	*(725+)*	9,826,500								
1867	*(625+)*	9,821,000								
1868	*(600+)*	10,266,500								
1869	*(600+)*	6,420,000								
1869, 9 Over 9										
1870, Shallow N	*(1,000+)*	5,275,000								
1870, Bold N										
1871, Shallow N	*(960+)*	3,929,500								
1871, Bold N										
1872, Shallow N	*(950+)*	4,042,000								
1872, Bold N										
1873, Close 3	*(1,100+)*									
1873, Doubled LIBERTY		11,676,500								
1873, Open 3										
1874	*(700)*	14,187,500								
1875	*(700)*	13,528,000								
1875, Dot Reverse										
1876	*(1,150)*	7,944,000								
1877	*(900)*	852,500								

Date		Quantity Minted	VG-8	F-12	VF-20	EF-40	MS-60	PF-63		Notes
1878	(2,350)	5,797,500								
1879	(3,200)	16,228,000								
1880	(3,955)	38,961,000								
1881	(3,575)	39,208,000								
1882	(3,100)	38,578,000								
1883	(6,609)	45,591,500								
1884	(3,942)	23,257,800								
1885	(3,790)	11,761,594								
1886, Variety 1	(4,290)	17,650,000								
1886, Variety 2										
1887	(2,960)	45,223,523								
1888	(4,582)	37,489,832								
1888, Last 8 Over 7										
1889	(3,336)	48,866,025								
1890	(2,740)	57,180,114								
1891	(2,350)	47,070,000								
1892	(2,745)	37,647,087								
1893	(2,195)	46,640,000								
1894	(2,632)	16,749,500								
1894, Doubled Date										
1895	(2,062)	38,341,574								
1896	(1,862)	39,055,431								
1897	(1,938)	50,464,392								
1898	(1,795)	49,821,284								
1899	(2,031)	53,598,000								
1900	(2,262)	66,831,502								
1901	(1,985)	79,609,158								
1902	(2,018)	87,374,704								
1903	(1,790)	85,092,703								
1904	(1,817)	61,326,198								
1905	(2,152)	80,717,011								
1906	(1,725)	96,020,530								
1907	(1,475)	108,137,143								
1908	(1,620)	32,326,367								
1908S		1,115,000								
1909	(2,175)	14,368,470								
1909S		309,000								

Lincoln, Wheat Ears Reverse, Variety 1, Bronze (1909–1942)

Check list on following page

Date		Quantity Minted	VG-8	F-12	VF-20	EF-40	MS-60	PF-63	Notes
1909, V.D.B.	(1,194)	27,995,000							
1909S, V.D.B.		484,000							
1909	(2,618)	72,702,618							
1909S		1,825,000							
1909S, S Over Horizontal S									
1910	(4,118)	146,801,218							
1910S		6,045,000							
1911	(1,725)	101,177,787							
1911D		12,672,000							
1911S		4,026,000							
1912	(2,172)	68,153,060							
1912D		10,411,000							
1912S		4,431,000							
1913	(2,983)	76,532,352							
1913D		15,804,000							
1913S		6,101,000							
1914	(1,365)	75,238,432							
1914D		1,193,000							
1914S		4,137,000							
1915	(1,150)	29,092,120							
1915D		22,050,000							
1915S		4,833,000							
1916	(1,050)	131,833,677							
1916D		35,956,000							
1916S		22,510,000							

Date	Quantity Minted	G-4	VG-8	F-12	VF-20	EF-40	MS-60	Notes
1917	196,429,785							
1917, Doubled-Die Obverse								
1917D	55,120,000							
1917S	32,620,000							
1918	288,104,634							
1918D	47,830,000							
1918S	34,680,000							
1919	392,021,000							
1919D	57,154,000							
1919S	139,760,000							
1920	310,165,000							
1920D	49,280,000							
1920S	46,220,000							
1921	39,157,000							
1921S	15,274,000							
1922D	7,160,000							
1922, No D								
1922, Weak D								

Date	Quantity Minted	G-4	VG-8	F-12	VF-20	EF-40	MS-60	Notes
1923	74,723,000							
1923S	8,700,000							
1924	75,178,000							
1924D	2,520,000							
1924S	11,696,000							
1925	139,949,000							
1925D	22,580,000							
1925S	26,380,000							
1926	157,088,000							
1926D	28,020,000							
1926S	4,550,000							
1927	144,440,000							
1927D	27,170,000							
1927S	14,276,000							
1928	134,116,000							
1928D	31,170,000							
1928S	17,266,000							
1929	185,262,000							
1929D	41,730,000							
1929S	50,148,000							
1930	157,415,000							
1930D	40,100,000							
1930S	24,286,000							
1931	19,396,000							
1931D	4,480,000							
1931S	866,000							
1932	9,062,000							
1932D	10,500,000							
1933	14,360,000							
1933D	6,200,000							
1934	219,080,000							
1934D	28,446,000							
1935	245,388,000							
1935D	47,000,000							
1935S	38,702,00							

Date	Quantity Minted	VG-8	F-12	VF-20	EF-40	MS-60	PF-63	Notes
1936 (5,569)	309,632,000							
1936, Doubled-Die Obverse								
1936D	40,620,000							
1936S	29,130,000							
1937 (9,320)	309,170,000							
1937D	50,430,000							

Date	Quantity Minted	VG-8	F-12	VF-20	EF-40	MS-60	PF-63	Notes
1937S	34,500,000							
1938	(14,734) 156,682,000							
1938D	20,010,000							
1938S	15,180,000							
1939	(13,520) 316,466,000							
1939D	15,160,000							
1939S	52,070,000							

Date	Quantity Minted	VG-8	F-12	VF-20	EF-40	MS-60	PF-65	Notes
1940	(15,872) 586,810,000							
1940D	81,390,000							
1940S	112,940,000							
1941	(21,100) 887,018,000							
1941D	128,700,000							
1941S	92,360,000							
1942	(32,600) 657,796,000							
1942D	206,698,000							
1942S	85,590,000							

Lincoln, Wheat Ears Reverse, Variety 2, Zinc-Coated Steel (1943)

Date	Quantity Minted	VG-8	F-12	VF-20	EF-40	MS-60	PF-65	Notes
1943	684,628,670							
1943D	217,660,000							
1943D, Boldly Doubled Mintmark								
1943S	191,550,000							

Lincoln, Wheat Ears Reverse, Variety 1 Resumed (1944–1958)

Date	Quantity Minted	VF-20	EF-40	AU-50	MS-60	MS-63	MS-65	Notes
1944	1,435,400,000							
1944D	430,578,000							
1944D, D Over S								
1944S	282,760,000							
1945	1,040,515,000							
1945D	266,268,000							
1945S	181,770,000							
1946	991,655,000							
1946D	315,690,000							
1946S	198,100,000							
1946S, S Over D								
1947	190,555,000							
1947D	194,750,000							
1947S	99,000,000							
1948	317,570,000							

Date	Quantity Minted	VF-20	EF-40	AU-50	MS-60	MS-63	MS-65	Notes
1948D	172,637,500							
1948S	81,735,000							
1949	217,775,000							
1949D	153,132,500							
1949S	64,290,000							

Date	Quantity Minted	EF-40	AU-50	MS-60	MS-63	MS-65	PF-65	Notes
1950	(51,386) 272,635,000							
1950D	334,950,000							
1950S	118,505,000							
1951	(57,500) 284,576,000							
1951D	625,355,000							
1951S	136,010,000							
1952	(81,980) 186,775,000							
1952D	746,130,000							
1952S	137,800,004							
1953	(128,800) 256,755,000							
1953D	700,515,000							
1953S	181,835,000							
1954	(233,300) 71,640,050							
1954D	251,552,500							
1954S	96,190,000							
1955 (378,200) 1955, DblDie Obv	330,958,200							
1955D	563,257,500							
1955S	44,610,000							
1956	(669,384) 420,745,000							
1956D 1956D, D Above Shadow D	1,098,201,100							
1957	(1,247,952) 282,540,000							
1957D	1,051,342,000							
1958 (875,652) 1958 DblDie Obv (3 known)	252,525,000							
1958D	800,953,300							

Lincoln, Memorial Reverse, Copper (1959–1982)

Date	Quantity Minted	EF-40	AU-50	MS-60	MS-63	MS-65	PF-65	Notes
1959	(1,149,291) 609,715,000							
1959D	1,279,760,000							
1960, Large Date (1,691,602) 1960, Small Date 1960, Large Over Small Date	586,405,000							

Date	Quantity Minted	EF-40	AU-50	MS-60	MS-63	MS-65	PF-65		Notes
1960D, Large Date									
1960D, Small Date	1,580,884,000								
1960, D/D, Sm/Lg Dt									
1961 (3,028,244)	753,345,000								
1961D	1,753,266,700								
1962 (3,218,019)	606,045,000								
1962D	1,793,148,140								
1963 (3,075,645)	754,110,000								
1963D	1,774,020,400								
1964 (3,950,762)	2,648,575,000								
1964D	3,799,071,500								
1965	1,497,224,900								
1966	2,188,147,783								
1967	3,048,667,100								
1968	1,707,880,970								
1968D	2,886,269,600								
1968S (3,041,506)	258,270,001								
1969	1,136,910,000								
1969D	4,002,832,200								
1969S (2,934,631)	544,375,000								
1969S DblDie Obv									
1970	1,898,315,000								
1970D	2,891,438,900								
1970S, SmDt (Hi 7) (2,632,810)	690,560,004								
1970S, LgDt (Lo 7)									
1970S DbleDie Obv									
1971	1,919,490,000								
1971, DblDie Obv									
1971D	2,911,045,600								
1971S (3,220,733)	525,133,459								
1971S, DblDie Obv									
1972	2,933,255,000								
1972, DblDie Obv									
1972D	2,665,071,400								
1972S (3,260,996)	376,939,108								
1973	3,728,245,000								
1973D	3,549,576,588								
1973S (2,760,339)	317,177,295								
1974	4,232,140,523								
1974D	4,235,098,000								
1974S (2,612,568)	409,426,660								
1975	5,451,476,142								
1975D	4,505,275,300								
1975S (2,845,450)									
1976	4,674,292,426								
1976D	4,221,592,455								

Date	Quantity Minted	EF-40	AU-50	MS-60	MS-63	MS-65	PF-65		Notes
1976S	(4,149,730)								
1977	4,469,930,000								
1977D	4,194,062,300								
1977S	(3,251,152)								
1978	5,558,605,000								
1978D	4,280,233,400								
1978S	(3,127,781)								
1979	6,018,515,000								
1979D	4,139,357,254								
1979S, Type 1	(3,677,175)								
1979S, Type 2									
1980	7,414,705,000								
1980D	5,140,098,660								
1980S	(3,554,806)								
1981	7,491,750,000								
1981D	5,373,235,677								
1981S, Type 1	(4,063,083)								
1981S, Type 2									
1982, Large Date*									
1982, Large Date**	10,712,525,000								
1982, Small Date*									
1982, Small Date**									
1982D*									
1982D, Large Dt**	6,012,979,368								
1982D, Small Dt**									
1982S*	(3,857,479)								

* Copper. ** Copper-plated zinc.

Lincoln, Memorial Reverse, Copper-Plated Zinc (1982–2008)

Date	Quantity Minted	MS-60	MS-63	MS-65	PF-65			Notes
1983	7,752,355,000							
1983, DblDie Rev								
1983D	6,467,199,428							
1983S	(3,279,126)							
1984	8,151,079,000							
1984, Doubled Ear								
1984D	5,569,238,906							
1984S	(3,065,110)							
1985	5,648,489,887							
1985D	5,287,339,926							
1985S	(3,362,821)							
1986	4,491,395,493							
1986D	4,442,866,698							
1986S	(3,010,497)							
1987	4,682,466,931							

Date	Quantity Minted	MS-60	MS-63	MS-65	PF-65				Notes
1987D	4,879,389,514								
1987S	(4,227,728)								
1988	6,092,810,000								
1988D	5,253,740,443								
1988S	(3,262,948)								
1989	7,261,535,000								
1989D	5,345,467,111								
1989S	(3,220,194)								
1990	6,851,765,000								
1990D	4,922,894,533								
1990S / 1990, Proof, No S	(3,299,559)								
1991	5,165,940,000								
1991D	4,158,446,076								
1991S	(2,867,787)								
1992 / 1992, Close AM	4,648,905,000								
1992D / 1992D, Close AM	4,448,673,300								
1992S	(4,176,560)								
1993	5,684,705,000								
1993D	6,426,650,571								
1993S	(3,394,792)								
1994	6,500,850,000								
1994D	7,131,765,000								
1994S	(3,269,923)								
1995 / 1995, DblDie Obv	6,411,440,000								
1995D	7,128,560,000								
1995S	(2,797,481)								
1996 / 1996, Wide AM	6,612,465,000								
1996D	6,510,795,000								
1996S	(2,525,265)								
1997	4,622,800,000								
1997D	4,576,555,000								
1997S	(2,796,678)								
1998 / 1998, Wide AM	5,032,155,000								
1998D	5,225,353,500								
1998S / 1998S, Close AM	(2,086,507)								
1999 / 1999, Wide AM	5,237,600,000								
1999D	6,360,065,000								

Date		Quantity Minted	MS-60	MS-63	MS-65	PF-65				Notes
1999S	(3,347,966)									
1999S, Close AM										
2000		5,503,200,000								
2000, Wide AM										
2000D		8,774,220,000								
2000S	(4,047,993)									
2001		4,959,600,000								
2001D		5,374,990,000								
2001S	(3,184,606)									
2002		3,260,800,000								
2002D		4,028,055,000								
2002S	(3,211,995)									
2003		3,300,000,000								
2003D		3,548,000,000								
2003S	(3,298,439)									
2004		3,379,600,000								
2004D		3,456,400,000								
2004S	(2,965,422)									
2005		3,935,600,000								
2005D		3,764,450,500								
2005S	(3,344,679)									
2006		4,290,000,000								
2006D		3,944,000,000								
2006S	(3,054,436)									
2007		3,762,400,000								
2007D		3,638,800,400								
2007S	(2,577,166)									
2008		2,558,800,000								
2008D		2,849,600,000								
2008S	(2,169,561)									

Lincoln, Bicentennial (2009)

Date	Quantity Minted	MS-60	MS-63	MS-65	PF-65				Notes
2009, Birth and Early Childhood	284,400,000								
2009, Birth and Early Childhood, copper, Satin finish									
2009D, Birth and Early Childhood	350,400,000								
2009D, Birth and Early Childhood, copper, Satin finish									
2009S, Birth and Early Childhood, copper	(2,995,615)								
2009, Formative Years	376,000,000								
2009, Formative Years, copper, Satin finish									
2009D, Formative Years	363,600,000								

Date	Quantity Minted	MS-60	MS-63	MS-65	PF-65				Notes
2009D, Formative Years, copper, Satin finish									
2009S, Formative Years, copper	(2,995,615)								
2009, Professional Life	316,000,000								
2009, Professional Life, copper, Satin finish									
2009D, Professional Life	336,000,000								
2009D, Professional Life, copper, Satin finish									
2009S, Professional Life, copper	(2,995,615)								
2009, Presidency	129,600,000								
2009, Presidency, copper, Satin finish									
2009D, Presidency	198,000,000								
2009D, Presidency, copper, Satin finish									
2009S, Presidency, copper	(2,995,615)								

Lincoln, Shield Reverse (2010 to Date)

Date	Quantity Minted	MS-60	MS-63	MS-65	PF-65				Notes
2010	1,963,630,000								
2010D	2,047,200,000								
2010S	(1,689,364)								
2011	2,006,800,000								
2011D	2,176,940,000								
2011S	(1,453,276)								
2012									
2012D									
2012S									

TWO-CENT PIECES

Two-Cent Piece (1864–1873)

Date		Quantity Minted	G-4	VG-8	F-12	EF-40	MS-60	PF-63	Notes
1864, Small Motto		19,822,500							
1864, Large Motto	(100+)								
1865	(500+)	13,640,000							
1866	(725+)	3,177,000							
1867	(625+)	2,938,750							
1867, Doubled-Die Obv									
1868	(600+)	2,803,750							
1869	(600+)	1,546,500							
1870	(1,000+)	861,250							
1871	(960+)	721,250							
1872	(950+)	65,000							
1873, Close 3, Pf only	(600)								
1873, Open 3, Restrike	(500)								

SILVER THREE-CENT PIECES (TRIMES)

Variety 1 (1851–1853)

Date	Quantity Minted	G-4	VG-8	F-12	EF-40	MS-60	PF-63	Notes
1851	5,447,400							
18510	720,000							
1852, 1 Over Inverted 2	18,663,500							
1852								
1853	11,400,000							

Variety 2 (1854–1858)

Check list on following page

Date		Quantity Minted	G-4	VG-8	F-12	EF-40	MS-60	PF-63		Notes
1854		671,000								
1855		139,000								
1856		1,458,000								
1857		1,042,000								
1858	(210)	1,603,700								

Variety 3 (1859–1873)

Date		Quantity Minted	G-4	VG-8	F-12	EF-40	MS-60	PF-63		Notes
1859	(800)	364,200								
1860	(1,000)	286,000								
1861	(1,000)	497,000								
1862, 2 Over 1		343,000								
1862	(550)									
1863, So-called 3/2		21,000								
1863	(460)									
1864	(470)	12,000								
1865	(500)	8,000								
1866	(725)	22,000								
1867	(625)	4,000								
1868	(600)	3,500								
1869	(600)	4,500								
1870	(1,000)	3,000								
1871	(960)	3,400								
1872	(950)	1,000								
1873 (Close 3, Pf only)	(600)									

NICKEL THREE-CENT PIECES

Nickel Three-Cent Piece (1865–1889)

Date		Quantity Minted	VG-8	F-12	VF-20	EF-40	MS-60	PF-63		Notes
1865	(500+)	11,382,000								
1866	(725+)	4,801,000								

Date		Quantity Minted	VG-8	F-12	VF-20	EF-40	MS-60	PF-63		Notes
1867	(625+)	3,915,000								
1868	(600+)	3,252,000								
1869	(600+)	1,604,000								
1870	(1,000+)	1,335,000								
1871	(960+)	604,000								
1872	(950+)	862,000								
1873, Close 3	(1,100+)	390,000								
1873, Open 3		783,000								
1874	(700+)	790,000								
1875	(700+)	228,000								
1876	(1,150+)	162,000								
1877, Proof only	(900)									
1878, Proof only	(2,350)									
1879	(3,200)	38,000								
1880	(3,955)	21,000								
1881	(3,575)	1,077,000								
1882	(3,100)	22,200								
1883	(6,609)	4,000								
1884	(3,942)	1,700								
1885	(3,790)	1,000								
1886, Proof only	(4,290)									
1887	(2,960)	5,001								
1887, 7 Over 6										
1888	(4,582)	36,501								
1889	(3,436)	18,125								

NICKEL FIVE-CENT PIECES

Shield (1866–1883)

Date		Quantity Minted	VG-8	F-12	VF-20	EF-40	MS-60	PF-60		Notes
1866, Rays	(600+)	14,742,500								
1866, Repunched Date										
1867, Rays	(25+)	2,019,000								
1867, No Rays	(600+)	28,890,500								
1868	(600+)	28,817,000								
1869	(600+)	16,395,000								
1870	(1,000+)	4,806,000								
1871	(960+)	561,000								
1872	(950+)	6,036,000								

Date		Quantity Minted	VG-8	F-12	VF-20	EF-40	MS-60	PF-63		Notes
1873, Close 3	(1,100+)	436,050								
1873, Open 3		4,113,950								
1873, Lg Over Sm 3										
1874	(700+)	3,538,000								
1875	(700+)	2,097,000								
1876	(1,150+)	2,530,000								
1877, Proof only	(900)									
1878, Proof only	(2,350)									
1879	(3,200)	25,900								
1879, 9 Over 8										
1880	(3,955)	16,000								
1881	(3,575)	68,800								
1882	(3,100)	11,472,900								
1883	(5,419)	1,451,500								
1883, 3 Over 2										

Liberty Head, Variety 1, Without CENTS (1883)

Date		Quantity Minted	VG-8	F-12	VF-20	EF-40	MS-60	PF-60		Notes
1883, Without CENTS	(5,219)	5,474,300								

Liberty Head, Variety 2, With CENTS (1883–1913)

Date		Quantity Minted	VG-8	F-12	VF-20	EF-40	MS-60	PF-60		Notes
1883, With CENTS	(6,783)	16,026,200								
1884	(3,942)	11,270,000								
1885	(3,790)	1,472,700								
1886	(4,290)	3,326,000								
1887	(2,960)	15,260,692								
1888	(4,582)	10,167,901								
1889	(3,336)	15,878,025								
1890	(2,740)	16,256,532								
1891	(2,350)	16,832,000								
1892	(2,745)	11,696,897								

Date		Quantity Minted	VG-8	F-12	VF-20	EF-40	MS-60	PF-60		Notes
1893	(2,195)	13,368,000								
1894	(2,632)	5,410,500								
1895	(2,062)	9,977,822								
1896	(1,862)	8,841,058								
1897	(1,938)	20,426,797								
1898	(1,795)	12,530,292								
1899	(2,031)	26,027,000								
1900	(2,262)	27,253,733								
1901	(1,985)	26,478,228								
1902	(2,018)	31,487,561								
1903	(1,790)	28,004,935								
1904	(1,817)	21,403,167								
1905	(2,152)	29,825,124								
1906	(1,725)	38,612,000								
1907	(1,475)	39,213,325								
1908	(1,620)	22,684,557								
1909	(4,763)	11,585,763								
1910	(2,405)	30,166,948								
1911	(1,733)	39,557,639								
1912	(2,145)	26,234,569								
1912D		8,474,000								
1912S		238,000								
1913, Liberty Head *(5 known)*										

Indian Head or Buffalo, Variety 1, FIVE CENTS on Raised Ground (1913)

Date		Quantity Minted	VG-8	F-12	VF-20	EF-40	MS-60	PF-60		Notes
1913, Variety 1	(1,520)	30,992,000								
1913D, Variety 1		5,337,000								
1913S, Variety 1		2,105,000								

Note: Nickel five-cent Proofs of 1913 through 1916 have a "Matte Proof" finish.

Indian Head or Buffalo, Variety 2, FIVE CENTS in Recess (1913–1938)

Date		Quantity Minted	VG-8	F-12	VF-20	EF-40	MS-60	PF-63		Notes
1913, Variety 2	(1,514)	29,857,186								

Note: Nickel five-cent Proofs of 1913 through 1916 have a "Matte Proof" finish.

Date	Quantity Minted	VG-8	F-12	VF-20	EF-40	MS-60	PF-60		Notes
1913D, Variety 2	4,156,000								
1913S, Variety 2	1,209,000								
1914 (1,275)	20,664,463								
1914, 4 Over 3									
1914D	3,912,000								
1914S	3,470,000								
1915 (1,050)	20,986,220								
1915D	7,569,000								
1915S	1,505,000								
1916 (600)	63,497,466								
1916, Doubled-Die Obverse									
1916D	13,333,000								
1916S	11,860,000								
1917	51,424,019								
1917D	9,910,000								
1917S	4,193,000								
1918	32,086,314								
1918D, 8 Over 7	8,362,000								
1918D									
1918S	4,882,000								
1919	60,868,000								
1919D	8,006,000								
1919S	7,521,000								
1920	63,093,000								
1920D	9,418,000								
1920S	9,689,000								
1921	10,663,000								
1921S	1,557,000								
1923	35,715,000								
1923S	6,142,000								
1924	21,620,000								
1924D	5,258,000								
1924S	1,437,000								
1925	35,565,100								
1925D	4,450,000								
1925S	6,256,000								
1926	44,693,000								
1926D	5,638,000								
1926S	970,000								
1927	37,981,000								
1927D	5,730,000								
1927S	3,430,000								
1928	23,411,000								
1928D	6,436,000								
1928S	6,936,000								

Note: Nickel five-cent Proofs of 1913 through 1916 have a "Matte Proof" finish.

Date		Quantity Minted	VG-8	F-12	VF-20	EF-40	MS-60	PF-63	Notes
1929		36,446,000							
1929D		8,370,000							
1929S		7,754,000							
1930		22,849,000							
1930S		5,435,000							
1931S		1,200,000							
1934		20,213,003							
1934D		7,480,000							
1935		58,264,000							
1935, Doubled-Die Reverse									
1935D		12,092,000							
1935S		10,300,000							
1936	(4,420)	118,997,000							
1936D		24,814,000							
1936D, 3-1/2 Legs									
1936S		14,930,000							
1937	(5,769)	79,480,000							
1937D		17,826,000							
1937D, 3-Legged									
1937S		5,635,000							
1938D		7,020,000							
1938D, D Over S									

Jefferson, Prewar Composition (1938–1942)

Date		Quantity Minted	VG-8	F-12	VF-20	EF-40	MS-63	PF-65	Notes
1938	(19,365)	19,496,000							
1938D		5,376,000							
1938S		4,105,000							
1939	(12,535)	120,615,000							
1939, Doubled MONTICELLO, FIVE CENTS									
1939D		3,514,000							
1939S		6,630,000							
1940	(14,158)	176,485,000							
1940D		43,540,000							
1940S		39,690,000							
1941	(18,720)	203,265,000							
1941D		53,432,000							

Date		Quantity Minted	VG-8	F-12	VF-20	EF-40	MS-60	PF-63	Notes
1941S		43,445,000							
1942	(29,600)	49,789,000							
1942D		13,938,000							
1942D Over Horizontal D									

Jefferson, Wartime Silver Alloy (1942–1945)

Date		Quantity Minted	VG-8	F-12	VF-20	EF-40	MS-63	PF-65	Notes
1942P	(27,600)	57,873,000							
1942S		32,900,000							
1943P, 3 Over 2									
1943P		271,165,000							
1943P, Doubled Eye									
1943D		15,294,000							
1943S		104,060,000							
1944P		119,150,000							
1944D		32,309,000							
1944S		21,640,000							
1945P		119,408,100							
1945P, Doubled-Die Reverse									
1945D		37,158,000							
1945S		58,939,000							

Jefferson, Prewar Composition Resumed (1946–1965)

Date		Quantity Minted	VF-20	EF-40	AU-50	MS-63	PF-65	Notes
1946		161,116,000						
1946D		45,292,200						
1946S		13,560,000						
1947		95,000,000						
1947D		37,822,000						
1947S		24,720,000						
1948		89,348,000						
1948D		44,734,000						
1948S		11,300,000						
1949		60,652,000						
1949D		36,498,000						
1949D, D Over S								
1949S		9,716,000						
1950	(51,386)	9,796,000						
1950D		2,630,030						
1951	(57,500)	28,552,000						
1951D		20,460,000						
1951S		7,776,000						
1952	(81,980)	63,988,000						
1952D		30,638,000						

Date		Quantity Minted	VF-20	EF-40	AU-50	MS-63	PF-65			Notes
1952S		20,572,000								
1953	(128,800)	46,644,000								
1953D		59,878,600								
1953S		19,210,900								
1954	(233,300)	47,684,050								
1954D		117,183,060								
1954S		29,384,000								
1954S, S Over D										
1955	(378,200)	7,888,000								
1955D		74,464,100								
1955D, D Over S										
1956	(669,384)	35,216,000								
1956D		67,222,940								
1957	(1,247,952)	38,408,000								
1957D		136,828,900								
1958	(875,652)	17,088,000								
1958D		168,249,120								
1959	(1,149,291)	27,248,000								
1959D		160,738,240								
1960	(1,691,602)	55,416,000								
1960D		192,582,180								
1961	(3,028,144)	73,640,100								
1961D		229,342,760								
1962	(3,218,019)	97,384,000								
1962D		280,195,720								
1963	(3,075,645)	175,776,000								
1963D		276,829,460								
1964	(3,950,762)	1,024,672,000								
1964D		1,787,297,160								
1965		136,131,380								

Jefferson, Designer's Initials Added (1966–2003)

Date		Quantity Minted	MS-63	MS-65	PF-65					Notes
1966		156,208,283								
1967		107,325,800								
1968D		91,227,880								
1968S	(3,041,506)	100,396,004								
1969D		202,807,500								
1969S	(2,934,631)	120,165,000								
1970D		515,485,380								
1970S	(2,632,810)	238,832,004								
1971		106,884,000								
1971D		316,144,800								
1971, No S	(3,220,733)									
1971S										
1972		202,036,000								

Date		Quantity Minted	MS-63	MS-65	PF-65					Notes
1972D		351,694,600								
1972S	(3,260,996)									
1973		384,396,000								
1973D		261,405,000								
1973S	(2,760,339)									
1974		601,752,000								
1974D		277,373,000								
1974S	(2,612,568)									
1975		181,772,000								
1975D		401,875,300								
1975S	(2,845,450)									
1976		367,124,000								
1976D		563,964,147								
1976S	(4,149,730)									
1977		585,376,000								
1977D		297,313,422								
1977S	(3,251,152)									
1978		391,308,000								
1978D		313,092,780								
1978S	(3,127,781)									
1979		463,188,000								
1979D		325,867,672								
1979S, Type 1	(3,677,175)									
1979S, Type 2										
1980P		593,004,000								
1980D		502,323,448								
1980S	(3,554,806)									
1981P		657,504,000								
1981D		364,801,843								
1981S, Type 1	(4,063,083)									
1981S, Type 2										
1982P		292,355,000								
1982D		373,726,544								
1982S	(3,857,479)									
1983P		561,615,000								
1983D		536,726,276								
1983S	(3,279,126)									
1984P		746,769,000								
1984D		517,675,146								
1984S	(3,065,110)									
1985P		647,114,962								
1985D		459,747,446								
1985S	(3,362,821)									
1986P		536,883,483								
1986D		361,819,140								
1986S	(3,010,497)									

Date		Quantity Minted	MS-63	MS-65	PF-65					Notes
1987P		371,499,481								
1987D		410,590,604								
1987S	(4,227,728)									
1988P		771,360,000								
1988D		663,771,652								
1988S	(3,262,948)									
1989P		898,812,000								
1989D		570,842,474								
1989S	(3,220,194)									
1990P		661,636,000								
1990D		663,938,503								
1990S	(3,299,559)									
1991P		614,104,000								
1991D		436,496,678								
1991S	(2,867,787)									
1992P		399,552,000								
1992D		450,565,113								
1992S	(4,176,560)									
1993P		412,076,000								
1993D		406,084,135								
1993S	(3,394,792)									
1994P		722,160,000								
1994P, Special Unc		167,703								
1994D		715,762,110								
1994S	(3,269,923)									
1995P		774,156,000								
1995D		888,112,000								
1995S	(2,797,481)									
1996P		829,332,000								
1996D		817,736,000								
1996S	(2,525,265)									
1997P		470,972,000								
1997P, Special Unc		25,000								
1997D		466,640,000								
1997S	(2,796,678)									
1998P		688,272,000								
1998D		635,360,000								
1998S	(2,086,507)									
1999P		1,212,000,000								
1999D		1,066,720,000								
1999S	(3,347,966)									
2000P		846,240,000								
2000D		1,509,520,000								
2000S	(4,047,993)									
2001P		675,704,000								
2001D		627,680,000								

Date	Quantity Minted	MS-63	MS-65	PF-65				Notes
2001S	(3,184,606)							
2002P	539,280,000							
2002D	691,200,000							
2002S	(3,211,995)							
2003P	441,840,000							
2003D	383,040,000							
2003S	(3,298,439)							

Westward Journey Nickels (2004–2006; 2006 Design Used to Date)

Date	Quantity Minted	MS-63	MS-65	PF-65	Notes	Date	Quantity Minted	MS-63	MS-65	PF-65	Notes
2004P, Peace Medal	361,440,000					2009D	46,800,000				
						2009S	(2,179,867)				
2004D, Peace Medal	372,000,000					2010P	260,640,000				
						2010D	229,920,000				
2004S, Peace Medal	(2,992,069)					2010S	(1,689,364)				
						2011P	379,440,000				
2004P, Keelboat	366,720,000					2011D	473,760,000				
2004D, Keelboat	344,880,000					2011S	(1,453,276)				
2004S, Keelboat	(2,965,422)					2012P					
2005P, American Bison	448,320,000					2012D					
2005D, American Bison	487,680,000					2012S					
2005S, American Bison	(3,344,679)										
2005P, Ocean in View	394,080,000										
2005D, Ocean in View	411,120,000										
2005S, Ocean in View	(3,344,679)										
2006P, Monticello	693,120,000										
2006D, Monticello	809,280,000										
2006S, Monticello	(3,054,436)										
2007P	571,680,000										
2007D	626,160,000										
2007S	(2,577,166)										
2008P	279,840,000										
2008D	345,600,000										
2008S	(2,169,561)										
2009P	39,840,000										

HALF DIMES

Flowing Hair (1794–1795)

Date	Quantity Minted	G-4	VG-8	F-12	VF-20	EF-40	MS-60	Notes
1794	86,416							
1795								

Draped Bust, Small Eagle Reverse (1796–1797)

Date	Quantity Minted	G-4	VG-8	F-12	VF-20	EF-40	MS-60	Notes
1796, 6 Over 5	10,230							
1796								
1796, LIKERTY								
1797, 15 Stars	44,527							
1797, 16 Stars								
1797, 13 Stars								

Draped Bust, Heraldic Eagle Reverse (1800–1805)

Date	Quantity Minted	G-4	VG-8	F-12	VF-20	EF-40	MS-60	Notes
1800	24,000							
1800, LIBEKTY	16,000							
1801	27,760							
1802	3,060							
1803, Large 8	37,850							
1803, Small 8								
1805	15,600							

Capped Bust (1829–1837)

Date	Quantity Minted	G-4	VG-8	F-12	VF-20	EF-40	MS-60		Notes
1829	1,230,000								
1830	1,240,000								
1831	1,242,700								
1832	965,000								
1833	1,370,000								
1834	1,480,000								
1834, 3 Over Inverted 3									
1835, Large Date and 5c	2,760,000								
1835, Large Date, Small 5c									
1835, Small Date, Large 5c									
1835, Small Date and 5c									
1836, Small 5c	1,900,000								
1836, Large 5c									
1836, 3 Over Inverted 3									
1837, Small 5c	871,000								
1837, Large 5c									

Liberty Seated, Variety 1, No Stars on Obverse (1837–1838)

Date	Quantity Minted	G-4	VG-8	F-12	VF-20	EF-40	MS-60		Notes
1837, Small Date	1,405,000								
1837, Large Date									
1838O, No Stars	70,000								

Liberty Seated, Variety 2, Stars on Obverse (1838–1853)

Date	Quantity Minted	G-4	VG-8	F-12	VF-20	EF-40	MS-60		Notes
1838, No Drapery, Large Stars	2,225,000								
1838, No Drapery, Small Stars									
1839, No Drapery	1,069,150								

Date	Quantity Minted	G-4	VG-8	F-12	VF-20	EF-40	MS-60	Notes
1839O, No Drapery	1,060,000							
1840, No Drapery	1,034,000							
1840O, No Drapery	695,000							
1840, Drapery	310,085							
1840O, Drapery	240,000							
1841	1,150,000							
1841O	815,000							
1842	815,000							
1842O	350,000							
1843	1,165,000							
1844	430,000							
1844O	220,000							
1845	1,564,000							
1846	27,000							
1847	1,274,000							
1848, Medium Date	668,000							
1848, Large Date								
1848O	600,000							
1849, 9 Over 6	1,309,000							
1849, 9 Over 8								
1849, Normal Date								
1849O	140,000							
1850	955,000							
1850O	690,000							
1851	781,000							
1851O	860,000							
1852	1,000,500							
1852O	260,000							
1853, No Arrows	135,000							
1853O, No Arrows	160,000							

Liberty Seated, Variety 3, Arrows at Date (1853–1855)

Date	Quantity Minted	VG-8	F-12	VF-20	EF-40	MS-60	PF-60	Notes
1853	13,210,020							
1853O	2,200,000							
1854	5,740,000							
1854O	1,560,000							
1855	1,750,000							
1855O	600,000							

Liberty Seated, Variety 2 Resumed, With Weight Standard of Variety 3 (1856–1859)

Date		Quantity Minted	VG-8	F-12	VF-20	EF-40	MS-60	PF-60		Notes
1856		4,880,000								
1856O		1,100,000								
1857		7,280,000								
1857O		1,380,000								
1858	(300)									
1858, Repunched High Dt		3,500,000								
1858, Over Inverted Date										
1858O		1,660,000								
1859	(800)	340,000								
1859O		560,000								

Transitional Patterns (1859 and 1860)

Date	Quantity Minted	MS-60	MS-63	PF-63				Notes
1859, Obverse of 1859, Reverse of 1860	20							
1860, Obverse of 1859 (With Stars), Reverse of 1860	100							

Liberty Seated, Variety 4, Legend on Obverse (1860–1873)

Date		Quantity Minted	VG-8	F-12	VF-20	EF-40	MS-60	PF-60		Notes
1860, Legend	(1,000)	798,000								
1860O		1,060,000								
1861	(1,000)									
1861, "1 Over 0"		3,360,000								
1862	(550)	1,492,000								
1863	(460)	18,000								
1863S		100,000								
1864	(470)	48,000								
1864S		90,000								
1865	(500)	13,000								
1865S		120,000								
1866	(725)	10,000								
1866S		120,000								
1867	(625)	8,000								
1867S		120,000								
1868	(600)	88,600								

Date		Quantity Minted	VG-8	F-12	VF-20	EF-40	MS-60	PF-60		Notes
1868S		280,000								
1869	(600)	208,000								
1869S		230,000								
1870	(1,000)	535,000								
1870S *(unique)*										
1871	(960)	1,873,000								
1871S		161,000								
1872	(950)	2,947,000								
1872S, Mintmk above bow		837,000								
1872S, Mintmk below bow										
1873 (Close 3 only)	(600)	712,000								
1873S (Close 3 only)		324,000								

DIMES

Draped Bust, Small Eagle Reverse (1796–1797)

Date	Quantity Minted	G-4	VG-8	F-12	VF-20	EF-40	MS-60		Notes
1796	22,135								
1797, 16 Stars	25,261								
1797, 13 Stars									

Draped Bust, Heraldic Eagle Reverse (1798–1807)

Date	Quantity Minted	G-4	VG-8	F-12	VF-20	EF-40	MS-60		Notes
1798, 8 Over 7, 16 Stars on Reverse	27,550								
1798, 8 Over 7, 13 Stars on Reverse									
1798									
1798, Small 8									
1800	21,760								
1801	34,640								
1802	10,975								
1803	33,040								
1804, 13 Stars on Reverse	8,265								
1804, 14 Stars on Reverse									

Date	Quantity Minted	G-4	VG-8	F-12	VF-20	EF-40	MS-60	Notes
1805, 4 Berries	120,780							
1805, 5 Berries								
1807	165,000							

Capped Bust, Variety 1, Wide Border (1809–1828)

Date	Quantity Minted	G-4	VG-8	F-12	VF-20	EF-40	MS-60	Notes
1809	51,065							
1811, 11 Over 09	65,180							
1814, Small Date	421,500							
1814, Large Date								
1814, STATESOFAMERICA								
1820, Large 0	942,587							
1820, Small 0								
1820, STATESOFAMERICA								
1821, Small Date	1,186,512							
1821, Large Date								
1822	100,000							
1823, 3 Over 2, Small E's	440,000							
1823, 3 Over 2, Large E's								
1824, 4 Over 2, Flat Top 1	510,000							
1824, 4 Over 2, Pointed Top 1								
1825								
1827	1,215,000							
1828, Large Date, Curl Base 2	125,000							
1828, Small Date, Square Base 2								

1829, Small 10c   1829, Large 10c
Capped Bust, Variety 2, Modified Design (1828–1837)

Date	Quantity Minted	G-4	VG-8	F-12	VF-20	EF-40	MS-60	Notes
1829, Curl Base 2	770,000							
1829, Small 10c								
1829, Medium 10c								
1829, Large 10c								
1830, 30 Over 29	510,000							
1830, Large 10c								
1830, Small 10c								

Date	Quantity Minted	G-4	VG-8	F-12	VF-20	EF-40	MS-60	Notes
1831	771,350							
1832	522,500							
1833	485,000							
1833, Last 3 High								
1834, Small 4	635,000							
1834, Large 4								
1835	1,410,000							
1836	1,190,000							
1837	359,500							

Liberty Seated, Variety 1, No Stars on Obverse (1837–1838)

Date	Quantity Minted	G-4	VG-8	F-12	VF-20	EF-40	MS-60	Notes
1837, Large Date	682,500							
1837, Small Date								
18380	406,034							

No Drapery, Small Stars   No Drapery, Large Stars   Drapery

Liberty Seated, Variety 2, Stars on Obverse (1838–1853)

Date	Quantity Minted	G-4	VG-8	F-12	VF-20	EF-40	MS-60	Notes
1838, Small Stars								
1838, Large Stars	1,992,500							
1838, Partial Drapery								
1839, No Drapery	1,053,115							
18390, No Drapery	1,291,600							
1840, No Drapery	981,500							
18400, No Drapery	1,175,000							
1840, Drapery	377,500							
1841	1,622,500							
18410	2,007,500							
1842	1,887,500							
18420	2,020,000							
1843	1,370,000							
18430	150,000							
1844	72,500							

Date	Quantity Minted	G-4	VG-8	F-12	VF-20	EF-40	MS-60	Notes
1845	1,755,000							
18450	230,000							
1846	31,300							
1847	245,000							
1848	451,500							
1849	839,000							
18490	300,000							
1850	1,931,500							
18500	510,000							
1851	1,026,500							
18510	400,000							
1852	1,535,500							
18520	430,000							
1853, No Arrows	95,000							

Liberty Seated, Variety 3, Arrows at Date (1853–1855)

Date	Quantity Minted	G-4	VG-8	F-12	VF-20	EF-40	MS-60	Notes
1853, With Arrows	12,078,010							
18530	1,100,000							
1854	4,470,000							
18540	1,770,000							
1855	2,075,000							

Liberty Seated, Variety 2 Resumed (1856–1860)

Date		Quantity Minted	VG-8	F-12	VF-20	EF-40	MS-60	PF-60	Notes
1856, Large Date		5,780,000							
1856, Small Date									
18560		1,180,000							
1856S		70,000							
1857		5,580,000							
18570		1,540,000							
1858	(300+)	1,540,000							
18580		290,000							
1858S		60,000							
1859	(800)	429,200							

Date	Quantity Minted	VG-8	F-12	VF-20	EF-40	MS-60	PF-60		Notes
1859O	480,000								
1859S	60,000								
1860S	140,000								

Liberty Seated, Variety 4, Legend on Obverse (1860–1873)

Date		Quantity Minted	VG-8	F-12	VF-20	EF-40	MS-60	PF-60		Notes
1859, Obverse of 1859 (With Stars), Reverse of 1860										
1860	(1,000)	606,000								
1860O		40,000								
1861	(1,000)	1,883,000								
1861S		172,500								
1862	(550)	847,000								
1862S		180,750								
1863	(460)	14,000								
1863S		157,500								
1864	(470)	11,000								
1864S		230,000								
1865	(500)	10,000								
1865S		175,000								
1866	(725)	8,000								
1866S		135,000								
1867	(625)	6,000								
1867S		140,000								
1868	(600)	464,000								
1868S		260,000								
1869	(600)	256,000								
1869S		450,000								
1870	(1,000)	470,500								
1870S		50,000								
1871	(960)	906,750								
1871CC		20,100								
1871S		320,000								
1872	(950)	2,395,500								
1872, Doubled-Die Rev *(rare)*										
1872CC		35,480								
1872S		190,000								
1873, Close 3	(1,100)	1,506,900								
1873, Open 3		60,000								
1873CC *(unique)*		12,400								

Liberty Seated, Variety 5, Arrows at Date (1873–1874)

Date	Quantity Minted	VG-8	F-12	VF-20	EF-40	MS-60	PF-60	Notes
1873 (800)	2,377,700							
1873, Doubled-Die Obverse								
1873CC	18,791							
1873S	455,000							
1874 (700)	2,939,300							
1874CC	10,817							
1874S	240,000							

Liberty Seated, Variety 4 Resumed (1875–1891)

Date	Quantity Minted	VG-8	F-12	VF-20	EF-40	MS-60	PF-60	Notes
1875 (700)	10,350,000							
1875CC, Above Bow	4,645,000							
1875CC, Below Bow								
1875S, Below Bow	9,070,000							
1875S, Above Bow								
1876 (1,150)	11,450,000							
1876CC	8,270,000							
1876S	10,420,000							
1877 (510)	7,310,000							
1877CC	7,700,000							
1877S	2,340,000							
1878 (800)	1,677,200							
1878CC	200,000							
1879 (1,100)	14,000							
1880 (1,355)	36,000							
1881 (975)	24,000							
1882 (1,100)	3,910,000							
1883 (1,039)	7,674,673							
1884 (875)	3,365,505							
1884S	564,969							
1885 (930)	2,532,497							
1885S	43,690							
1886 (886)	6,376,684							
1886S	206,524							
1887 (710)	11,283,229							
1887S	4,454,450							
1888 (832)	5,495,655							

Date		Quantity Minted	VG-8	F-12	VF-20	EF-40	MS-60	PF-60	Notes
1888S		1,720,000							
1889	(711)	7,380,000							
1889S		972,678							
1890	(590)	9,910,951							
1890S, Large S		1,423,076							
1890S, Small S *(rare)*									
1891	(600)	15,310,000							
1891O		4,540,000							
1891O, O Over Horizontal O									
1891S		3,196,116							

Barber or Liberty Head (1892–1916)

Date		Quantity Minted	VG-8	F-12	VF-20	EF-40	MS-60	PF-63	Notes
1892	(1,245)	12,120,000							
1892O		3,841,700							
1892S		990,710							
1893, "3 Over 2"		3,339,940							
1893	(792)								
1893O		1,760,000							
1893S		2,491,401							
1894	(972)	1,330,000							
1894O		720,000							
1894S		24							
1895	(880)	690,000							
1895O		440,000							
1895S		1,120,000							
1896	(762)	2,000,000							
1896O		610,000							
1896S		575,056							
1897	(731)	10,868,533							
1897O		666,000							
1897S		1,342,844							
1898	(735)	16,320,000							
1898O		2,130,000							
1898S		1,702,507							
1899	(846)	19,580,000							
1899O		2,650,000							
1899S		1,867,493							
1900	(912)	17,600,000							
1900O		2,010,000							

Date		Quantity Minted	VG-8	F-12	VF-20	EF-40	MS-60	PF-63		Notes
1900S		5,168,270								
1901	(813)	18,859,665								
19010		5,620,000								
1901S		593,022								
1902	(777)	21,380,000								
19020		4,500,000								
1902S		2,070,000								
1903	(755)	19,500,000								
19030		8,180,000								
1903S		613,300								
1904	(670)	14,600,357								
1904S		800,000								
1905	(727)	14,551,623								
19050										
19050, Micro 0		3,400,000								
1905S		6,855,199								
1906	(675)	19,957,731								
1906D		4,060,000								
19060		2,610,000								
1906S		3,136,640								
1907	(575)	22,220,000								
1907D		4,080,000								
19070		5,058,000								
1907S		3,178,470								
1908	(545)	10,600,000								
1908D		7,490,000								
19080		1,789,000								
1908S		3,220,000								
1909	(650)	10,240,000								
1909D		954,000								
19090		2,287,000								
1909S		1,000,000								
1910	(551)	11,520,000								
1910D		3,490,000								
1910S		1,240,000								
1911	(543)	18,870,000								
1911D		11,209,000								
1911S		3,520,000								
1912	(700)	19,349,300								
1912D		11,760,000								
1912S		3,420,000								
1913	(622)	19,760,000								
1913S		510,000								
1914	(425)	17,360,230								
1914D		11,908,000								
1914S		2,100,000								

Date	Quantity Minted		VG-8	F-12	VF-20	EF-40	MS-60	PF-63		Notes
1915	(450)	5,620,000								
1915S		960,000								
1916		18,490,000								
1916S		5,820,000								

Winged Liberty Head or "Mercury" (1916–1945)

Date	Quantity Minted	VG-8	F-12	VF-20	EF-40	MS-60	MS-65		Notes
1916	22,180,080								
1916D	264,000								
1916S	10,450,000								
1917	55,230,000								
1917D	9,402,000								
1917S	27,330,000								
1918	26,680,000								
1918D	22,674,800								
1918S	19,300,000								
1919	35,740,000								
1919D	9,939,000								
1919S	8,850,000								
1920	59,030,000								
1920D	19,171,000								
1920S	13,820,000								
1921	1,230,000								
1921D	1,080,000								
1923	50,130,000								
1923S	6,440,000								
1924	24,010,000								
1924D	6,810,000								
1924S	7,120,000								
1925	25,610,000								
1925D	5,117,000								
1925S	5,850,000								
1926	32,160,000								
1926D	6,828,000								
1926S	1,520,000								
1927	28,080,000								
1927D	4,812,000								
1927S	4,770,000								
1928	19,480,000								
1928D	4,161,000								

Date	Quantity Minted	VG-8	F-12	VF-20	EF-40	MS-60	MS-65		Notes
1928S	7,400,000								
1929	25,970,000								
1929D	5,034,000								
1929S	4,730,000								
1930	6,770,000								
1930S	1,843,000								
1931	3,150,000								
1931D	1,260,000								
1931S	1,800,000								

Date	Quantity Minted	F-12	VF-20	EF-40	MS-60	MS-65	PF-65		Notes
1934	24,080,000								
1934D	6,772,000								
1935	58,830,000								
1935D	10,477,000								
1935S	15,840,000								
1936 (4,130)	87,500,000								
1936D	16,132,000								
1936S	9,210,000								
1937 (5,756)	56,860,000								
1937D	14,146,000								
1937S	9,740,000								
1938 (8,728)	22,190,000								
1938D	5,537,000								
1938S	8,090,000								
1939 (9,321)	67,740,000								
1939D	24,394,000								
1939S	10,540,000								
1940 (11,827)	65,350,000								
1940D	21,198,000								
1940S	21,560,000								
1941 (16,557)	175,090,000								
1941D	45,634,000								
1941S	43,090,000								
1942, 42 Over 41 / 1942 (22,329)	205,410,000								
1942D, 42 Over 41 / 1942D	60,740,000								
1942S	49,300,000								
1943	191,710,000								
1943D	71,949,000								
1943S	60,400,000								
1944	231,410,000								
1944D	62,224,000								
1944S	49,490,000								

Date	Quantity Minted	F-12	VF-20	EF-40	MS-60	MS-65	PF-65	Notes
1945	159,130,000							
1945D	40,245,000							
1945S	41,920,000							
1945S, Micro S								

Roosevelt, Silver Coinage (1946–1964)

Date	Quantity Minted	EF-40	AU-50	MS-60	MS-63	MS-65	PF-65	Notes
1946	255,250,000							
1946D	61,043,500							
1946S	27,900,000							
1947	121,520,000							
1947D	46,835,000							
1947S	34,840,000							
1948	74,950,000							
1948D	52,841,000							
1948S	35,520,000							
1949	30,940,000							
1949D	26,034,000							
1949S	13,510,000							
1950	(51,386) 50,130,114							
1950D	46,803,000							
1950S	20,440,000							
1951	(57,500) 103,880,102							
1951D	56,529,000							
1951S	31,630,000							
1952	(81,980) 99,040,093							
1952D	122,100,000							
1952S	44,419,500							
1953	(128,800) 53,490,120							
1953D	136,433,000							
1953S	39,180,000							
1954	(233,300) 114,010,203							
1954D	106,397,000							
1954S	22,860,000							
1955	(378,200) 12,450,181							
1955D	13,959,000							
1955S	18,510,000							
1956	(669,384) 108,640,000							
1956D	108,015,100							
1957	(1,247,952) 160,160,000							

Date		Quantity Minted	EF-40	AU-50	MS-60	MS-63	MS-65	PF-65	Notes
1957D		113,354,330							
1958	(875,652)	31,910,000							
1958D		136,564,600							
1959	(1,149,291)	85,780,000							
1959D		164,919,790							
1960	(1,691,602)	70,390,000							
1960, DblDie Obv									
1960D		200,160,400							
1961	(3,028,244)	93,730,000							
1961D		209,146,550							
1962	(3,218,019)	72,450,000							
1962D		334,948,380							
1963	(3,075,645)	123,650,000							
1963, DblDie Rev									
1963D		421,476,530							
1964	(3,950,762)	929,360,000							
1964D		1,357,517,180							
1964D, DblDie Rev									

Roosevelt, Clad Coinage and Silver Proofs (1965 to Date)

Date		Quantity Minted	AU-50	MS-60	MS-63	MS-65	PF-65	Notes
1965		1,652,140,570						
1966		1,382,734,540						
1967		2,244,007,320						
1968		424,470,400						
1968D		480,748,280						
1968S	(3,041,506)							
1969		145,790,000						
1969D		563,323,870						
1969S	(2,394,631)							
1970		345,570,000						
1970D		754,942,100						
1970S	(2,632,810)							
1971		162,690,000						
1971D		377,914,240						
1971S	(3,220,733)							
1972		431,540,000						
1972D		330,290,000						
1972S	(3,260,996)							
1973		315,670,000						
1973D		455,032,426						
1973S	(2,760,339)							
1974		470,248,000						
1974D		571,083,000						
1974S	(2,612,568)							

Date	Quantity Minted	AU-50	MS-60	MS-63	MS-65	PF-65				Notes
1975	585,673,900									
1975D	313,705,300									
1975S	(2,845,450)									
1976	568,760,000									
1976D	695,222,774									
1976S	(4,149,730)									
1977	796,930,000									
1977D	376,607,228									
1977S	(3,251,152)									
1978	663,980,000									
1978D	282,847,540									
1978S	(3,127,781)									
1979	315,440,000									
1979D	390,921,184									
1979S, Type 1	(3,677,175)									
1979S, Type 2										
1980P	735,170,000									
1980D	719,354,321									
1980S	(3,554,806)									
1981P	676,650,000									
1981D	712,284,143									
1981S, Type 1	(4,063,083)									
1982S, Type 2										
1982, No Mintmark										
1982P	519,475,000									
1982D	542,713,584									
1982S	(3,857,479)									
1983P	647,025,000									
1983D	730,129,224									
1983S	(3,279,126)									
1984P	856,669,000									
1984D	704,803,976									
1984S	(3,065,110)									
1985P	705,200,962									
1985D	587,979,970									
1985S	(3,362,821)									
1986P	682,649,693									
1986D	473,326,970									
1986S	(3,010,497)									
1987P	762,709,481									
1987D	653,203,402									
1987S	(4,227,728)									
1988P	1,030,550,000									
1988D	962,385,489									
1988S	(3,262,948)									
1989P	1,298,400,000									

Date	Quantity Minted	AU-50	MS-60	MS-63	MS-65	PF-65			Notes
1989D	896,535,597								
1989S	(3,220,194)					.			
1990P	1,034,340,000								
1990D	839,995,824								
1990S	(3,299,559)								
1991P	927,220,000								
1991D	601,241,114								
1991S	(2,867,787)								
1992P	593,500,000								
1992D	616,273,932								
1992S	(2,858,981)								
1992S, Silver	(1,317,579)								
1993P	766,180,000								
1993D	750,110,166								
1993S	(2,633,439)								
1993S, Silver	(761,353)								
1994P	1,189,000,000								
1994D	1,303,268,110								
1994S	(2,484,594)								
1994S, Silver	(785,329)								
1995P	1,125,500,000								
1995D	1,274,890,000								
1995S	(2,117,496)								
1995S, Silver	(679,985)								
1996P	1,421,163,000								
1996D	1,400,300,000								
1996W	1,457,000								
1996S	(1,750,244)								
1996S, Silver	(775,021)								
1997P	991,640,000								
1997D	979,810,000								
1997S	(2,055,000)								
1997S, Silver	(741,678)								
1998P	1,163,000,000								
1998D	1,172,250,000								
1998S	(2,086,507)								
1998S, Silver	(878,792)								
1999P	2,164,000,000								
1999D	1,397,750,000								
1999S	(2,543,401)								
1999S, Silver	(804,565)								
2000P	1,842,500,000								
2000D	1,818,700,000								
2000S	(3,082,572)								
2000S, Silver	(965,421)								

Date	Quantity Minted	AU-50	MS-60	MS-63	MS-65	PF-65			Notes
2001P	1,369,590,000								
2001D	1,412,800,000								
2001S	(2,294,909)								
2001S, Silver	(889,697)								
2002P	1,187,500,000								
2002D	1,379,500,000								
2002S	(2,319,766)								
2002S, Silver	(892,229)								
2003P	1,085,500,000								
2003D	986,500,000								
2003S	(2,172,684)								
2003S, Silver	(1,125,755)								
2004P	1,328,000,000								
2004D	1,159,500,000								
2004S	(1,789,488)								
2004S, Silver	(1,175,934)								
2005P	1,412,000,000								
2005D	1,423,500,000								
2005S	(2,275,000)								
2005S, Silver	(1,069,679)								
2006P	1,381,000,000								
2006D	1,447,000,000								
2006S	(2,000,428)								
2006S, Silver	(1,054,008)								
2007P	1,047,500,000								
2007D	1,042,000,000								
2007S	(1,702,116)								
2007S, Silver	(875,050)								
2008P	391,000,000								
2008D	624,500,000								
2008S	(1,405,674)								
2008S, Silver	(763,887)								
2009P	96,500,000								
2009D	49,500,000								
2009S	(1,482,502)								
2009S, Silver	(697,365)								
2010P	557,000,000								
2010D	562,000,000								
2010S	(1,103,950)								
2010S, Silver	(585,414)								
2011P	664,000,000								
2011D	664,000,000								
2011S	(952,881)								
2011S, Silver	(500,395)								

Date	Quantity Minted	AU-50	MS-60	MS-63	MS-65	PF-65	Notes
2012P							
2012D							
2012S							
2012S, Silver							

TWENTY-CENT PIECES

Liberty Seated (1875–1878)

Date	Quantity Minted		VG-8	F-12	VF-20	EF-40	MS-60	PF-63	Notes
1875	(2,790)	36,910							
1875CC		133,290							
1875S		1,155,000							
1876	(1,260)	14,640							
1876CC		10,000							
1877	(510)								
1878	(600)								

QUARTER DOLLARS

Draped Bust, Small Eagle Reverse (1796)

Date	Quantity Minted	G-4	VG-8	F-12	VF-20	EF-40	MS-60	Notes
1796	6,146							

Draped Bust, Heraldic Eagle Reverse (1804–1807)

Date	Quantity Minted	G-4	VG-8	F-12	VF-20	EF-40	MS-60	Notes
1804	6,738							
1805	121,394							
1806, 6 Over 5	206,124							
1806								
1807	220,643							

Capped Bust, Variety 1, Large Diameter (1815–1828)

Date	Quantity Minted	G-4	VG-8	F-12	VF-20	EF-40	MS-60	Notes
1815	89,235							
1818, 8 Over 5	361,174							
1818, Normal Date								

Date	Quantity Minted	G-4	VG-8	F-12	VF-20	EF-40	MS-60	Notes
1819, Small 9	144,000							
1819, Large 9								
1820, Small 0	127,444							
1820, Large 0								
1821	216,851							
1822	64,080							
1822, 25 Over 50c								
1823, 3 Over 2	17,800							
1824, 4 Over 2	168,000							
1825, 5 Over 2								
1825, 5 Over 4								
1827, Original (Curl Base 2 in 25c)	4,000							
1827, Restrike (Sq Base 2 in 25c)								
1828	102,000							
1828, 25 Over 50c								

Capped Bust, Variety 2, Reduced Diameter (1831–1838), Motto Removed

Date	Quantity Minted	G-4	VG-8	F-12	VF-20	EF-40	MS-60	Notes
1831, Small Letters	398,000							
1831, Large Letters								
1832	320,000							
1833	156,000							
1834	286,000							
1834, O Over F in OF								
1835	1,952,000							
1836	472,000							
1837	252,400							
1838	366,000							

Liberty Seated, Variety 1, No Motto Above Eagle (1838–1853)

Date	Quantity Minted	G-4	VG-8	F-12	VF-20	EF-40	MS-60	Notes
1838, No Drapery	466,000							
1839, No Drapery	491,146							
1840O, No Drapery	382,200							
1840, Drapery	188,127							
1840O, Drapery	43,000							
1841	120,000							
1841O	452,000							
1842, Small Date (Proof only)								
1842, Large Date	88,000							
1842O, Small Date	769,000							
1842O, Large Date								
1843	645,600							
1843O	968,000							
1844	421,200							
1844O	740,000							
1845	922,000							
1846	510,000							
1847	734,000							
1847O	368,000							
1848	146,000							
1849	340,000							
1849O	*							
1850	190,800							
1850O	412,000							
1851	160,000							
1851O	88,000							
1852	177,060							
1852O	96,000							
1853, Recut Date, No Arrows or Rays	44,200							

* Included in 1850-O mintage.

Liberty Seated, Variety 2, Arrows at Date, Rays Around Eagle (1853)

Date	Quantity Minted	G-4	VG-8	F-12	VF-20	EF-40	MS-60	Notes
1853	15,210,020							
1853, 3 Over 4								
1853O	1,332,000							

Liberty Seated, Variety 3, Arrows at Date, No Rays (1854–1855)

Date	Quantity Minted	G-4	VG-8	F-12	VF-20	EF-40	MS-60	Notes
1854	12,380,000							
1854O	1,484,000							
1854O, Huge O								
1855	2,857,000							
1855O	176,000							
1855S	396,400							

Liberty Seated, Variety 1 Resumed, With Weight Standard of Variety 2 (1856–1865)

Date		Quantity Minted	G-4	VG-8	F-12	VF-20	EF-40	MS-60	Notes
1856		7,264,000							
1856O		968,000							
1856S		286,000							
1856S, S Over Small S									
1857		9,644,000							
1857O		1,180,000							
1857S		82,000							
1858	*(300)*	7,368,000							
1858O		520,000							
1858S		121,000							
1859	*(800)*	1,343,200							
1859O		260,000							
1859S		80,000							
1860	*(1,000)*	804,400							
1860O		388,000							
1860S		56,000							
1861	*(1,000)*	4,853,600							
1861S		96,000							
1862	*(550)*	932,000							
1862S		67,000							
1863	*(460)*	191,600							
1864	*(470)*	93,600							
1864S		20,000							
1865	*(500)*	58,800							
1865S		41,000							
1866 *(unique, not a regular issue)*									

Liberty Seated, Variety 4, Motto Above Eagle (1866–1873)

Date		Quantity Minted	VG-8	F-12	VF-20	EF-40	MS-60	PF-60		Notes
1866	(725)	16,800								
1866S		28,000								
1867	(625)	20,000								
1867S		48,000								
1868	(600)	29,400								
1868S		96,000								
1869	(600)	16,000								
1869S		76,000								
1870	(1,000)	86,400								
1870CC		8,340								
1871	(960)	118,200								
1871CC		10,890								
1871S		30,900								
1872	(950)	182,000								
1872CC		22,850								
1872S		83,000								
1873, Close 3	(600)	40,000								
1873, Open 3		172,000								
1873CC (5 known)		4,000								

Liberty Seated, Variety 5, Arrows at Date (1873–1874)

Date		Quantity Minted	VG-8	F-12	VF-20	EF-40	MS-60	PF-60		Notes
1873	(540)	1,271,160								
1873CC		12,462								
1873S		156,000								
1874	(700)	471,200								
1874S		392,000								

Liberty Seated, Variety 4 Resumed, With Weight Standard of Variety 5 (1875–1891)

Date		Quantity Minted	VG-8	F-12	VF-20	EF-40	MS-60	PF-60	Notes
1875	(700)	4,292,800							
1875CC		140,000							
1875S		680,000							
1876	(1,150)	17,816,000							
1876CC		4,944,000							
1876S		8,596,000							
1877	(510)	10,911,200							
1877CC		4,192,000							
1877S 1877S, S Over Horizontal S		8,996,000							
1878	(800)	2,260,000							
1878CC		996,000							
1878S		140,000							
1879	(1,100)	13,600							
1880	(1,355)	13,600							
1881	(975)	12,000							
1882	(1,100)	15,200							
1883	(1,039)	14,400							
1884	(875)	8,000							
1885	(930)	13,600							
1886	(886)	5,000							
1887	(710)	10,000							
1888	(832)	10,001							
1888S		1,216,000							
1889	(711)	12,000							
1890	(590)	80,000							
1891	(600)	3,920,000							
18910		6,800							
1891S		2,216,000							

Barber or Liberty Head (1892–1916)

Date	Quantity Minted		VG-8	F-12	VF-20	EF-40	MS-60	PF-63	Notes
1892	(1,245)	8,236,000							
1892O		2,460,000							
1892S		964,079							
1893	(792)	5,444,023							
1893O		3,396,000							
1893S		1,454,535							
1894	(972)	3,432,000							
1894O		2,852,000							
1894S		2,648,821							
1895	(880)	4,440,000							
1895O		2,816,000							
1895S		1,764,681							
1896	(762)	3,874,000							
1896O		1,484,000							
1896S		188,039							
1897	(731)	8,140,000							
1897O		1,414,800							
1897S		542,229							
1898	(735)	11,100,000							
1898O		1,868,000							
1898S		1,020,592							
1899	(846)	12,624,000							
1899O		2,644,000							
1899S		708,000							
1900	(912)	10,016,000							
1900O		3,416,000							
1900S		1,858,585							
1901	(813)	8,892,000							
1901O		1,612,000							
1901S		72,664							
1902	(777)	12,196,967							
1902O		4,748,000							
1902S		1,524,612							
1903	(755)	9,759,309							
1903O		3,500,000							
1903S		1,036,000							

Date		Quantity Minted	VG-8	F-12	VF-20	EF-40	MS-60	PF-63		Notes
1904	(670)	9,588,143								
1904O		2,456,000								
1905	(727)	4,967,523								
1905O		1,230,000								
1905S		1,884,000								
1906	(675)	3,655,760								
1906D		3,280,000								
1906O		2,056,000								
1907	(575)	7,132,000								
1907D		2,484,000								
1907O		4,560,000								
1907S		1,360,000								
1908	(545)	4,232,000								
1908D		5,788,000								
1908O		6,244,000								
1908S		784,000								
1909	(650)	9,268,000								
1909D		5,114,000								
1909O		712,000								
1909S		1,348,000								
1910	(551)	2,244,000								
1910D		1,500,000								
1911	(543)	3,720,000								
1911D		933,600								
1911S		988,000								
1912	(700)	4,400,000								
1912S		708,000								
1913	(613)	484,000								
1913D		1,450,800								
1913S		40,000								
1914	(380)	6,244,230								
1914D		3,046,000								
1914S		264,000								
1915	(450)	3,480,000								
1915D		3,694,000								
1915S		704,000								
1916		1,788,000								
1916D		6,540,800								

Standing Liberty, Variety 1, No Stars Below Eagle (1916–1917)

Date	Quantity Minted	VG-8	F-12	VF-20	EF-40	MS-60	PF-63	Notes
1916	52,000							
1917, Variety 1	8,740,000							
1917D, Variety 1	1,509,200							
1917S, Variety 1	1,952,000							

Standing Liberty, Variety 2, Stars Below Eagle, Pedestal Date (1917–1924)

Date	Quantity Minted	VG-8	F-12	VF-20	EF-40	MS-60	PF-63	Notes
1917, Variety 2	13,880,000							
1917D, Variety 2	6,224,400							
1917S, Variety 2	5,552,000							
1918	14,240,000							
1918D	7,380,000							
1918S, Normal Date	11,072,000							
1918S, 8 Over 7								
1919	11,324,000							
1919D	1,944,000							
1919S	1,836,000							
1920	27,860,000							
1920D	3,586,400							
1920S	6,380,000							
1921	1,916,000							
1923	9,716,000							
1923S	1,360,000							
1924	10,920,000							
1924D	3,112,000							
1924S	2,860,000							

Date	Quantity Minted	F-12	VF-20	EF-40	MS-60	MS-65	PF-65	Notes
1952S	13,707,800							
1953	(128,800) 18,536,120							
1953D	56,112,400							
1953S	14,016,000							
1954	(233,300) 54,412,203							
1954D	42,305,500							
1954S	11,834,722							
1955	(378,200) 18,180,181							
1955D	3,182,400							
1956	(669,384) 44,144,000							
1956D	32,334,500							
1957	(1,247,952) 46,532,000							
1957D	77,924,160							
1958	(875,652) 6,360,000							
1958D	78,124,900							
1959	(1,149,291) 24,384,000							
1959D	62,054,232							
1960	(1,691,602) 29,164,000							
1960D	63,000,324							
1961	(3,028,244) 37,036,000							
1961D	83,656,928							
1962	(3,218,019) 36,156,000							
1962D	127,554,756							
1963	(3,075,645) 74,316,000							
1963D	135,288,184							
1964	(3,950,762) 560,390,585							
1964D	704,135,528							

Washington, Clad Coinage (1965–1974)

Date	Quantity Minted	VF-20	EF-40	MS-60	MS-65	PF-65	Notes
1965	1,819,717,540						
1966	821,101,500						
1967	1,524,031,848						
1968	220,731,500						
1968D	101,534,000						
1968S	(3,041,506)						
1969	176,212,000						
1969D	114,372,000						
1969S	(2,934,631)						
1970	136,420,000						
1970D	417,341,364						
1970S	(2,632,810)						
1971	109,284,000						
1971D	258,634,428						
1971S	(3,220,733)						

Date	Quantity Minted	VF-20	EF-40	MS-60	MS-65	PF-65			Notes
1972	215,048,000								
1972D	311,067,732								
1972S	(3,260,996)								
1973	346,924,000								
1973D	232,977,400								
1973S	(2,760,339)								
1974	801,456,000								
1974D	353,160,300								
1974S	(2,612,568)								

Washington, Bicentennial Coinage (Dated 1776–1976)

Date	Quantity Minted	VF-20	EF-40	MS-60	MS-65	PF-65			Notes
1776–1976, C-N Clad	809,784,016								
1776–1976D, C-N Clad	860,118,839								
1776–1976S, C-N Clad	(7,059,099)								
1776–1976S, Slv Clad	(11,000,000)								
1776–1976S, Slv Clad	(4,000,000)								

Washington, Eagle Reverse Resumed (1977–1998)

Date	Quantity Minted	AU-50	MS-60	MS-65	PF-65			Notes
1977	468,556,000							
1977D	256,524,978							
1977S	(3,251,152)							
1978	521,452,000							
1978D	287,373,152							
1978S	(3,127,781)							
1979	515,708,000							
1979D	489,789,780							
1979S, Type 1	(3,677,175)							
1979S, Type 2								
1980P	635,832,000							
1980D	518,327,487							
1980S	(3,554,806)							
1981P	601,716,000							
1981D	575,722,833							
1981S, Type 1	(4,063,083)							
1981S, Type 2								
1982P	500,931,000							

Date	Quantity Minted	MS-63	MS-65	PF-65			Notes
1999S, Connecticut	(3,713,359)						
1999S, Connecticut, Silver	(804,565)						

Date	Quantity Minted	MS-63	MS-65	PF-65			Notes
2000P, Massachusetts	628,600,000						
2000D, Massachusetts	535,184,000						
2000S, Massachusetts	(4,020,172)						
2000S, Massachusetts, Silver	(965,421)						
2000P, Maryland	678,200,000						
2000D, Maryland	556,532,000						
2000S, Maryland	(4,020,172)						
2000S, Maryland, Silver	(965,421)						
2000P, South Carolina	742,576,000						
2000D, South Carolina	566,208,000						
2000S, South Carolina	(4,020,172)						
2000S, South Carolina, Silver	(965,421)						
2000P, New Hampshire	673,040,000						
2000D, New Hampshire	495,976,000						
2000S, New Hampshire	(4,020,172)						
2000S, New Hampshire, Silver	(965,421)						
2000P, Virginia	943,000,000						
2000D, Virginia	651,616,000						
2000S, Virginia	(4,020,172)						
2000S, Virginia, Silver	(965,421)						

Date	Quantity Minted	MS-63	MS-65	PF-65			Notes
2001P, New York	655,400,000						
2001D, New York	619,640,000						
2001S, New York	(3,094,140)						
2001S, New York, Silver	(889,697)						
2001P, North Carolina	627,600,000						
2001D, North Carolina	427,876,000						

Date		Quantity Minted	MS-63	MS-65	PF-65				Notes
2001S, North Carolina	(3,094,140)								
2001S, North Carolina, Silver	(889,697)								
2001P, Rhode Island		423,000,000							
2001D, Rhode Island		447,100,000							
2001S, Rhode Island	(3,094,140)								
2001S, Rhode Island, Silver	(889,697)								
2001P, Vermont		423,400,000							
2001D, Vermont		459,404,000							
2001S, Vermont	(3,094,140)								
2001S, Vermont, Silver	(889,697)								
2001P, Kentucky		353,000,000							
2001D, Kentucky		370,564,000							
2001S, Kentucky	(3,094,140)								
2001S, Kentucky, Silver	(889,697)								

Date		Quantity Minted	MS-63	MS-65	PF-65				Notes
2002P, Tennessee		361,600,000							
2002D, Tennessee		286,468,000							
2002S, Tennessee	(3,084,245)								
2002S, Tennessee, Silver	(892,229)								
2002P, Ohio		217,200,000							
2002D, Ohio		414,832,000							
2002S, Ohio	(3,084,245)								
2002S, Ohio, Silver	(892,229)								
2002P, Louisiana		362,000,000							
2002D, Louisiana		402,204,000							
2002S, Louisiana	(3,084,245)								
2002S, Louisiana, Silver	(892,229)								
2002P, Indiana		362,600,000							
2002D, Indiana		327,200,000							
2002S, Indiana	(3,084,245)								
2002S, Indiana, Silver	(892,229)								
2002P, Mississippi		290,000,000							
2002D, Mississippi		289,600,000							
2002S, Mississippi	(3,084,245)								
2002S, Mississippi, Silver	(892,229)								

Date	Quantity Minted	MS-63	MS-65	PF-65				Notes
2006P, Nevada	277,000,000							
2006D, Nevada	312,800,000							
2006S, Nevada	(2,882,428)							
2006S, Nevada, Silver	(1,585,008)							
2006P, Nebraska	318,000,000							
2006D, Nebraska	273,000,000							
2006S, Nebraska	(2,882,428)							
2006S, Nebraska, Silver	(1,585,008)							
2006P, Colorado	274,800,000							
2006D, Colorado	294,200,000							
2006S, Colorado	(2,882,428)							
2006S, Colorado, Silver	(1,585,008)							
2006P, North Dakota	305,800,000							
2006D, North Dakota	359,000,000							
2006S, North Dakota	(2,882,428)							
2006S, North Dakota, Silver	(1,585,008)							
2006P, South Dakota	245,000,000							
2006D, South Dakota	265,800,000							
2006S, South Dakota	(2,882,428)							
2006S, South Dakota, Silver	(1,585,008)							

Date	Quantity Minted	MS-63	MS-65	PF-65				Notes
2007P, Montana	257,000,000							
2007D, Montana	256,240,000							
2007S, Montana	(2,374,778)							
2007S, Montana, Silver	(1,313,481)							
2007P, Washington	265,200,000							
2007D, Washington	280,000,000							
2007S, Washington	(2,374,778)							
2007S, Washington, Silver	(1,313,481)							
2007P, Idaho	294,600,000							
2007D, Idaho	286,800,000							
2007S, Idaho	(2,374,778)							
2007S, Idaho, Silver	(1,313,481)							
2007P, Wyoming	243,600,000							
2007D, Wyoming	320,800,000							
2007S, Wyoming	(2,374,778)							
2007S, Wyoming, Silver	(1,313,481)							

Date	Quantity Minted	MS-63	MS-65	PF-65				Notes
2007P, Utah	255,000,000							
2007D, Utah	253,200,000							
2007S, Utah	(2,374,778)							
2007S, Utah, Silver	(1,313,481)							

Date	Quantity Minted	MS-63	MS-65	PF-65				Notes
2008P, Oklahoma	222,000,000							
2008D, Oklahoma	194,600,000							
2008S, Oklahoma	(2,078,112)							
2008S, Oklahoma, Silver	(1,192,908)							
2008P, New Mexico	244,200,000							
2008D, New Mexico	244,400,000							
2008S, New Mexico	(2,078,112)							
2008S, New Mexico, Silver	(1,192,908)							
2008P, Arizona	244,600,000							
2008D, Arizona	265,000,000							
2008S, Arizona	(2,078,112)							
2008S, Arizona, Silver	(1,192,908)							
2008P, Alaska	251,800,000							
2008D, Alaska	254,000,000							
2008S, Alaska	(2,078,112)							
2008S, Alaska, Silver	(1,192,908)							
2008P, Hawaii	254,000,000							
2008D, Hawaii	263,600,000							
2008S, Hawaii	(2,078,112)							
2008S, Hawaii, Silver	(1,192,908)							

District of Columbia and U.S. Territories (2009)

Date	Quantity Minted	MS-63	MS-65	PF-65				Notes
2012P, El Yunque National Forest (PR)								
2012D, El Yunque National Forest (PR)								
2012S, El Yunque National Forest (PR)								
2012S, El Yunque Nat'l Forest (PR), Silver								
2012P, Chaco Culture Nat'l Hist Park (NM)								
2012D, Chaco Culture Nat'l Hist Park (NM)								
2012S, Chaco Culture Nat'l Hist Park (NM)								
2012S, Chaco Culture Nat'l Hist Park (NM), Silver								
2012P, Acadia National Park (ME)								
2012D, Acadia National Park (ME)								
2012S, Acadia National Park (ME)								
2012S, Acadia National Park (ME), Silver								
2012P, Hawai'i Volcanoes Nat'l Park (HI)								
2012D, Hawai'i Volcanoes Nat'l Park (HI)								
2012S, Hawai'i Volcanoes Nat'l Park (HI)								
2012S, Hawai'i Volcanoes Nat'l Park (HI), Silver								
2012P, Denali Nat'l Park and Preserve (AK)								
2012D, Denali Nat'l Park and Preserve (AK)								
2012S, Denali Nat'l Park and Preserve (AK)								
2012S, Denali Nat'l Park and Preserve (AK), Silver								

HALF DOLLARS

Flowing Hair (1794–1795)

Date	Quantity Minted	AG-3	G-4	VG-8	F-12	VF-20	EF-40		Notes
1794	23,464								
1795, Normal Date									
1795, Recut Date	299,680								
1795, 3 Leaves Under Each Wing									

Draped Bust, Small Eagle Reverse (1796–1797)

Date	Quantity Minted	AG-3	G-4	VG-8	F-12	VF-20	EF-40	Notes
1796, 15 Stars								
1796, 16 Stars	3,918							
1797, 15 Stars								

Draped Bust, Heraldic Eagle Reverse (1801–1807)

Date	Quantity Minted	G-4	VG-8	F-12	VF-20	EF-40	MS-60	Notes
1801	30,289							
1802	29,890							
1803, Small 3	188,234							
1803, Large 3								
1805, 5 Over 4	211,722							
1805, Normal Date								
1806, 6 Over 5								
1806, 6 Over Inverted 6								
1806, Knobbed 6, Large Stars (Traces of Overdate)								
1806, Knobbed 6, Small Stars								
1806, Knobbed 6, Stem Not Through Claw	839,576							
1806, Pointed 6, Stem Through Claw								
1806, E Over A in STATES								
1806, Pointed 6, Stem Not Through Claw								
1807	301,076							

Capped Bust, Lettered Edge, First Style (1807–1808)

Date	Quantity Minted	G-4	VG-8	F-12	VF-20	EF-40	MS-60		Notes
1807, Small Stars									
1807, Large Stars	750,500								
1807, Large Stars, 50 Over 20									
1807, "Bearded" Liberty									
1808, 8 Over 7	1,368,600								
1808									

Capped Bust, Lettered Edge, Remodeled Portrait and Eagle (1809–1836)

Date	Quantity Minted	G-4	VG-8	F-12	VF-20	EF-40	MS-60		Notes
1809, Normal Edge									
1809, xxxx Edge	1,405,810								
1809, lllll Edge									
1810	1,276,276								
1811, (18.11), 11 Over 10									
1811, Small 8	1,203,644								
1811, Large 8									
1812, 2 Over 1, Small 8									
1812, 2 Over 1, Large 8	1,628,059								
1812									
1812, Single Leaf Below Wing									
1813	1,241,903								
1813, 50 C. Over UNI									
1814, 4 Over 3									
1814, E Over A in STATES	1,039,075								
1814									
1814, Single Leaf Below Wing									

Date	Quantity Minted	G-4	VG-8	F-12	VF-20	EF-40	MS-60	Notes
1815, 5 Over 2	47,150							
1817, 7 Over 3								
1817, 7 Over 4 (8 known)								
1817, Dated 181.7	1,215,567							
1817								
1817, Single Leaf Below Wing								
1818, 8 Over 7, Small 8								
1818, 8 Over 7, Large 8	1,960,322							
1818								
1819, Small 9 Over 8								
1819, Large 9 Over 8	2,208,000							
1819								
1820, 20 Over 19, Square 2								
1820, 20 Over 19, Curl Base 2								
1820, Curl Base 2, Small Date								
1820, Square Base Knob 2, Large Date	751,122							
1820, Square Base No Knob 2, Large Date								
1820, No Serifs on E's								
1821	1,305,797							
1822	1,559,573							
1822, 2 Over 1								
1823, Broken 3								
1823, Patched 3	1,694,200							
1823, Ugly 3								
1823, Normal								
1824, 4 Over Various Dates								
1824, 4 Over 1	3,504,954							
1824, 4 Over 4 (2 varieties)								
1824, Normal								
1825	2,943,166							
1826	4,004,180							
1827, 7 Over 6								
1827, Square Base 2	5,493,400							
1827, Curl Base 2								
1828, Curl Base No Knob 2								
1828, Curl Base Knob 2								
1828, Square Base 2, Large 8's								
1828, Square Base 2, Small 8's, Large Letters	3,075,200							
1828, Square Base 2, Small 8's and Letters								
1829, 9 Over 7								
1829	3,712,156							
1829, Large Letters								

Date	Quantity Minted	G-4	VG-8	F-12	VF-20	EF-40	MS-60	Notes
1830, Small 0								
1830, Large 0	4,764,800							
1830, Large Letters								
1831	5,873,660							
1832	4,797,000							
1832, Large Letters								
1833	5,206,000							
1834, Large Date and Letters								
1834, Large Date, Small Letters	6,412,004							
1834, Small Date, Stars, Letters								
1835	5,352,006							
1836								
1836 Over 1336	6,545,000							
1836, 50 Over 00								
1836, Beaded Border on Rev								

Capped Bust, Reeded Edge, Reverse 50 CENTS (1836–1837)

Date	Quantity Minted	G-4	VG-8	F-12	VF-20	EF-40	MS-60	Notes
1836	*1,200+*							
1837	3,629,820							

Capped Bust, Reeded Edge, Reverse HALF DOL. (1838–1839)

Date	Quantity Minted	G-4	VG-8	F-12	VF-20	EF-40	MS-60	Notes
1838	3,546,000							
18380	20							
1839	1,392,976							

Date	Quantity Minted	G-4	VG-8	F-12	VF-20	EF-40	MS-60	Notes
1839, Small Letters Reverse *(extremely rare)*								
18390	116,000							

Liberty Seated, Variety 1, No Motto Above Eagle (1839–1853)

Date	Quantity Minted	G-4	VG-8	F-12	VF-20	EF-40	MS-60	Notes
1839, No Drapery From Elbow	1,972,400							
1839, Drapery From Elbow								
1840, Small Letters	1,435,008							
1840, Medium Letters								
18400	855,100							
1841	310,000							
18410	401,000							
1842, Small Date, Small Letters	*							
18420, Small Date, Small Letters	203,000							
1842, Medium Date	2,012,764							
1842, Small Date								
18420, Medium Date	754,000							
1843	3,844,000							
18430	2,268,000							
1844	1,766,000							
18440	2,005,000							
18440, Doubled Date								
1845	589,000							
18450	2,094,000							
18450, No Drapery								
1846, Medium Date	2,210,000							
1846, Tall Date								
1846, 6 Over Horizontal 6								
18460, Medium Date	2,304,000							
18460, Tall Date								
1847, 7 Over 6	1,156,000							
1847								
18470	2,584,000							
1848	580,000							
18480	3,180,000							
1849	1,252,000							

* Included in 1842, Medium Date mintage.

Date	Quantity Minted	G-4	VG-8	F-12	VF-20	EF-40	MS-60		Notes
18490	2,310,000								
1850	227,000								
18500	2,456,000								
1851	200,750								
18510	402,000								
1852	77,130								
18520	144,000								
18530 *(3 known)*									

Liberty Seated, Variety 2, Arrows at Date, Rays Around Eagle (1853)

Date	Quantity Minted	G-4	VG-8	F-12	VF-20	EF-40	MS-60		Notes
1853	3,532,708								
18530	1,328,000								

Liberty Seated, Variety 3, Arrows at Date, No Rays (1854–1855)

Date	Quantity Minted	G-4	VG-8	F-12	VF-20	EF-40	MS-60		Notes
1854	2,982,000								
18540	5,240,000								
1855 Over 1854	759,500								
1855, Normal Date									
18550	3,688,000								
1855S	129,950								

Liberty Seated, Variety 1 Resumed, With Weight Standard of Variety 2 (1856–1866)

Date	Quantity Minted	VG-8	F-12	VF-20	EF-40	MS-60	PF-60		Notes
1856	938,000								
18560	2,658,000								
1856S	211,000								
1857	1,988,000								
18570	818,000								
1857S	158,000								
1858 *(300+)*	4,225,700								
18580	7,294,000								
1858S	476,000								

Date		Quantity Minted	VG-8	F-12	VF-20	EF-40	MS-60	PF-60		Notes
1859	(800)	747,200								
1859O		2,834,000								
1859S		566,000								
1860	(1,000)	302,700								
1860O		1,290,000								
1860S		472,000								
1861	(1,000)	2,887,400								
1861O		2,532,633								
1861O, Cracked Obverse										
1861S		939,500								
1862	(550)	253,000								
1862S		1,352,000								
1863	(460)	503,200								
1863S		916,000								
1864	(470)	379,100								
1864S		658,000								
1865	(500)	511,400								
1865S		675,000								
1866S, No Motto		60,000								
1866 *(unique, not a regular issue)*										

Liberty Seated, Variety 4, Motto Above Eagle (1866–1873)

Date		Quantity Minted	VG-8	F-12	VF-20	EF-40	MS-60	PF-63		Notes
1866	(725)	744,900								
1866S		994,000								
1867	(625)	449,300								
1867S		1,196,000								
1868	(600)	417,600								
1868S		1,160,000								
1869	(600)	795,300								
1869S		656,000								
1870	(1,000)	633,900								
1870CC		54,617								
1870S		1,004,000								
1871	(960)	1,203,600								
1871CC		153,950								
1871S		2,178,000								

Date		Quantity Minted	VG-8	F-12	VF-20	EF-40	MS-60	PF-63		Notes
1872	(950)	880,600								
1872CC		257,000								
1872S		580,000								
1873, Close 3	(600)	587,000								
1873, Open 3		214,200								
1873CC		122,500								
1873S, No Arrows *(unknown in any collection)*		5,000								

Liberty Seated, Variety 5, Arrows at Date (1873–1874)

Date		Quantity Minted	VG-8	F-12	VF-20	EF-40	MS-60	PF-63		Notes
1873	(550)	1,815,150								
1873CC		214,560								
1873S		228,000								
1874	(700)	2,359,600								
1874CC		59,000								
1874S		394,000								

Liberty Seated, Variety 4 Resumed, With Weight Standard of Variety 5 (1875–1891)

Date		Quantity Minted	VG-8	F-12	VF-20	EF-40	MS-60	PF-63		Notes
1875	(700)	6,026,800								
1875CC		1,008,000								
1875S		3,200,000								
1876	(1,150)	8,418,000								
1876CC		1,956,000								
1876S		4,528,000								
1877	(510)	8,304,000								
1877, 7 Over 6										
1877CC		1,420,000								
1877S		5,356,000								
1878	(800)	1,377,600								
1878CC		62,000								
1878S		12,000								
1879	(1,100)	4,800								
1880	(1,355)	8,400								
1881	(975)	10,000								

Date	Quantity Minted		VG-8	F-12	VF-20	EF-40	MS-60	PF-63	Notes
1882	(1,100)	4,400							
1883	(1,039)	8,000							
1884	(875)	4,400							
1885	(930)	5,200							
1886	(886)	5,000							
1887	(710)	5,000							
1888	(832)	12,001							
1889	(711)	12,000							
1890	(590)	12,000							
1891	(600)	200,000							

Barber or Liberty Head (1892–1915)

Date	Quantity Minted		VG-8	F-12	VF-20	EF-40	MS-60	PF-63	Notes
1892	(1,245)	934,000							
1892O		390,000							
1892O, Micro O									
1892S		1,029,028							
1893	(792)	1,826,000							
1893O		1,389,000							
1893S		740,000							
1894	(972)	1,148,000							
1894O		2,138,000							
1894S		4,048,690							
1895	(880)	1,834,338							
1895O		1,766,000							
1895S		1,108,086							
1896	(762)	950,000							
1896O		924,000							
1896S		1,140,948							
1897	(731)	2,480,000							
1897O		632,000							
1897S		933,900							
1898	(735)	2,956,000							
1898O		874,000							
1898S		2,358,550							
1899	(846)	5,538,000							
1899O		1,724,000							

Date		Quantity Minted	VG-8	F-12	VF-20	EF-40	MS-60	PF-63		Notes
1899S		1,686,411								
1900	(912)	4,762,000								
1900O		2,744,000								
1900S		2,560,322								
1901	(813)	4,268,000								
1901O		1,124,000								
1901S		847,044								
1902	(777)	4,922,000								
1902O		2,526,000								
1902S		1,460,670								
1903	(755)	2,278,000								
1903O		2,100,000								
1903S		1,920,772								
1904	(670)	2,992,000								
1904O		1,117,600								
1904S		553,038								
1905	(727)	662,000								
1905O		505,000								
1905S		2,494,000								
1906	(675)	2,638,000								
1906D		4,028,000								
1906O		2,446,000								
1906S		1,740,154								
1907	(575)	2,598,000								
1907D		3,856,000								
1907O		3,946,600								
1907S		1,250,000								
1908	(545)	1,354,000								
1908D		3,280,000								
1908O		5,360,000								
1908S		1,644,828								
1909	(650)	2,368,000								
1909O		925,400								
1909S		1,764,000								
1910	(551)	418,000								
1910S		1,948,000								
1911	(543)	1,406,000								
1911D		695,080								
1911S		1,272,000								
1912	(700)	1,550,000								
1912D		2,300,800								
1912S		1,370,000								
1913	(627)	188,000								
1913D		534,000								
1913S		604,000								
1914	(380)	124,230								

Date		Quantity Minted	VG-8	F-12	VF-20	EF-40	MS-60	PF-63	Notes
1914S		992,000							
1915	(450)	138,000							
1915D		1,170,400							
1915S		1,604,000							

Liberty Walking (1916–1947)

Date	Quantity Minted	VG-8	F-12	VF-20	EF-40	MS-60	PF-63	Notes
1916	608,000							
1916D, Obverse Mintmark	1,014,400							
1916S, Obverse Mintmark	508,000							
1917	12,292,000							
1917D, Obverse Mintmark	765,400							
1917D, Reverse Mintmark	1,940,000							
1917S, Obverse Mintmark	952,000							
1917S, Reverse Mintmark	5,554,000							
1918	6,634,000							
1918D	3,853,040							
1918S	10,282,000							
1919	962,000							
1919D	1,165,000							
1919S	1,552,000							
1920	6,372,000							
1920D	1,551,000							
1920S	4,624,000							
1921	246,000							
1921D	208,000							
1921S	548,000							
1923S	2,178,000							
1927S	2,392,000							
1928S	1,940,000							
1929D	1,001,200							
1929S	1,902,000							
1933S	1,786,000							
1934	6,964,000							
1934D	2,361,000							
1934S	3,652,000							
1935	9,162,000							

Date		Quantity Minted	VG-8	F-12	VF-20	EF-40	MS-60	PF-63		Notes
1935D		3,003,800								
1935S		3,854,000								
1936	(3,901)	12,614,000								
1936D		4,252,400								
1936S		3,884,000								
1937	(5,728)	9,522,000								
1937D		1,676,000								
1937S		2,090,000								
1938	(8,152)	4,110,000								
1938D		491,600								
1939	(8,808)	6,812,000								
1939D		4,267,800								
1939S		2,552,000								
1940	(11,279)	9,156,000								
1940S		4,550,000								
1941	(15,412)	24,192,000								
1941D		11,248,400								
1941S		8,098,000								
1942	(21,120)	47,818,000								
1942D		10,973,800								
1942S		12,708,000								
1943		53,190,000								
1943D		11,346,000								
1943S		13,450,000								
1944		28,206,000								
1944D		9,769,000								
1944S		8,904,000								
1945		31,502,000								
1945D		9,966,800								
1945S		10,156,000								
1946		12,118,000								
1946, Doubled-Die Reverse										
1946D		2,151,000								
1946S		3,724,000								
1947		4,094,000								
1947D		3,900,600								

Franklin (1948–1963)

Date	Quantity Minted	VF-20	EF-40	MS-60	MS-63	MS-65	PF-65	Notes
1948	3,006,814							
1948D	4,028,600							
1949	5,614,000							
1949D	4,120,600							
1949S	3,744,000							
1950	(51,386) 7,742,123							
1950D	8,031,600							
1951	(57,500) 16,802,102							
1951D	9,475,200							
1951S	13,696,000							
1952	(81,980) 21,192,093							
1952D	25,395,600							
1952S	5,526,000							
1953	(128,800) 2,668,120							
1953D	20,900,400							
1953S	4,148,000							
1954	(233,300) 13,188,202							
1954D	25,445,580							
1954S	4,993,400							
1955	(378,200) 2,498,181							
1956	(669,384) 4,032,000							
1957	(1,247,952) 5,114,000							
1957D	19,966,850							
1958	(875,652) 4,042,000							
1958D	23,962,412							
1959	(1,149,291) 6,200,000							
1959D	13,053,750							
1960	(1,691,602) 6,024,000							
1960D	18,215,812							
1961	8,290,000							
1961, Doubled-Die Proof	(3,028,244)							
1961D	20,276,442							
1962	(3,218,019) 9,714,000							
1962D	35,473,281							

Date		Quantity Minted	VF-20	EF-40	MS-60	MS-63	MS-65	PF-65		Notes
1963	(3,075,645)	22,164,000								
1963D		67,069,292								

Kennedy, Silver Coinage (1964)

Date		Quantity Minted	MS-60	MS-63	MS-65	PF-65				Notes
1964	(3,950,762)	273,304,004								
1964, Hv Acc Hair										
1964D		156,205,446								

Kennedy, Silver Clad Coinage (1965–1970)

Date		Quantity Minted	MS-60	MS-63	MS-65	PF-65				Notes
1965		65,879,366								
1966		108,984,932								
1967		295,046,978								
1968D		246,951,930								
1968S	(3,041,506)									
1969D		129,881,800								
1969S	(2,934,631)									
1970D		2,150,000								
1970S	(2,632,810)									

Kennedy, Copper-Nickel Clad Coinage (1971–1974)

Date		Quantity Minted	MS-60	MS-63	MS-65	PF-65				Notes
1971		155,164,000								
1971D		302,097,424								
1971S	(3,220,733)									
1972		153,180,000								
1972D		141,890,000								
1972S	(3,260,996)									
1973		64,964,000								
1973D		83,171,400								
1973S	(2,760,339)									
1974		201,596,000								
1974D		79,066,300								
1974D, DblDie Obv										
1974S	(2,612,568)									

Kennedy, Bicentennial Coinage, Dated 1776–1976

Date		Quantity Minted	MS-60	MS-63	MS-65	PF-65				Notes
1976		234,308,000								
1976D		287,565,248								
1976S	(7,059,099)									
1976S, Silver Clad		*11,000,000*								
1976S, Silver Clad	*(4,000,000)*									

Kennedy, Eagle Reverse Resumed (1977 to Date)

Date		Quantity Minted	MS-60	MS-63	MS-65	PF-65				Notes
1977		43,598,000								
1977D		31,449,106								
1977S	(3,251,152)									
1978		14,350,000								
1978D		13,765,799								
1978S	(3,127,781)									
1979		68,312,000								
1979D		15,815,422								
1979S, Type 1	(3,677,175)									
1979S, Type 2										
1980P		44,134,000								
1980D		33,456,449								
1980S	(3,554,806)									
1981P		29,544,000								
1981D		27,839,533								
1981S, Type 1	(4,063,083)									
1981S, Type 2										
1982P		10,819,000								
1982D		13,140,102								
1982S	(3,857,479)									
1983P		34,139,000								
1983D		32,472,244								
1983S	(3,279,126)									
1984P		26,029,000								
1984D		26,262,158								
1984S	(3,065,110)									

Date	Quantity Minted	MS-60	MS-63	MS-65	PF-65					Notes
1985P	18,706,962									
1985D	19,814,034									
1985S	(3,362,821)									
1986P	13,107,633									
1986D	15,336,145									
1986S	(3,010,497)									
1987P	2,890,758									
1987D	2,890,758									
1987S	(4,227,728)									
1988P	13,626,000									
1988D	12,000,096									
1988S	(3,262,948)									
1989P	24,542,000									
1989D	23,000,216									
1989S	(3,220,194)									
1990P	22,278,000									
1990D	20,096,242									
1990S	(3,299,559)									
1991P	14,874,000									
1991D	15,054,678									
1991S	(2,867,787)									
1992P	17,628,000									
1992D	17,000,106									
1992S	(2,858,981)									
1992S, Silver	(1,317,579)									
1993P	15,510,000									
1993D	15,000,006									
1993S	(2,633,439)									
1993S, Silver	(761,353)									
1994P	23,718,000									
1994D	23,828,110									
1994S	(2,484,594)									
1994S, Silver	(785,329)									
1995P	26,496,000									
1995D	26,288,000									
1995S	(2,117,496)									
1995S, Silver	(679,985)									
1996P	24,442,000									
1996D	24,744,000									
1996S	(1,750,244)									
1996S, Silver	(775,021)									
1997P	20,882,000									
1997D	19,876,000									
1997S	(2,055,000)									
1997S, Silver	(741,678)									
1998P	15,646,000									

Date		Quantity Minted	MS-60	MS-63	MS-65	PF-65				Notes
1998D		15,064,000								
1998S	(2,086,507)									
1998S, Silver		878,792								
1998S, Silver, Matte Finish										
1999P		8,900,000								
1999D		10,682,000								
1999S	(2,543,401)									
1999S, Silver	(804,565)									
2000P		22,600,000								
2000D		19,466,000								
2000S	(3,082,483)									
2000S, Silver	(965,421)									
2001P		21,200,000								
2001D		19,504,000								
2001S	(2,294,909)									
2001S, Silver	(889,697)									
2002P		3,100,000								
2002D		2,500,000								
2002S	(2,319,766)									
2002S, Silver	(892,229)									
2003P		2,500,000								
2003D		2,500,000								
2003S	(2,172,684)									
2003S, Silver	(1,125,755)									
2004P		2,900,000								
2004D		2,900,000								
2004S	(1,789,488)									
2004S, Silver	(1,175,934)									
2005P		3,800,000								
2005D		3,500,000								
2005S	(2,275,000)									
2005S, Silver	(1,069,679)									
2006P		2,400,000								
2006D		2,000,000								
2006S	(2,000,428)									
2006S, Silver	(1,054,008)									
2007P		2,400,000								
2007D		2,400,000								
2007S	(1,702,116)									
2007S, Silver	(875,050)									
2008P		1,700,000								
2008D		1,700,000								
2008S	(1,405,674)									
2008S, Silver	(763,887)									
2009P		1,900,000								
2009D		1,900,000								

Date	Quantity Minted	MS-60	MS-63	MS-65	PF-65			Notes
2009S	(1,482,502)							
2009S, Silver	(697,365)							
2010P	1,800,000							
2010D	1,700,000							
2010S	(1,103,950)							
2010S, Silver	(585,414)							
2011P	1,750,000							
2011D	1,700,000							
2011S	(952,881)							
2011S, Silver	(500,395)							
2012P								
2012D								
2012S								
2012S, Silver								

SILVER AND RELATED DOLLARS

Flowing Hair (1794–1795)

Date	Quantity Minted	G-4	VG-8	F-12	VF-20	EF-40	MS-60		Notes
1794	1,758								
1794, Silver Plug (unique)									
1795, Two Leaves	160,295								
1795, Three Leaves									
1795, Silver Plug									

Draped Bust, Small Eagle Reverse (1795–1798)

Date	Quantity Minted	G-4	VG-8	F-12	VF-20	EF-40	MS-60	Notes
1795, Off-Center Bust	42,738							
1795, Centered Bust								
1796, Small Date, Small Letters (3 varieties)	79,920							
1796, Small Date, Large Letters								
1796, Large Date, Small Letters								
1797, 10 Stars Left, 6 Right	7,776							
1797, 9 Stars Left, 7 Right, Large Letters								
1797, 9 Stars Left, 7 Right, Small Letters								
1798, 15 Stars on Obverse	327,536							
1798, 13 Stars on Obverse								

Draped Bust, Heraldic Eagle Reverse (1798–1804)

Date	Quantity Minted	G-4	VG-8	F-12	VF-20	EF-40	MS-60	Notes
1798, Knob 9, 5 Vertical Lines								
1798, Knob 9, 4 Vertical Lines								
1798, Knob 9, 10 Arrows								
1798, Pointed 9, Close Date								
1798, Pointed 9, Wide Date								
1798, Pointed 9, 5 Vertical Lines								
1798, Pointed 9, 10 Arrows								
1798, Pointed 9, 4 Berries								

Date	Quantity Minted	G-4	VG-8	F-12	VF-20	EF-40	MS-60	Notes
1799, 99 Over 98, 15-Star Reverse								
1799, 99 Over 98, 13-Star Reverse								
1799, Irregular Date, 15-Star Reverse	423,515							
1799, Irregular Date, 13-Star Reverse								
1799, Normal Date								
1799, 8 Stars Left, 5 Right								
1800, Very Wide Date, Low 8								
1800, "Dotted Date" *(from die breaks)*	220,920							
1800, Only 12 Arrows								
1800, Normal Dies								
1800, AMERICAI								
1801	54,454							
1801, Proof Restrike *(reverse struck from first die of 1804 dollar) (2 known)*								
1802, 2 Over 1, Narrow Date								
1802, 2 Over 1, Wide Date								
1802, Narrow Normal Date	41,650							
1802, Wide Normal Date								
1802, Proof Restrike *(4 known)*								
1803, Small 3								
1803, Large 3	85,634							
1803, Proof Restrike *(4 known)*								
1804, 1st Rev, Orig *(8 known)*								
1804, 2nd Rev, Rstrk *(6 known)*								
1804, Second Reverse, Restrike With Plain Edge *(unique)*								
1804, Mint-Made Electrotype of Plain-Edge Specimen *(4 known)*								

Gobrecht (1836–1839)

Date	Quantity Minted	G-4	VG-8	F-12	VF-20	EF-40	MS-60	Notes
1836, All kinds								
1838, All kinds								
1839, All kinds								

Liberty Seated, No Motto (1840–1865)

Date	Quantity Minted		VG-8	F-12	VF-20	EF-40	MS-60	PF-63	Notes
1840	61,005								
1841	173,000								
1842	184,618								
1843	165,100								
1844	20,000								
1845	24,500								
1846	110,600								
18460	59,000								
1847	140,750								
1848	15,000								
1849	62,600								
1850	7,500								
18500	40,000								
1851, Original, High Date	1,300								
1851, Restrike, Date Centered									
1852, Original	1,100								
1852, Restrike									
1853	46,110								
1854	33,140								
1855	26,000								
1856	63,500								
1857	94,000								
1858	(300)								
1859	(800) 255,700								
18590	360,000								
1859S	20,000								
1860	(1,330) 217,600								
18600	515,000								

Date		Quantity Minted	VG-8	F-12	VF-20	EF-40	MS-60	PF-63		Notes
1861	(1,000)	77,500								
1862	(550)	11,540								
1863	(460)	27,200								
1864	(470)	30,700								
1865	(500)	46,500								
1866, No Motto *(2 known)*										

Liberty Seated, With Motto (1866–1873)

Date		Quantity Minted	VG-8	F-12	VF-20	EF-40	MS-60	PF-63		Notes
1866	(725)	48,900								
1867	(625)	46,900								
1868	(600)	162,100								
1869	(600)	423,700								
1870	(1,000)	415,000								
1870CC		11,758								
1870S										
1871	(960)	1,073,800								
1871CC		1,376								
1872	(950)	1,105,500								
1872CC		3,150								
1872S		9,000								
1873	(600)	293,000								
1873CC		2,300								
1873S *(unknown in any collection)*		700								

Trade Dollars
(1873–1885)

Date		Quantity Minted	VG-8	F-12	EF-40	MS-60	MS-63	PF-63	Notes
1873	(865)	396,635							
1873CC		124,500							
1873S		703,000							
1874	(700)	987,100							
1874CC		1,373,200							
1874S		2,549,000							
1875	(700)	218,200							
1875, Reverse 2									
1875CC		1,573,700							
1875CC, Reverse 2									
1875S		4,487,000							
1875S, Reverse 2									
1875S, S Over CC									
1876	(1,150)	455,000							
1876, Obv 2, Rev 2 *(extremely rare)*									
1876, Reverse 2									
1876CC		509,000							
1876CC, Reverse 1									
1876CC, DblDie Rev									
1876S		5,227,000							
1876S, Reverse 2									
1876S, Obv 2, Rev 2									
1877	(510)	3,039,200							
1877CC		534,000							
1877S		9,519,000							
1878	(900)								
1878CC		97,000							
1878S		4,162,000							
1879	(1,541)								
1880	(1,987)								
1881	(960)								
1882	(1,097)								
1883	(979)								
1884	(10)								
1885	(5)								

Morgan (1878–1921)

Date		Quantity Minted	VF-20	EF-40	AU-50	MS-60	MS-63	PF-63	Notes
1878, 8 Feathers	(500)	*749,500*							
1878, 7 Feathers									
1878, 7 Over 8 Clear Doubled Feathers									
1878, 7 Feathers, 2nd Reverse	(250)	*9,759,300*							
1878, 7 Feathers, 3rd Reverse									
1878CC		2,212,000							
1878S		9,774,000							
1879	(1,100)	14,806,000							
1879CC, CC Over CC		756,000							
1879CC, Clear CC									
18790		2,887,000							
1879S, 2nd Reverse		9,110,000							
1879S, 3rd Reverse									
1880	(1,355)	12,600,000							
1880, 80 Over 79									
1880CC, 80/79, 2nd Rev		591,000							
1880CC, 8/7, 2nd Rev									
1880CC, 8/High 7, 3rd Rev									
1880CC, 8/Low 7, 3rd Rev									
1880CC, 3rd Reverse									
18800, 80 Over 79		5,305,000							
18800									
1880S, 80 Over 79		8,900,000							
1880S, 0 Over 9									
1880S									
1881	(984)	9,163,000							
1881CC		296,000							
18810		5,708,000							
1881S		12,760,000							
1882	(1,100)	11,100,000							

Date		Quantity Minted	VF-20	EF-40	AU-50	MS-60	MS-63	PF-63		Notes
1882CC		1,133,000								
1882O		6,090,000								
1882O, O Over S										
1882S		9,250,000								
1883	(1,039)	12,290,000								
1883CC		1,204,000								
1883O		8,725,000								
1883S		6,250,000								
1884	(875)	14,070,000								
1884CC		1,136,000								
1884O		9,730,000								
1884S		3,200,000								
1885	(930)	17,787,000								
1885CC		228,000								
1885O		9,185,000								
1885S		1,497,000								
1886	(886)	19,963,000								
1886O		10,710,000								
1886S		750,000								
1887, 7 Over 6		20,290,000								
1887	(710)									
1887O, 7 Over 6		11,550,000								
1887O										
1887S		1,771,000								
1888	(833)	19,183,000								
1888O		12,150,000								
1888O, Doubled-Die Obv										
1888S		657,000								
1889	(811)	21,726,000								
1889CC		350,000								
1889O		11,875,000								
1889S		700,000								
1890	(590)	16,802,000								
1890CC		2,309,041								
1890O		10,701,000								
1890S		8,230,373								
1891	(650)	8,693,556								
1891CC		1,618,000								
1891O		7,954,529								
1891S		5,296,000								
1892	(1,245)	1,036,000								
1892CC		1,352,000								
1892O		2,744,000								
1892S		1,200,000								
1893	(792)	378,000								
1893CC		677,000								

Date		Quantity Minted	VF-20	EF-40	AU-50	MS-60	MS-63	PF-63		Notes
1893O		300,000								
1893S		100,000								
1894	(972)	110,000								
1894O		1,723,000								
1894S		1,260,000								
1895, Proof	(880)									
1895O		450,000								
1895S		400,000								
1896	(762)	9,976,000								
1896O		4,900,000								
1896S		5,000,000								
1897	(731)	2,822,000								
1897O		4,004,000								
1897S		5,825,000								
1898	(735)	5,884,000								
1898O		4,440,000								
1898S		4,102,000								
1899	(846)	330,000								
1899O		12,290,000								
1899S		2,562,000								
1900	(912)	8,830,000								
1900O		12,590,000								
1900O, O Over CC										
1900S		3,540,000								
1901	(813)	6,962,000								
1901, Doubled-Die Reverse										
1901O		13,320,000								
1901S		2,284,000								
1902	(777)	7,994,000								
1902O		8,636,000								
1902S		1,530,000								
1903	(755)	4,652,000								
1903O		4,450,000								
1903S		1,241,000								
1904	(650)	2,788,000								
1904O		3,720,000								
1904S		2,304,000								
1921		44,690,000								
1921D		20,345,000								
1921S		21,695,000								

Peace (1921–1935)

Date	Quantity Minted	VF-20	EF-40	AU-50	MS-60	MS-63			Notes
1921, High Relief	1,006,473								
1922, High Relief	35,401								
1922, Normal Relief	51,737,000								
1922D	15,063,000								
1922S	17,475,000								
1923	30,800,000								
1923D	6,811,000								
1923S	19,020,000								
1924	11,811,000								
1924S	1,728,000								
1925	10,198,000								
1925S	1,610,000								
1926	1,939,000								
1926D	2,348,700								
1926S	6,980,000								
1927	848,000								
1927D	1,268,900								
1927S	866,000								
1928	360,649								
1928S	1,632,000								
1934	954,057								
1934D	1,569,500								
1934D, Doubled-Die Obverse									
1934S	1,011,000								
1935	1,576,000								
1935S	1,964,000								

Eisenhower, Eagle Reverse (1971–1974)

Date		Quantity Minted	VF-20	EF-40	AU-50	MS-60	MS-63	PF-65	Notes
1971, Copper-Nickel Clad		47,799,000							
1971D, Copper-Nickel Clad		68,587,424							
1971S, Silver Clad	(4,265,234)	6,868,530							
1972, Copper-Nickel Clad, Variety I									
1972 , Copper-Nickel Clad, Variety II		75,890,000							
1972, Copper-Nickel Clad, Variety III									
1972D, Copper-Nickel Clad		92,548,511							
1972S, Silver Clad	(1,811,631)	2,193,056							
1973, Copper-Nickel Clad		2,000,056							
1973D, Copper-Nickel Clad		2,000,000							
1973S, Copper-Nickel Clad	(2,760,339)								
1973S, Silver Clad	(1,013,646)	1,883,140							
1974, Copper-Nickel Clad		27,366,000							
1974D, Copper-Nickel Clad		45,517,000							
1974S, Copper-Nickel Clad	(2,612,568)								
1974S, Silver Clad	(1,306,579)	1,900,156							

Eisenhower, Bicentennial Coinage Dated 1776–1976

Date	Quantity Minted	VF-20	EF-40	AU-50	MS-60	MS-63	PF-65	Notes
1776–1976, Copper-Nickel Clad, Variety 1	4,019,000							
1776–1976, Copper-Nickel Clad, Variety 2	113,318,000							
1776–1976D, Copper-Nickel Clad, Variety 1	21,048,710							
1776–1976D, Copper-Nickel Clad, Variety 2	82,179,564							
1776–1976S, Copper-Nickel Clad, Variety 1	(2,845,450)							
1776–1976S, Copper-Nickel Clad, Variety 2	(4,149,730)							
1776–1976, Silver Clad, Variety 2								
1776–1976S, Silver Clad, Variety 1	11,000,000							
1776–1976S, Silver Clad, Variety 1	(4,000,000)							

Eisenhower, Eagle Reverse Resumed (1977–1978)

Date	Quantity Minted	MS-63	MS-65	PF-65	Notes
1977, Copper-Nickel Clad	12,596,000				
1977D, Copper-Nickel Clad	32,983,006				
1977S, Copper-Nickel Clad	(3,251,152)				
1978, Copper-Nickel Clad	25,702,000				
1978D, Copper-Nickel Clad	33,012,890				
1978S, Copper-Nickel Clad	(3,127,781)				

Susan B. Anthony (1979–1999)

Date	Quantity Minted	MS-63	MS-65	PF-65					Notes
1979P, Narrow Rim	360,222,000								
1979P, Wide Rim									
1979D	288,015,744								
1979S	109,576,000								
1979S, Proof, Type 1	(3,677,175)								
1979S, Proof, Type 2									
1980P	27,610,000								
1980D	41,628,708								
1980S	20,422,000								
1980S, Proof	(3,554,806)								
1981P	3,000,000								
1981D	3,250,000								
1981S	3,492,000								
1981S, Proof, Type 1	(4,063,083)								
1981S, Proof, Type 2									
1999P	29,592,000								
1999P, Proof									
1999D	11,776,000								

Sacagawea (2000–2008)

Date	Quantity Minted	MS-63	MS-65	PF-65					Notes
2000P	767,140,000								
2000P, Goodacre Presentation Finish	5,000								
2000P, Boldly Detailed Tail Feathers	5,500								
2000D	518,916,000								
2000S	(4,047,904)								

Date	Quantity Minted	MS-63	MS-65	PF-65					Notes
2001P	62,468,000								
2001D	70,939,500								
2001S	(3,183,740)								
2002P	3,865,610								
2002D	3,732,000								
2002S	(3,211,995)								
2003P	3,080,000								
2003D	3,080,000								
2003S	(3,298,439)								
2004P	2,660,000								
2004D	2,660,000								
2004S	(2,965,422)								
2005P	2,520,000								
2005D	2,520,000								
2005S	(3,344,679)								
2006P	4,900,000								
2006D	2,800,000								
2006S	(3,054,436)								
2007P	3,640,000								
2007D	3,920,000								
2007S	(2,577,166)								
2008P	9,800,000								
2008D	14,840,000								
2008S	(2,169,561)								

Native American Dollars (2009 to Date)

Date	Quantity Minted	MS-65	PF-65						Notes
2009P, Three Sisters	37,380,000								
2009D, Three Sisters	33,880,000								
2009S, Three Sisters	(2,179,867)								
2010P, Great Law	32,060,000								
2010D, Great Law	32,060,000								
2010S, Great Law	(1,689,364)								
2011P, Wampanoag Treaty	22,260,000								
2011D, Wampanoag Treaty	23,100,000								
2011S, Wampanoag Treaty	(1,453,276)								
2012P, Trade Routes									
2012D, Trade Routes									
2012S, Trade Routes									

Reverse

Date, Mintmark, and
Mottos Incused on Edge

Presidential (2007–2016)

Date		Quantity Minted	MS-65	PF-65					Notes
2007P, Washington		176,680,000							
2007D, Washington		163,680,000							
2007S, Washington	(3,965,989)								
2007P, J. Adams		112,420,000							
2007D, J. Adams		112,140,000							
2007S, J. Adams	(3,965,989)								
2007P, Jefferson		100,800,000							
2007D, Jefferson		102,810,000							
2007S, Jefferson	(3,965,989)								
2007P, Madison		84,560,000							
2007D, Madison		87,780,000							
2007S, Madison	(3,965,989)								

Date		Quantity Minted	MS-65	PF-65					Notes
2008P, Monroe		64,260,000							
2008D, Monroe		60,230,000							
2008S, Monroe	(3,083,940)								
2008P, J.Q. Adams		57,540,000							
2008D, J.Q. Adams		57,720,000							
2008S, J.Q. Adams	(3,083,940)								
2008P, Jackson		61,180,000							
2008D, Jackson		61,070,000							
2008S, Jackson	(3,083,940)								
2008P, Van Buren		51,520,000							
2008D, Van Buren		50,960,000							
2008S, Van Buren	(3,083,940)								

Date	Quantity Minted	MS-65	PF-65						Notes
2009P, W.H. Harrison	43,260,000								
2009D, W.H. Harrison	55,160,000								
2009S, W.H. Harrison (2,809,452)									
2009P, Tyler	43,540,000								
2009D, Tyler	43,540,000								
2009S, Tyler (2,809,452)									
2009P, Polk	46,620,000								
2009D, Polk	41,720,000								
2009S, Polk (2,809,452)									
2009P, Taylor	41,580,000								
2009D, Taylor	36,680,000								
2009S, Taylor (2,809,452)									

Date	Quantity Minted	MS-65	PF-65						Notes
2010P, Fillmore	37,520,000								
2010D, Fillmore	36,960,000								
2010S, Fillmore (2,224,827)									
2010P, Pierce	38,220,000								
2010D, Pierce	38,360,000								
2010S, Pierce (2,224,827)									
2010P, Buchanan	36,820,000								
2010D, Buchanan	36,540,000								
2010S, Buchanan (2,224,827)									
2010P, Lincoln	49,000,000								
2010D, Lincoln	48,020,000								
2010S, Lincoln (2,224,827)									

Date	Quantity Minted	MS-65	PF-65							Notes
2011P, Johnson	146,300,000									
2011D, Johnson	148,960,000									
2011S, Johnson	(1,706,916)									
2011P, Grant	146,300,000									
2011D, Grant	148,960,000									
2011S, Grant	(1,706,916)									
2011P, Hayes	146,300,000									
2011D, Hayes	148,960,000									
2011S, Hayes	(1,706,916)									
2011P, Garfield	146,300,000									
2011D, Garfield	148,960,000									
2011S, Garfield	(1,706,916)									

Date	Quantity Minted	MS-65	PF-65							Notes
2012P, Arthur										
2012D, Arthur										
2012S, Arthur										
2012P, Cleveland, Var 1										
2012D, Cleveland, Var 1										
2012S, Cleveland, Var 1										
2012P, B. Harrison										
2012D, B. Harrison										
2012S, B. Harrison										
2012P, Cleveland, Var 2										
2012D, Cleveland, Var 2										
2012S, Cleveland, Var 2										

Date	Quantity Minted	MS-65	PF-65						Notes

GOLD DOLLARS

Liberty Head (Type 1) (1849–1854)

Date	Quantity Minted	VF-20	EF-40	AU-50	MS-60	MS-63			Notes
1849, Open Wreath, No L									
1849, Small Head, With L	688,567								
1849, Close Wreath (Ends Closer to Numeral)									
1849C, Close Wreath	11,634								
1849C, Open Wreath *(ex. rare)*									
1849D, Open Wreath	21,588								
1849O, Open Wreath	215,000								
1850	481,953								
1850C	6,966								
1850D	8,382								

Date	Quantity Minted	VF-20	EF-40	AU-50	MS-60	MS-63		Notes
18500	14,000							
1851	3,317,671							
1851C	41,267							
1851D	9,882							
18510	290,000							
1852	2,045,351							
1852C	9,434							
1852D	6,360							
18520	140,000							
1853	4,076,051							
1853C	11,515							
1853D	6,583							
18530	290,000							
1854	855,502							
1854D	2,935							
1854S	14,632							

Indian Princess Head, Small Head (Type 2) (1854–1856)

Date	Quantity Minted	VF-20	EF-40	AU-50	MS-60	MS-63		Notes
1854	783,943							
1855	758,269							
1855C	9,803							
1855D	1,811							
18550	55,000							
1856S	24,600							

Indian Princess Head, Large Head (Type 3) (1856–1889)

Date	Quantity Minted	VF-20	EF-40	AU-50	MS-60	MS-63	PF-63	Notes
1856, Upright 5	1,762,936							
1856, Slant 5								
1856D	1,460							
1857	774,789							
1857C	13,280							
1857D	3,533							
1857S	10,000							
1858	117,995							

Date		Quantity Minted	VF-20	EF-40	AU-50	MS-60	MS-63			Notes
1858D		3,477								
1858S		10,000								
1859	(80)	168,244								
1859C		5,235								
1859D		4,952								
1859S		15,000								
1860	(154)	36,514								
1860D		1,566								
1860S		13,000								
1861	(349)	527,150								
1861D		*1,250*								
1862	(35)	1,361,355								
1863	(50)	6,200								
1864	(50)	5,900								
1865	(25)	3,725								
1866	(30)	7,100								
1867	(50)	5,200								
1868	(25)	10,500								
1869	(25)	5,900								
1870	(35)	6,300								
1870S		3,000								
1871	(30)	3,900								
1872	(30)	3,500								
1873, Close 3	(25)	1,800								
1873, Open 3		123,300								
1874	(20)	198,800								
1875	(20)	400								
1876	(45)	3,200								
1877	(20)	3,900								
1878	(20)	3,000								
1879	(30)	3,000								
1880	(36)	1,600								
1881	(87)	7,620								
1882	(125)	5,000								
1883	(207)	10,800								
1884	(1,006)	5,230								
1885	(1,105)	11,156								
1886	(1,016)	5,000								
1887	(1,043)	7,500								
1888	(1,079)	15,501								
1889	(1,779)	28,950								

QUARTER EAGLES

Capped Bust to Right (1796–1807)

Date	Quantity Minted	F-12	VF-20	EF-40	AU-50	MS-60			Notes
1796, No Stars on Obverse	963								
1796, Stars on Obverse	432								
1797	427								
1798	1,094								
1802, 2 Over 1	3,035								
1804, 13-Star Reverse	3,327								
1804, 14-Star Reverse									
1805	1,781								
1806, 6/4, 8 Stars Left, 5 Right	1,136								
1806, 6/5, 7 Stars Left, 6 Right	480								
1807	6,812								

Capped Bust to Left, Large Size (1808)

Date	Quantity Minted	F-12	VF-20	EF-40	AU-50	MS-60			Notes
1808	2,710								

Capped Head to Left, Large Diameter (1821–1827)

Date	Quantity Minted	F-12	VF-20	EF-40	AU-50	MS-60			Notes
1821	6,448								
1824, 4 Over 1	2,600								
1825	4,434								
1826, 6 Over 6	760								
1827	2,800								

Capped Head to Left, Reduced Diameter (1829–1834)

Date	Quantity Minted	VF-20	EF-40	AU-50	MS-60			Notes
1829	3,403							
1830	4,540							
1831	4,520							
1832	4,400							
1833	4,160							
1834, With Motto	4,000							

Classic Head, No Motto on Reverse (1834–1839)

Date	Quantity Minted	VF-20	EF-40	AU-50	MS-60			Notes
1834, No Motto	112,234							
1835	131,402							
1836, Script 8	547,986							
1836, Block 8								
1837	45,080							
1838	47,030							
1838C	7,880							
1839	27,021							
1839C	18,140							
1839D	13,674							
1839O	17,781							

Liberty Head (1840–1907)

Date	Quantity Minted	VF-20	EF-40	AU-50	MS-60			Notes
1840	18,859							
1840C	12,822							
1840D	3,532							
1840O	33,580							

Date	Quantity Minted	VF-20	EF-40	AU-50	MS-60				Notes
1841	(unknown)								
1841C	10,281								
1841D	4,164								
1842	2,823								
1842C	6,729								
1842D	4,643								
1842O	19,800								
1843	100,546								
1843C, Small Date, Crosslet 4	2,988								
1843C, Large Date, Plain 4	23,076								
1843D, Small Date, Crosslet 4	36,209								
1843O, Small Date, Crosslet 4	288,002								
1843O, Large Date, Plain 4	76,000								
1844	6,784								
1844C	11,622								
1844D	17,332								
1845	91,051								
1845D	19,460								
1845O	4,000								
1846	21,598								
1846C	4,808								
1846D	19,303								
1846O	62,000								
1847	29,814								
1847C	23,226								
1847D	15,784								
1847O	124,000								
1848	6,500								
1848, CAL. Above Eagle	1,389								
1848C	16,788								
1848D	13,771								
1849	23,294								
1849C	10,220								
1849D	10,945								
1850	252,923								
1850C	9,148								
1850D	12,148								
1850O	84,000								
1851	1,372,748								
1851C	14,923								
1851D	11,264								
1851O	148,000								
1852	1,159,681								
1852C	9,772								
1852D	4,078								
1852O	140,000								

Date		Quantity Minted	VF-20	EF-40	AU-50	MS-60				Notes
1853		1,404,668								
1853D		3,178								
1854		596,258								
1854C		7,295								
1854D		1,760								
1854O		153,000								
1854S		246								
1855		235,480								
1855C		3,677								
1855D		1,123								
1856		384,240								
1856C		7,913								
1856D		874								
1856O		21,100								
1856S		72,120								
1857		214,130								
1857D		2,364								
1857O		34,000								
1857S		69,200								
1858		47,377								
1858C		9,056								
1859, Old Reverse	(80)	39,364								
1859, New Reverse										
1859D		2,244								
1859S		15,200								
1860, Old Reverse	(112)	22,563								
1860, New Reverse										
1860C		7,469								
1860S		35,600								
1861, Old Reverse	(90)	1,283,788								
1861, New Reverse										
1861S		24,000								
1862, 2 Over 1		98,508								
1862	(35)									
1862S		8,000								
1863, Proof only	(30)									
1863S		10,800								
1864	(50)	2,824								
1865	(25)	1,520								
1865S		23,376								
1866	(30)	3,080								
1866S		38,960								
1867	(50)	3,200								
1867S		28,000								
1868	(25)	3,600								
1868S		34,000								

Date		Quantity Minted	VF-20	EF-40	AU-50	MS-60				Notes
1869	(25)	4,320								
1869S		29,500								
1870	(35)	4,520								
1870S		16,000								
1871	(30)	5,320								
1871S		22,000								
1872	(30)	3,000								
1872S		18,000								
1873, Close 3	(25)	55,200								
1873, Open 3		122,800								
1873S		27,000								
1874	(20)	3,920								
1875	(20)	400								
1875S		11,600								
1876	(45)	4,176								
1876S		5,000								
1877	(20)	1,632								
1877S		35,400								
1878	(20)	286,240								
1878S		178,000								
1879	(30)	88,960								
1879S		43,500								
1880	(36)	2,960								
1881	(51)	640								
1882	(67)	4,000								
1883	(82)	1,920								
1884	(73)	1,950								
1885	(87)	800								
1886	(88)	4,000								
1887	(122)	6,160								
1888	(97)	16,001								
1889	(48)	17,600								
1890	(93)	8,720								
1891	(80)	10,960								
1892	(105)	2,440								
1893	(106)	30,000								
1894	(122)	4,000								
1895	(119)	6,000								
1896	(132)	19,070								
1897	(136)	29,768								
1898	(165)	24,000								
1899	(150)	27,200								
1900	(205)	67,000								
1901	(223)	91,100								
1902	(193)	133,540								
1903	(197)	201,060								

Date		Quantity Minted	VF-20	EF-40	AU-50	MS-60		Notes
1904	(170)	160,790						
1905	(144)	217,800						
1906	(160)	176,330						
1907	(154)	336,294						

Indian Head (1908–1929)

Date		Quantity Minted	VF-20	EF-40	AU-50	MS-60	PF-63		Notes
1908	(236)	564,821							
1909	(139)	441,760							
1910	(682)	492,000							
1911	(191)	704,000							
1911D		55,680							
1912	(197)	616,000							
1913	(165)	722,000							
1914	(117)	240,000							
1914D		448,000							
1915	(100)	606,000							
1925D		578,000							
1926		446,000							
1927		388,000							
1928		416,000							
1929		532,000							

THREE-DOLLAR GOLD PIECES

Indian Princess Head (1854–1889)

Date	Quantity Minted	VF-20	EF-40	AU-50	MS-60	PF-63		Notes
1854	138,618							
1854D	1,120							
1854O	24,000							
1855	50,555							
1855S	6,600							
1856	26,010							

Date		Quantity Minted	VF-20	EF-40	AU-50	MS-60	PF-63			Notes
1856S		34,500								
1857		20,891								
1857S		14,000								
1858		2,133								
1859	(80)	15,558								
1860	(119)	7,036								
1860S		7,000								
1861	(113)	5,959								
1862	(35)	5,750								
1863	(39)	5,000								
1864	(50)	2,630								
1865	(25)	1,140								
1866	(30)	4,000								
1867	(50)	2,600								
1868	(25)	4,850								
1869	(25)	2,500								
1870	(35)	3,500								
1870S *(unique)*										
1871	(30)	1,300								
1872	(30)	2,000								
1873, Open 3 (Original)	(25)									
1873, Close 3		*(unknown)*								
1874	(20)	41,800								
1875, Proof only	(20)									
1876, Proof only	(45)									
1877	(20)	1,468								
1878	(20)	82,304								
1879	(30)	3,000								
1880	(36)	1,000								
1881	(54)	500								
1882	(76)	1,500								
1883	(89)	900								
1884	(106)	1,000								
1885	(109)	801								
1886	(142)	1,000								
1887	(160)	6,000								
1888	(291)	5,000								
1889	(129)	2,300								

FOUR-DOLLAR GOLD PIECES

Stella (1879–1880)

Date	Quantity Minted	VF-20	EF-40	AU-50	MS-60	PF-63		Notes
1879, Flowing Hair	(425+)							
1879, Coiled Hair (12 known)								
1880, Flowing Hair (17 known)								
1880, Coiled Hair (8 known)								

HALF EAGLES

Capped Bust to Right, Small Eagle (1795–1798)

Date	Quantity Minted	F-12	VF-20	EF-40	AU-50	MS-60		Notes
1795, Small Eagle	8,707							
1796, 6 Over 5	6,196							
1797, 15 Stars	3,609							
1797, 16 Stars								
1798, Small Eagle (7 known)								

Capped Bust to Right, Heraldic Eagle (1795–1807)

Date	Quantity Minted	F-12	VF-20	EF-40	AU-50	MS-60			Notes
1795, Heraldic Eagle*									
1797, 7 Over 5*									
1797, 16-Star Obverse* (unique, in Smithsonian)									
1797, 15-Star Obverse* (unique, in Smithsonian)	24,867								
1798, Small 8									
1798, Large 8, 13-Star Reverse									
1798, Large 8, 14-Star Reverse									
1799	7,451								
1800	37,628								
1802, 2 Over 1	53,176								
1803, 3 Over 2	33,506								
1804, Small 8	30,475								
1804, Small 8 Over Large 8									
1805	33,183								
1806, Pointed-Top 6	9,676								
1806, Round-Top 6	54,417								
1807	32,488								

* Thought to have been struck in 1798 and included in the mintage figure for that year.

Capped Bust to Left (1807–1812)

Date	Quantity Minted	F-12	VF-20	EF-40	AU-50	MS-60			Notes
1807	51,605								
1808, 8 Over 7	55,578								
1808									
1809, 9 Over 8	33,875								

Date	Quantity Minted	F-12	VF-20	EF-40	AU-50	MS-60			Notes
1810, Small Date, Small 5									
1810, Small Date, Tall 5	100,287								
1810, Large Date, Small 5									
1810, Large Date, Large 5									
1811, Small 5	99,581								
1811, Tall 5									
1812	58,087								

Capped Head to Left, Large Diameter (1813–1829)

Date	Quantity Minted	F-12	VF-20	EF-40	AU-50	MS-60			Notes
1813	95,428								
1814, 4 Over 3	15,454								
1815 *(11 known)*	635								
1818									
1818, STATESOF one word	48,588								
1818, 5D Over 50									
1819	51,723								
1819, 5D Over 50									
1820, Curved-Base 2, Small Letters									
1820, Curved-Base 2, Large Letters	263,806								
1820, Square-Base 2									
1821	34,641								
1822 *(3 known)*	17,796								
1823	14,485								
1824	17,340								
1825, 5 Over Partial 4	29,060								
1825, 5 Over 4 *(2 known)*									
1826	18,069								
1827	24,913								
1828, 8 Over 7 *(5 known)*	28,029								
1828									
1829, Large Date	57,442								
1829, Small Date*									

* Reduced diameter.

Capped Head to Left, Reduced Diameter (1829–1834)

Date	Quantity Minted	F-12	VF-20	EF-40	AU-50	MS-60		Notes
1830, Small or Large 5D	126,351							
1831, Small or Large 5D	140,594							
1832, Curved-Base 2, 12 Stars *(5 known)*	157,487							
1832, Square-Base 2, 13 Stars								
1833, Large Date	193,630							
1833, Small Date								
1834, Plain 4	50,141							
1834, Crosslet 4								

Classic Head (1834–1838)

Date	Quantity Minted	F-12	VF-20	EF-40	AU-50	MS-60		Notes
1834, Plain 4	657,460							
1834, Crosslet 4								
1835	371,534							
1836	553,147							
1837	207,121							
1838	286,588							
1838C	17,179							
1838D	20,583							

Liberty Head, Variety 1, No Motto Above Eagle (1839–1866)

Date	Quantity Minted	F-12	VF-20	EF-40	AU-50	MS-60	PF-63	Notes
1839	118,143							
1839C	17,205							
1839D	18,939							
1840	137,382							
1840C	18,992							
1840D	22,896							
1840O	40,120							
1841	15,833							
1841C	21,467							
1841D	29,392							
1841O *(not known to exist)*	50							
1842, Small Letters	27,578							
1842, Large Letters								
1842C, Small Date	27,432							
1842C, Large Date								
1842D, Small Date	59,608							
1842D, Large Date								
1842O	16,400							
1843	611,205							
1843C	44,277							
1843D	98,452							
1843O, Small Letters	19,075							
1843O, Large Letters	82,000							
1844	340,330							
1844C	23,631							
1844D	88,982							
1844O	364,600							
1845	417,099							
1845D	90,629							
1845O	41,000							
1846, Large Date	395,942							
1846, Small Date								
1846C	12,995							
1846D	80,294							
1846D, High 2nd D Over D								
1846O	58,000							
1847	915,981							
1847, Top of Extra 7 Very Low at Border								

Date	Quantity Minted	F-12	VF-20	EF-40	AU-50	MS-60	PF-63		Notes
1847C	84,151								
1847D	64,405								
1847O	12,000								
1848	260,775								
1848C	64,472								
1848D	47,465								
1849	133,070								
1849C	64,823								
1849D	39,036								
1850	64,491								
1850C	63,591								
1850D	43,984								
1851	377,505								
1851C	49,176								
1851D	62,710								
1851O	41,000								
1852	573,901								
1852C	72,574								
1852D	91,584								
1853	305,770								
1853C	65,571								
1853D	89,678								
1854	160,675								
1854C	39,283								
1854D	56,413								
1854O	46,000								
1854S *(3 known)*	268								
1855	117,098								
1855C	39,788								
1855D	22,432								
1855O	11,100								
1855S	61,000								
1856	197,990								
1856C	28,457								
1856D	19,786								
1856O	10,000								
1856S	105,100								
1857	98,188								
1857C	31,360								
1857D	17,046								
1857O	13,000								
1857S	87,000								
1858	15,136								
1858C	38,856								

Date		Quantity Minted	F-12	VF-20	EF-40	AU-50	MS-60	PF-63		Notes
1858D		15,362								
1858S		18,600								
1859	(80)	16,734								
1859C		31,847								
1859D		10,366								
1859S		13,220								
1860	(62)	19,763								
1860C		14,813								
1860D		14,635								
1860S		21,200								
1861	(66)	688,084								
1861C		6,879								
1861D		1,597								
1861S		18,000								
1862	(35)	4,430								
1862S		9,500								
1863	(30)	2,442								
1863S		17,000								
1864	(50)	4,170								
1864S		3,888								
1865	(25)	1,270								
1865S		27,612								
1866S, No Motto		9,000								

Liberty Head, Variety 2, Motto Above Eagle (1866–1908)

Date		Quantity Minted	VF-20	EF-40	AU-50	MS-60	PF-63		Notes
1866	(30)	6,700							
1866S		34,920							
1867	(50)	6,870							
1867S		29,000							
1868	(25)	5,700							
1868S		52,000							
1869	(25)	1,760							
1869S		31,000							
1870	(35)	4,000							
1870CC		7,675							
1870S		17,000							
1871	(30)	3,200							
1871CC		20,770							

Date		Quantity Minted	VF-20	EF-40	AU-50	MS-60	PF-63			Notes
1871S		25,000								
1872	(30)	1,660								
1872CC		16,980								
1872S		36,400								
1873, Close 3	(25)	112,480								
1873, Open 3		112,505								
1873CC		7,416								
1873S		31,000								
1874	(20)	3,488								
1874CC		21,198								
1874S		16,000								
1875	(20)	200								
1875CC		11,828								
1875S		9,000								
1876	(45)	1,432								
1876CC		6,887								
1876S		4,000								
1877	(20)	1,132								
1877CC		8,680								
1877S		26,700								
1878	(20)	131,720								
1878CC		9,054								
1878S		144,700								
1879	(30)	301,920								
1879CC		17,281								
1879S		426,200								
1880	(36)	3,166,400								
1880CC		51,017								
1880S		1,348,900								
1881, Final 1 Over 0		5,708,802								
1881	(42)									
1881CC		13,886								
1881S		969,000								
1882	(48)	2,514,520								
1882CC		82,817								
1882S		969,000								
1883	(61)	233,400								
1883CC		12,598								
1883S		83,200								
1884	(48)	191,030								
1884CC		16,402								
1884S		177,000								
1885	(66)	601,440								
1885S		1,211,500								
1886	(72)	388,360								
1886S		3,268,000								

Date	Quantity Minted		VF-20	EF-40	AU-50	MS-60	PF-63			Notes
1887, Proof only	(87)									
1887S		1,912,000								
1888	(95)	18,201								
1888S		293,900								
1889	(45)	7,520								
1890	(88)	4,240								
1890CC		53,800								
1891	(53)	61,360								
1891CC		208,000								
1892	(92)	753,480								
1892CC		82,968								
1892O		10,000								
1892S		298,400								
1893	(77)	1,528,120								
1893CC		60,000								
1893O		110,000								
1893S		224,000								
1894	(75)	957,880								
1894O		16,600								
1894S		55,900								
1895	(81)	1,345,855								
1895S		112,000								
1896	(103)	58,960								
1896S		155,400								
1897	(83)	867,800								
1897S		354,000								
1898	(75)	633,420								
1898S		1,397,400								
1899	(99)	1,710,630								
1899S		1,545,000								
1900	(230)	1,405,500								
1900S		329,000								
1901	(140)	615,900								
1901S, Final 1 Over 0		3,648,000								
1901S										
1902	(162)	172,400								
1902S		939,000								
1903	(154)	226,870								
1903S		1,855,000								
1904	(136)	392,000								
1904S		97,000								
1905	(108)	302,200								
1905S		880,700								
1906	(85)	348,735								
1906D		320,000								
1906S		598,000								

Date		Quantity Minted	VF-20	EF-40	AU-50	MS-60	PF-63		Notes
1907	(92)	626,100							
1907D		888,000							
1908		421,874							

Indian Head (1908–1929)

Date		Quantity Minted	VF-20	EF-40	AU-50	MS-60	PF-63		Notes
1908	(167)	577,845							
1908D		148,000							
1908S		82,000							
1909	(78)	627,060							
1909D		3,423,560							
19090		34,200							
1909S		297,200							
1910	(250)	604,000							
1910D		193,600							
1910S		770,200							
1911	(139)	915,000							
1911D		72,500							
1911S		1,416,000							
1912	(144)	790,000							
1912S		392,000							
1913	(99)	915,901							
1913S		408,000							
1914	(125)	247,000							
1914D		247,000							
1914S		263,000							
1915*	(75)	588,000							
1915S		164,000							
1916S		240,000							
1929		662,000							

* Pieces dated 1915-D are counterfeit.

EAGLES

Capped Bust to Right, Small Eagle (1795–1797)

Date	Quantity Minted	F-12	VF-20	EF-40	AU-50	MS-60		Notes
1795, 13 Leaves Below Eagle	5,583							
1795, 9 Leaves Below Eagle								
1796	4,146							
1797, Small Eagle	3,615							

Capped Bust to Right, Heraldic Eagle (1797–1804)

Date	Quantity Minted	F-12	VF-20	EF-40	AU-50	MS-60		Notes
1797, Large Eagle	10,940							
1798, 8 Over 7, 9 Stars Left, 4 Right	900							
1798, 8 Over 7, 7 Stars Left, 6 Right	842							
1799, Small Obverse Stars	37,449							
1799, Large Obverse Stars								
1800	5,999							
1801	44,344							
1803, Small Reverse Stars	15,017							
1803, Large Reverse Stars								
1804, Crosslet 4	3,757							
1804, Plain 4, Proof, Restrike *(4 known)*								

Liberty Head, No Motto Above Eagle (1838–1866)

Date	Quantity Minted	VF-20	EF-40	AU-50	MS-60	PF-63			Notes
1838	7,200								
1839, Large Letters	25,801								
1839, 9 Over 8, Type of 1838									
1839, Small Letters	12,447								
1840	47,338								
1841	63,131								
18410	2,500								
1842, Small Date, Plain 4	18,623								
1842, Large Date, Crosslet 4	62,884								
18420	27,400								
1843	75,462								
18430	175,162								
1844	6,361								
18440	118,700								
1845	26,153								
18450	47,500								
1846	20,095								
18460 / 18460, 6 Over 5	81,780								
1847	862,258								
18470	571,500								
1848	145,484								
18480	35,850								
1849	653,618								
18490	23,900								
1850, Large Date / 1850, Small Date	291,451								
18500	57,500								
1851	176,328								
18510	263,000								
1852	263,106								
18520	18,000								
1853, 3 Over 2 / 1853	201,253								
18530	51,000								
1854	54,250								

Date		Quantity Minted	VF-20	EF-40	AU-50	MS-60	PF-63		Notes
18540, Large or Small Date		52,500							
1854S		123,826							
1855		121,701							
18550		18,000							
1855S		9,000							
1856		60,490							
18560		14,500							
1856S		68,000							
1857		16,606							
18570		5,500							
1857S		26,000							
1858		2,521							
18580		20,000							
1858S		11,800							
1859	(80)	16,013							
18590		2,300							
1859S		7,000							
1860	(50)	15,055							
18600		11,100							
1860S		5,000							
1861	(69)	113,164							
1861S		15,500							
1862	(35)	10,960							
1862S		12,500							
1863	(30)	1,218							
1863S		10,000							
1864	(50)	3,530							
1864S		2,500							
1865	(25)	3,980							
1865S		16,700							
1865S, 865 Over Inverted 186									
1866S		8,500							

Liberty Head, Motto Above Eagle (1866–1907)

Date		Quantity Minted	VF-20	EF-40	AU-50	MS-60	PF-63		Notes
1866	(30)	3,750							
1866S		11,500							
1867	(50)	3,090							

Date		Quantity Minted	VF-20	EF-40	AU-50	MS-60	PF-63			Notes
1867S		9,000								
1868	(25)	10,630								
1868S		13,500								
1869	(25)	1,830								
1869S		6,430								
1870	(35)	3,990								
1870CC		5,908								
1870S		8,000								
1871	(30)	1,790								
1871CC		8,085								
1871S		16,500								
1872	(30)	1,620								
1872CC		4,600								
1872S		17,300								
1873	(25)	800								
1873CC		4,543								
1873S		12,000								
1874	(20)	53,140								
1874CC		16,767								
1874S		10,000								
1875	(20)	100								
1875CC		7,715								
1876	(45)	687								
1876CC		4,696								
1876S		5,000								
1877	(20)	797								
1877CC		3,332								
1877S		17,000								
1878	(20)	73,780								
1878CC		3,244								
1878S		26,100								
1879	(30)	384,740								
1879CC		1,762								
18790		1,500								
1879S		224,000								
1880	(36)	1,644,840								
1880CC		11,190								
18800		9,200								
1880S		506,250								
1881	(40)	3,877,220								
1881CC		24,015								
18810		8,350								
1881S		970,000								
1882	(40)	2,324,440								
1882CC		6,764								
18820		10,820								

Date		Quantity Minted	VF-20	EF-40	AU-50	MS-60	PF-63			Notes
1882S		132,000								
1883	(40)	208,700								
1883CC		12,000								
1883O		800								
1883S		38,000								
1884	(45)	76,860								
1884CC		9,925								
1884S		124,250								
1885	(65)	253,462								
1885S		228,000								
1886	(60)	236,100								
1886S		826,000								
1887	(80)	53,600								
1887S		817,000								
1888	(75)	132,921								
1888O		21,335								
1888S		648,700								
1889	(45)	4,440								
1889S		425,400								
1890	(63)	57,980								
1890CC		17,500								
1891	(48)	91,820								
1891CC		103,732								
1892	(72)	797,480								
1892CC		40,000								
1892O		28,688								
1892S		115,500								
1893	(55)	1,840,840								
1893CC		14,000								
1893O		17,000								
1893S		141,350								
1894	(43)	2,470,735								
1894O		107,500								
1894S		25,000								
1895	(56)	567,770								
1895O		98,000								
1895S		49,000								
1896	(78)	76,270								
1896S		123,750								
1897	(69)	1,000,090								
1897O		42,500								
1897S		234,750								
1898	(67)	812,130								
1898S		473,600								
1899	(86)	1,262,219								
1899O		37,047								

Date		Quantity Minted	VF-20	EF-40	AU-50	MS-60	PF-63			Notes
1899S		841,000								
1900	(120)	293,840								
1900S		81,000								
1901	(85)	1,718,740								
19010		72,041								
1901S		2,812,750								
1902	(113)	82,400								
1902S		469,500								
1903	(96)	125,830								
19030		112,771								
1903S		538,000								
1904	(108)	161,930								
19040		108,950								
1905	(86)	200,992								
1905S		369,250								
1906	(77)	165,420								
1906D		981,000								
19060		86,895								
1906S		457,000								
1907	(74)	1,203,899								
1907D		1,030,000								
1907S		210,500								

Indian Head, Variety 1, No Motto on Reverse (1907–1908)

Date	Quantity Minted	VF-20	EF-40	AU-50	MS-60	PF-63			Notes
1907, Wire Rim, Periods	500								
1907, Rounded Rim, Periods Before and After •E•PLURIBUS•UNUM•	50								
1907, No Periods	239,406								
1908, No Motto	33,500								
1908D, No Motto	210,000								

Indian Head, Variety 2, Motto on Reverse (1908–1933)

Date		Quantity Minted	VF-20	EF-40	AU-50	MS-60	MS-63	PF-63		Notes
1908	(116)	341,370								
1908D		836,500								
1908S		59,850								
1909	(74)	184,789								
1909D		121,540								
1909S		292,350								
1910	(204)	318,500								
1910D		2,356,640								
1910S		811,000								
1911	(95)	505,500								
1911D		30,100								
1911S		51,000								
1912	(83)	405,000								
1912S		300,000								
1913	(71)	442,000								
1913S		66,000								
1914	(50)	151,000								
1914D		343,500								
1914S		208,000								
1915	(75)	351,000								
1915S		59,000								
1916S		138,500								
1920S		126,500								
1926		1,014,000								
1930S		96,000								
1932		4,463,000								
1933		312,500								

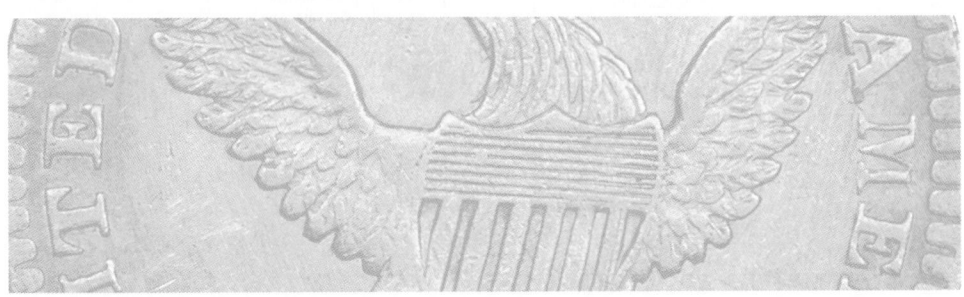

DOUBLE EAGLES

Liberty Head, Without Motto on Reverse (1849–1866)

Date	Quantity Minted	VF-20	EF-40	AU-50	MS-60	PF-63		Notes
1849 *(pattern; in Smithsonian)*	1							
1850	1,170,261							
18500	141,000							
1851	2,087,155							
18510	315,000							
1852	2,053,026							
18520	190,000							
1853, "3 Over 2"	1,261,326							
1853								
18530	71,000							
1854, Small Date	757,899							
1854, Large Date								
18540	3,250							
1854S	141,468							
1855	364,666							
18550	8,000							
1855S	879,675							
1856	329,878							
18560	2,250							
1856S	1,189,750							
1857	439,375							
18570	30,000							
1857S	970,500							
1858	211,714							
18580	35,250							
1858S	846,710							
1859 (80)	43,597							
18590	9,100							
1859S	636,445							
1860 (59)	577,670							
18600	6,600							

Date		Quantity Minted	VF-20	EF-40	AU-50	MS-60	PF-63			Notes
1860S		544,950								
1861	(66)	2,976,453								
18610		17,741								
1861S		768,000								
1861, Paquet Reverse (Tall Letters)										
1861S, Paquet Reverse (Tall Letters)		19,250								
1862	(35)	92,133								
1862S		854,173								
1863	(30)	142,790								
1863S		966,570								
1864	(50)	204,235								
1864S		793,660								
1865	(25)	351,175								
1865S		1,042,500								
1866S		120,000								

Liberty Head, Motto Above Eagle, Value TWENTY D. (1866–1876)

Date		Quantity Minted	VF-20	EF-40	AU-50	MS-60	PF-63			Notes
1866	(30)	698,745								
1866S		842,250								
1867	(50)	251,015								
1867S		920,750								
1868	(25)	98,575								
1868S		837,500								
1869	(25)	175,130								
1869S		686,750								
1870	(35)	155,150								
1870CC		3,789								
1870S		982,000								
1871	(30)	80,120								
1871CC		17,387								
1871S		928,000								
1872	(30)	251,850								
1872CC		26,900								

Date		Quantity Minted	VF-20	EF-40	AU-50	MS-60	PF-63		Notes
1872S		780,000							
1873, Close 3	(25)	1,709,825							
1873, Open 3									
1873CC, Close 3		22,410							
1873S, Close 3		1,040,600							
1873S, Open 3									
1874	(20)	366,780							
1874CC		115,085							
1874S		1,214,000							
1875	(20)	295,720							
1875CC		111,151							
1875S		1,230,000							
1876	(45)	583,860							
1876CC		138,441							
1876S		1,597,000							

Liberty Head, Motto Above Eagle, Value TWENTY DOLLARS (1877–1907)

Date		Quantity Minted	VF-20	EF-40	AU-50	MS-60	PF-63		Notes
1877	(20)	397,650							
1877CC		42,565							
1877S		1,735,000							
1878	(20)	543,625							
1878CC		13,180							
1878S		1,739,000							
1879	(30)	207,600							
1879CC		10,708							
1879O		2,325							
1879S		1,223,800							
1880	(36)	51,420							
1880S		836,000							
1881	(61)	2,199							
1881S		727,000							
1882	(59)	571							
1882CC		39,140							
1882S		1,125,000							
1883, Proof only	(92)								

Date		Quantity Minted	VF-20	EF-40	AU-50	MS-60	PF-63			Notes
1883CC		59,962								
1883S		1,189,000								
1884, Proof only	(71)									
1884CC		81,139								
1884S		916,000								
1885	(77)	751								
1885CC		9,450								
1885S		683,500								
1886	(106)	1,000								
1887, Proof only	(121)									
1887S		283,000								
1888	(105)	226,161								
1888S		859,600								
1889	(41)	44,070								
1889CC		30,945								
1889S		774,700								
1890	(55)	75,940								
1890CC		91,209								
1890S		802,750								
1891	(52)	1,390								
1891CC		5,000								
1891S		1,288,125								
1892	(93)	4,430								
1892CC		27,265								
1892S		930,150								
1893	(59)	344,280								
1893CC		18,402								
1893S		996,175								
1894	(50)	1,368,940								
1894S		1,048,550								
1895	(51)	1,114,605								
1895S		1,143,500								
1896	(128)	792,535								
1896S		1,403,925								
1897	(86)	1,383,175								
1897S		1,470,250								
1898	(75)	170,395								
1898S		2,575,175								
1899	(84)	1,669,300								
1899S		2,010,300								
1900	(124)	1,874,460								
1900S		2,459,500								
1901	(96)	111,430								
1901S		1,596,000								
1902	(114)	31,140								
1902S		1,753,625								

Date		Quantity Minted	VF-20	EF-40	AU-50	MS-60	PF-63		Notes
1903	(158)	287,270							
1903S		954,000							
1904	(98)	6,256,699							
1904S		5,134,175							
1905	(92)	58,919							
1905S		1,813,000							
1906	(94)	69,596							
1906D		620,250							
1906S		2,065,750							
1907	(78)	1,451,786							
1907D		842,250							
1907S		2,165,800							

Saint-Gaudens, Ultra High Relief Pattern, MCMVII (1907)

Date	Quantity Minted	PF-67						Notes
1907, Ultra High Relief, Plain Edge *(unique)*								
1907, Ultra High Relief, Lettered Edge								

Saint-Gaudens, Without Motto, High Relief, MCMVII (1907)

Date	Quantity Minted	VF-20	EF-40	AU-50	MS-60			Notes
1907, High Relief, Roman Numerals (MCMVII), Wire Rim	12,367							
1907, Same, Flat Rim								

Saint-Gaudens, Without Motto, Arabic Numerals (1907–1908)

Date	Quantity Minted	VF-20	EF-40	AU-50	MS-60			Notes
1907, Arabic Numerals	361,667							
1908	4,271,551							
1908D	663,750							

Saint-Gaudens, With Motto IN GOD WE TRUST (1908–1933)

Date		Quantity Minted	VF-20	EF-40	AU-50	MS-60	PF-63			Notes
1908	(101)	156,258								
1908D		349,500								
1908S		22,000								
1909, 9 Over 8		161,282								
1909	(67)									
1909D		52,500								
1909S		2,774,925								
1910	(167)	482,000								
1910D		429,000								
1910S		2,128,250								
1911	(100)	197,250								
1911D		846,500								
1911S		775,750								
1912	(74)	149,750								
1913	(58)	168,780								
1913D		393,500								
1913S		34,000								

Date	Quantity Minted	VF-20	EF-40	AU-50	MS-60	PF-63			Notes
1914	(70) 95,250								
1914D	453,000								
1914S	1,498,000								
1915	(50) 152,000								
1915S	567,500								
1916S	796,000								
1920	228,250								
1920S	558,000								
1921	528,500								
1922	1,375,500								
1922S	2,658,000								
1923	566,000								
1923D	1,702,250								
1924	4,323,500								
1924D	3,049,500								
1924S	2,927,500								
1925	2,831,750								
1925D	2,938,500								
1925S	3,776,500								
1926	816,750								
1926D	481,000								
1926S	2,041,500								
1927	2,946,750								
1927D	180,000								
1927S	3,107,000								
1928	8,816,000								
1929	1,779,750								
1930S	74,000								
1931	2,938,250								
1931D	106,500								
1932	1,101,750								
1933 *(extremely rare)*	445,500								

COMMEMORATIVES

Classic Commemorative Silver and Gold

Date	Distribution	AU-50	MS-60	MS-65		Notes
1892, World's Columbian Exposition half dollar	950,000					
1893, Same type	1,550,405					
1893, World's Columbian Exposition quarter	24,214					
1900, Lafayette	36,026					
1903, Louisiana Purchase / Thomas Jefferson	17,500					
1903, Louisiana Purchase / William McKinley	17,500					
1904, Lewis and Clark Exposition	10,025					
1905, Lewis and Clark Exposition	10,041					
1915S, Panama-Pacific Exposition half dollar	27,134					
1915S, Panama-Pacific Exposition dollar	15,000					
1915S, Panama-Pacific Exposition $2.50	6,749					
1915S, Panama-Pacific Exposition $50, Round	483					

Date	Distribution	AU-50	MS-60	MS-65		Notes
1915S, Panama-Pacific Exposition $50, Octagonal	645					
1916, McKinley Memorial	*15,000*					
1917, McKinley Memorial	*5,000*					
1918, Illinois Centennial	100,058					
1920, Maine Centennial	50,028					
1920, Pilgrim Tercentenary	152,112					
1921, Same, With Date Added in Field	20,053					
1921, Missouri Centennial, "2 ★ 4" in Field	9,400					
1921, Missouri Centennial, Plain	11,400					
1921, Alabama Centennial, Plain	*35,000*					
1921, Alabama Centennial, With "2X2" in Field of Obverse	*30,000*					
1922, Grant Memorial half dollar, With Star	4,256					
1922, Same type, No Star	67,405					
1922, Grant Memorial dollar, With Star	5,016					
1922, Grant Memorial dollar, No Star	5,016					
1923S, Monroe Doctrine Centennial	274,077					
1924, Huguenot-Walloon Tercentenary	142,080					
1925, Lexington-Concord Sesquicentennial	162,013					
1925, Stone Mountain Memorial	1,314,709					
1925S, California Diamond Jubilee	86,594					
1925, Fort Vancouver Centennial	14,994					
1926, Sesquicentennial of American Independence half dollar	141,120					
1926, Sesquicentennial of American Independence $2.50	46,019					
1926, Oregon Trail Memorial	47,955					
1926S, Same type, S Mint	83,055					
1928, Oregon Trail Memorial (same as 1926)	6,028					
1933D, Oregon Trail Memorial	5,008					
1934D, Oregon Trail Memorial	7,006					
1936, Oregon Trail Memorial	10,006					
1936S, Same type, S Mint	5,006					
1937D, Oregon Trail Memorial	12,008					
1938, Oregon Trail Memorial (same as 1926)	6,006					
1938D, Same type, D Mint	6,005					
1938S, Same type, S Mint	6,006					
1939, Oregon Trail Memorial (same as 1926)	3,004					
1939D, Same type, D Mint	3,004					
1939S, Same type, S Mint	3,005					
1927, Vermont Sesquicentennial	28,142					
1928, Hawaiian Sesquicentennial	10,008					
1928, Hawaiian Sesquicentennial Sandblast Proof Presentation Piece	(50)					
1934, Maryland Tercentenary	25,015					
1934, Texas Independence Centennial	61,463					

Date	Distribution	AU-50	MS-60	MS-65		Notes
1935, Texas Independence Centennial (same as 1934)	9,996					
1935D, Same type, D Mint	10,007					
1935S, Same type, S Mint	10,008					
1936, Texas Independence Centennial (same as 1934)	8,911					
1936D, Same type, D Mint	9,039					
1936S, Same type, S Mint	9,055					
1937, Texas Independence Centennial (same as 1934)	6,571					
1937D, Same type, D Mint	6,605					
1937S, Same type, S Mint	6,637					
1938, Texas Independence Centennial (same as 1934)	3,780					
1938D, Same type, D Mint	3,775					
1938S, Same type, S Mint	3,814					
1934, Daniel Boone Bicentennial	10,007					
1935, Same type	10,010					
1935D, Same type, D Mint	5,005					
1935S, Same type, S Mint	5,005					
1935, Same as 1934, Same 1934 on Reverse	10,008					
1935D, Same type, D Mint	2,003					
1935S, Same type, S Mint	2,004					
1936, Daniel Boone Bicentennial (same as above)	12,012					
1936D, Same type, D Mint	5,005					
1936S, Same type, S Mint	5,006					
1937, Daniel Boone Bicentennial (same as above)	9,810					
1937D, Same type, D Mint	2,506					
1937S, Same type, S Mint	2,506					
1938, Daniel Boone Bicentennial (same as above)	2,100					
1938D, Same type, D Mint	2,100					
1938S, Same type, S Mint	2,100					
1935, Connecticut Tercentenary	25,018					
1935, Arkansas Centennial	13,012					
1935D, Same type, D Mint	5,505					
1935, Same type, S Mint	5,506					
1936, Arkansas Centennial (same as 1935; date 1936 on reverse)	9,660					
1936, Same type, D Mint	9,660					
1936S, Same type, S Mint	9,662					
1937, Arkansas Centennial (same as 1935)	5,505					
1937, Same type, D Mint	5,505					
1937S, Same type S Mint	5,506					
1938, Arkansas Centennial (same as 1935)	3,156					
1938, Same type, D Mint	3,155					
1938S, Same type, S Mint	3,156					
1939, Arkansas Centennial (same as 1935)	2,104					
1939, Same type, D Mint	2,104					
1939, Same type, S Mint	2,105					
1936, Arkansas Centennial (Robinson)	25,265					

Date	Distribution	AU-50	MS-60	MS-65		Notes
1935, Hudson, New York, Sesquicentennial	10,008					
1935S, California Pacific International Exposition	70,132					
1936D, California Pacific International Exposition	30,092					
1935, Old Spanish Trail	10,008					
1936, Providence, Rhode Island, Tercentenary	20,013					
1936D, Same type, D Mint	15,010					
1936S, Same type, S Mint	15,011					
1936, Cleveland Centennial / Great Lakes Exposition	50,030					
1936, Wisconsin Territorial Centennial	25,015					
1936, Cincinnati Music Center	5,005					
1936D, Same type, D Mint	5,005					
1936S, Same type, S Mint	5,006					
1936, Long Island Tercentenary	81,826					
1936, York County, Maine, Tercentenary	25,015					
1936, Bridgeport, Connecticut, Centennial	25,015					
1936, Lynchburg, Virginia, Sesquicentennial	20,013					
1936, Elgin, Illinois, Centennial	20,015					
1936, Albany, New York, Charter	17,671					
1936S, San Francisco–Oakland Bay Bridge Opening	71,424					
1936, Columbia, South Carolina, Sesquicentennial	9,007					
1936D, Same type, D Mint	8,009					
1936S, Same type, S Mint	8,007					
1936, Delaware Tercentenary	20,993					
1936, Battle of Gettysburg Anniversary	26,928					
1936, Norfolk, Virginia, Bicentennial	16,936					
1937, Roanoke Island, North Carolina, 350th Anniversary	29,030					
1937, Battle of Antietam Anniversary	18,028					
1938, New Rochelle, New York, 250th Anniversary	15,266					
1946, Iowa Centennial	100,057					
1946, Booker T. Washington Memorial	700,546					
1946D, Same type, D Mint	50,000					
1946S, Same type, S Mint	500,279					
1947, Same type as 1946	6,000					
1947D, Same type, D Mint	6,000					
1947S, Same type, S Mint	6,000					
1948, Same type as 1946	8,005					
1948D, Same type, D Mint	8,005					
1948S, Same type, S Mint	8,005					
1949, Same type as 1946	6,004					
1949D, Same type, D Mint	6,004					
1949S, Same type, S Mint	6,004					
1950, Same type as 1946	6,004					
1950D, Same type, D Mint	6,004					
1950S, Same type, S Mint	62,091					

Date	Distribution	AU-50	MS-60	MS-65		Notes
1951, Same type as 1946	210,082					
1951D, Same type, D Mint	7,004					
1951S, Same type, S Mint	7,004					
1951, Carver/Washington	20,018					
1951D, Same type, D Mint	10,004					
1951S, Same type, S Mint	10,004					
1952, Same type as 1951	1,106,292					
1952D, Same type, D Mint	8,006					
1952S, Same type, S Mint	8,006					
1953, Same type as 1951	8,003					
1953D, Same type, D Mint	8,003					
1953S, Same type, S Mint	88,020					
1954, Same type as 1951	12,006					
1954D, Same type, D Mint	12,006					
1954S, Same type, S Mint	42,024					

Modern Commemoratives

Date	Distribution		MS-67	PF-67			Notes
1982D, George Washington, 250th Anniversary half dollar	2,210,458						
1982S, Same type, Proof	(4,894,044)						
1983P, Los Angeles Olympiad, Discus Thrower silver dollar	294,543						

Date		Distribution	MS-67	PF-67			Notes
1983D, Same type, D Mint		174,014					
1983S, Same type, S Mint	(1,577,025)	174,014					
1984P, Olympic Coliseum silver dollar		217,954					
1984D, Same type, D Mint		116,675					
1984S, Same type, S Mint	(1,801,210)	116,675					
1984P, Olympic Torch Bearers gold $10	(33,309)						
1984D, Same type, D Mint	(34,533)						
1984S, Same type, S Mint	(48,551)						
1984W, Same type, W Mint	(381,085)	75,886					
1986D, Statue of Liberty half dollar		928,008					
1986S, Same type, S Mint, Proof	(6,925,627)						
1986P, Statue of Liberty silver dollar		723,635					
1986S, Same type, S Mint, Proof	(6,414,638)						
1986W, Statue of Liberty gold $5	(404,013)	95,248					
1987P, U.S. Constitution silver dollar		451,629					
1987S, Same type, S Mint, Proof	(2,747,116)						
1987W, U.S. Constitution gold $5	(651,659)	214,225					
1988D, Seoul Olympiad silver dollar		191,368					
1988S, Same type, S Mint, Proof	(1,359,366)						
1988W, Seoul Olympiad gold $5	(281,465)	62,913					
1989D, Congress Bicentennial half dollar		163,753					
1989S, Same type, S Mint, Proof	(767,897)						
1989D, Congress Bicentennial silver dollar		135,203					
1989S, Same type, S Mint, Proof	(762,198)						
1989W, Congress Bicentennial gold $5	(164,690)	46,899					
1990W, Eisenhower Centennial silver dollar		241,669					
1990P, Same type, P Mint, Proof	(1,144,461)						
1991D, Mount Rushmore half dollar		172,754					
1991S, Same type, S Mint, Proof	(753,257)						
1991P, Mount Rushmore silver dollar		133,139					
1991S, Same type, S Mint, Proof	(738,419)						
1991W, Mount Rushmore gold $5	(111,991)	31,959					
1991D, Korean War silver dollar		213,049					
1991P, Same type, P Mint, Proof	(618,488)						
1991D USO silver dollar		124,958					
1991S, Same type, S Mint, Proof	(321,275)						
1992P, XXV Olympiad clad half dollar		161,607					
1992S, Same type, S Mint, Proof	(519,645)						
1992D, XXV Olympiad silver dollar		187,552					
1992S, Same type, S Mint, Proof	(504,505)						
1992W, XXV Olympiad gold $5	(77,313)	27,732					
1992D, White House silver dollar		123,803					
1992W, Same type, W Mint, Proof	(375,851)						

Date		Distribution	MS-67	PF-67			Notes
1992D, Columbus Quincentenary half dollar		135,702					
1992S, Same type, S Mint, Proof	(390,154)						
1992D, Columbus Quincentenary silver dollar		106,949					
1992P, Same type, P Mint, Proof	(385,241)						
1992W, Columbus Quincentenary gold $5	(79,730)	24,329					
1993W, Bill of Rights silver half dollar		193,346					
1993S, Same type, S Mint, Proof	(586,315)						
1993D, Bill of Rights silver dollar		98,383					
1993S, Same type, S Mint, Proof	(534,001)						
1993W, Bill of Rights gold $5	(78,651)	23,266					
(1993P) 1991–1995 World War II clad half dollar	(317,396)	197,072					
(1993D) 1991–1995 World War II silver dollar		107,240					
(1993W) Same type, W Mint, Proof	(342,041)						
(1993W) 1991–1995 World War II gold $5	(67,026)	23,672					
1994D, World Cup Tournament clad half dollar		168,208					
1994P, Same type, P Mint, Proof	(609,354)						
1994D, World Cup Tournament silver dollar		81,524					
1994S, Same type, S Mint, Proof	(577,090)						
1994W, World Cup Tournament gold $5	(89,614)	22,447					
1993 (1994) Thomas Jefferson silver dollar, P Mint		266,927					
1993 (1994) Same type, S Mint, Proof	(332,891)						
1994W, Vietnam Veterans Memorial silver dollar		57,290					
1994P, Same type, P Mint, Proof	(227,671)						
1994W, U.S. POW Museum silver dollar		54,893					
1994P, Same type, P Mint, Proof	(224,449)						
1994W, Women in Military Service Memorial silver dollar		69,860					
1994P, Same type, P Mint, Proof	(241,278)						
1994D, U.S. Capitol Bicentennial silver dollar		68,332					
1994S, Same type, S Mint, Proof	(279,579)						
1995S, Civil War Battlefield Preservation clad half dollar		119,520					
1995S, Same type, S Mint, Proof	(330,002)						
1995P, Civil War Battlefield Preservation silver dollar		45,866					

Date		Distribution	MS-67	PF-67			Notes
1995S, Same type, S Mint, Proof	(437,114)						
1995W, Civil War Battlefield Preservation gold $5		12,735					
1995W, Same type, W Mint, Proof	(55,246)						
1995S, XXVI Olympiad, Basketball clad half dollar		171,001					
1995S, Same type, S Mint, Proof	(169,655)						
1995S, XXVI Olympiad, Baseball clad half dollar		164,605					
1995S, Same type, S Mint, Proof	(118,087)						
1996S, XXVI Olympiad, Swimming clad half dollar		49,533					
1996S, Same type, S Mint, Proof	(114,315)						
1996S, XXVI Olympiad, Soccer clad half dollar		52,836					
1996S, Same type, S Mint, Proof	(112,412)						
1995D, XXVI Olympiad, Gymnastics silver dollar		42,497					
1995P, Same type, P Mint, Proof	(182,676)						
1995D, XXVI Olympiad, Paralympics silver dollar		28,649					
1995P, Same type, P Mint, Proof	(138,337)						
1995D, XXVI Olympiad, Track and Field silver dollar		24,976					
1995P, Same type, P Mint, Proof	(136,935)						
1995D, XXVI Olympiad, Cycling silver dollar		19,662					
1995P, Same type, P Mint, Proof	(118,795)						
1996D, XXVI Olympiad, Tennis silver $1		15,983					
1996P, Same type, P Mint, Proof	(92,016)						
1996D, XXVI Olympiad, Paralympics silver dollar		14,497					
1996P, Same type, P Mint, Proof	(84,280)						
1996D, XXVI Olympiad, Rowing silver $1		16,258					
1996P, Same type, P Mint, Proof	(151,890)						
1996D, XXVI Olympiad, High Jump silver dollar		15,697					
1996P, Same type, P Mint, Proof	(124,502)						
1995W, XXVI Olympiad, Torch Runner gold $5		14,675					
1995W, Same type, W Mint, Proof	(57,442)						
1995W, XXVI Olympiad, Stadium gold $5		10,579					
1995W, Same type, W Mint, Proof	(43,124)						
1996W, XXVI Olympiad, Flag Bearer gold $5		9,174					
1996W, Same type, W Mint, Proof	(32,886)						

Date		Distribution	MS-67	PF-67			Notes
1996W, XXVI Olympiad, Cauldron gold $5		9,210					
1996W, Same type, W Mint, Proof	(38,555)						
1995W, Special Olympics silver dollar		89,301					
1995P, Same type, P Mint, Proof	(351,764)						
1996S, National Community Service silver dollar		23,500					
1996S, Same type, S Mint, Proof	(101,543)						
1996D, Smithsonian silver dollar		31,320					
1996P, Same type, P Mint, Proof	(129,152)						
1996W, Smithsonian gold $5		9,068					
1996W, Same type, W Mint, Proof	(21,772)						
1997P, Botanic Garden silver dollar		58,505					
1997P, Same type, P Mint, Proof	(189,671)						
1997S, Jackie Robinson silver dollar		30,180					
1997S, Same type, S Mint, Proof	(110,002)						
1997W, Jackie Robinson gold $5		5,174					
1997W, Same type, W Mint, Proof	(24,072)						
1997W, Franklin D. Roosevelt gold $5		11,894					
1997W, Same type, W Mint, Proof	(29,474)						
1997P, Law Enforcement silver dollar		28,575					
1997P, Same type, P Mint, Proof	(110,428)						
1998S, Robert F. Kennedy silver dollar		106,422					
1998S, Same type, S Mint, Proof	(99,020)						
1998S, Black Patriots silver dollar		37,210					
1998S, Same type, S Mint, Proof	(75,070)						
1999P, Dolley Madison silver dollar		89,104					
1999P, Same type, P Mint, Proof	(224,403)						
1999W, George Washington gold $5		22,511					
1999W, Same type, W Mint, Proof	(41,693)						
1999P, Yellowstone silver dollar		23,614					
1999P, Same type, S Mint, Proof	(128,646)						
2000P, Library of Congress silver dollar		53,264					
2000P, Same type, P Mint, Proof	(198,503)						
2000W, Library of Congress bimetallic (gold/platinum) $10		7,261					
2000W, Same type, W Mint, Proof	(27,445)						
2000P, Leif Ericson silver dollar		28,150					
2000P, Same type, P Mint, Proof	(144,748)						
2001D, American Buffalo silver dollar		227,131					
2001P, Same type, P Mint, Proof	(272,869)						
2001P, U.S. Capitol Visitor Center clad half dollar		99,157					
2001P, Same type, P Mint, Proof	(77,962)						
2001P, U.S. Capitol Visitor Center silver dollar		35,380					
2001P, Same type, P Mint, Proof	(143,793)						

Date		Distribution	MS-67	PF-67				Notes
2001W, U.S. Capitol Visitor Center gold $5		6,761						
2001W, Same type, W Mint, Proof	(27,652)							
2002D, Salt Lake City Olympics silv dollar		40,257						
2002P, Same type, P Mint, Proof	(166,864)							
2002W, Salt Lake City Olympics gold $5		10,585						
2002W, Same type, W Mint, Proof	(32,877)							
2002W, West Point Bicentennial silver dollar		103,201						
2002W, Same type, W Mint, Proof	(288,293)							
2003P, First Flight Centennial clad half dollar		57,122						
2003P, Same type, P Mint, Proof	(109,710)							
2003P, First Flight Centennial silver dollar		53,533						
2003P, Same type, P Mint, Proof	(190,240)							
2003W, First Flight Centennial gold $10		10,009						
2003W, Same type, W Mint, Proof	(21,676)							
2004P, Thomas Edison silver dollar		92,510						
2004P, Same type, P Mint, Proof	(211,055)							
2004P, Lewis and Clark silver dollar		142,015						
2004P, Same type, P Mint, Proof	(351,989)							
2005P, John Marshall silver dollar		67,096						
2005P, Same type, P Mint, Proof	(196,753)							
2005P, Marine Corps 230th Anniversary silver dollar		49,671						
2005P, Same type, P Mint, Proof	(548,810)							
2006P, Benjamin Franklin "Scientist" silver dollar		58,000						
2006P, Same type, P Mint, Proof	(142,000)							
2006P, Benjamin Franklin "Founding Father" silver dollar		58,000						
2006P, Same type, P Mint, Proof	(142,000)							
2006S, San Francisco Old Mint silver dollar		67,100						
2006S, Same type, S Mint, Proof	(160,870)							
2006S, San Francisco Old Mint gold $5		17,500						
2006S, Same type, S Mint, Proof	(44,174)							
2007P, Jamestown 400th Anniversary silver dollar								
2007P, Same type, P Mint, Proof								
2007W, Jamestown 400th Anniversary gold $5								
2007W, Same type, W Mint, Proof								
2007P, Little Rock Central High School Desegregation silver dollar		124,678						
2007S, Same type, P Mint, Proof	(66,093)							

Date	Distribution	MS-67	PF-67				Notes
2008S, Bald Eagle clad half dollar	120,180						
2008S, Same type, S Mint, Proof	(220,577)						
2008P, Bald Eagle silver dollar	119,204						
2008P, Same type, P Mint, Proof	(294,601)						
2008W, Bald Eagle gold $5	15,009						
2008W, Same type, W Mint, Proof	(59,269)						
2009P, Louis Braille Bicentennial silver dollar	82,639						
2009P, Same type, P Mint, Proof	(135,235)						
2009P, Abraham Lincoln Bicentennial silver dollar	125,000						
2009P, Same type, P Mint, Proof	(325,000)						
2010W, American Veterans Disabled for Life silver dollar	77,859						
2010W, Same type, W Mint, Proof	(189,881)						
2010P, Boy Scouts Centennial silver dollar	105,000						
2010P, Same type, P Mint, Proof	(245,000)						
2011P, Medal of Honor silver dollar							
2011S, Same type, S Mint, Proof							
2011P, Medal of Honor gold $5							
2011S, Same type, P Mint, Proof							
2011P, U.S. Army clad half dollar							
2011S, Same type, S Mint, Proof							
2011P, U.S. Army silver dollar							
2011S, Same type, S Mint, Proof							
2011P, U.S. Army gold $5							
2011S, Same type, S Mint, Proof							
2012P, Infantry Soldier silver dollar							
2012S, Same type, S Mint, Proof							
2012P, Star-Spangled Banner silver dollar							
2012S, Same type, S Mint, Proof							
2012P, Star-Spangled Banner gold $5							
2012S, Same type, S Mint, Proof							

GOVERNMENT COMMEMORATIVE SETS

		Notes
(1983–1984) LOS ANGELES OLYMPIAD		
1983 and 1984 Proof dollars		
1983 and 1984 6-coin set. One each of 1983 and 1984 dollars, both Proof and Uncirculated gold $10		
1983 3-piece collector set. 1983 P, D, and S Uncirculated dollars		
1984 3-piece collector set. 1984 P, D, and S Uncirculated dollars		
1983 and 1984 gold and silver Uncirculated set. One each of 1983 and 1984 Uncirculated dollar and one 1984 Uncirculated gold $10		
1983 and 1984 gold and silver Proof set. One each of 1983 and 1984 Proof dollars and one 1984 Proof gold $10		

		Notes
(1986) STATUE OF LIBERTY		
2-coin set. Proof silver dollar and clad half dollar		
3-coin set. Proof silver dollar, clad half dollar, and gold $5		
2-coin set. Uncirculated silver dollar and clad half dollar		
2-coin set. Uncirculated and Proof gold $5		
3-coin set. Uncirculated silver dollar, clad half dollar, and gold $5		
6-coin set. One each of Proof and Uncirculated half dollar, silver dollar, and gold $5		
(1987) CONSTITUTION		
2-coin set. Uncirculated silver dollar and gold $5		
2-coin set. Proof silver dollar and gold $5		
4-coin set. One each of Proof and Uncirculated silver dollar and gold $5		
(1988) SEOUL OLYMPIAD		
2-coin set. Uncirculated silver dollar and gold $5		
2-coin set. Proof silver dollar and gold $5		
4-coin set. One each of Proof and Uncirculated silver dollar and gold $5		
(1989) CONGRESS		
2-coin set. Proof clad half dollar and silver dollar		
3-coin set. Proof clad half dollar, silver dollar, and gold $5		
2-coin set. Uncirculated clad half dollar and silver dollar		
3-coin set. Uncirculated clad half dollar, silver dollar, and gold $5		
6-coin set. One each of Proof and Uncirculated clad half dollar, silver dollar, and gold $5		
(1991) MOUNT RUSHMORE		
2-coin set. Uncirculated clad half dollar and silver dollar		
2-coin set. Proof clad half dollar and silver dollar		
3-coin set. Uncirculated clad half dollar, silver dollar, and gold $5		
3 coin set. Proof half dollar, silver dollar, and gold $5		
6-coin set. One each of Proof and Uncirculated clad half dollar, silver dollar, and gold $5		
(1992) XXV OLYMPIAD		
2-coin set. Uncirculated clad half dollar and silver dollar		
2-coin set. Proof clad half dollar and silver dollar		
3-coin set. Uncirculated clad half dollar, silver dollar, and gold $5		
3-coin set. Proof half dollar, silver dollar, and gold $5		
6-coin set. One each of Proof and Uncirculated clad half dollar, silver dollar, and gold $5		
(1992) CHRISTOPHER COLUMBUS		
2-coin set. Uncirculated clad half dollar and silver dollar		
2-coin set. Proof clad half dollar and silver dollar		
3-coin set. Uncirculated clad half dollar, silver dollar, and gold $5		
3-coin set. Proof silver half dollar, silver dollar, and gold $5		
6-coin set. One each of Proof and Uncirculated clad half dollar, silver dollar, and gold $5		
(1993) BILL OF RIGHTS		
2-coin set. Uncirculated silver half dollar and silver dollar		
2-coin set. Proof silver half dollar and silver dollar		
3-coin set. Uncirculated silver half dollar, silver dollar, and gold $5		
3-coin set. Proof silver half dollar, silver dollar, and gold $5		
6-coin set. One each of Proof and Uncirculated silver half dollar, silver dollar, and gold $5		
"Young Collector" set. Silver half dollar		

	Notes

Educational set. Silver half dollar and James Madison medal

Proof silver half dollar and 25-cent stamp

(1993) WORLD WAR II

2-coin set. Uncirculated clad half dollar and silver dollar

2-coin set. Proof clad half dollar and silver dollar

3-coin set. Uncirculated clad half dollar, silver dollar, and gold $5

3-coin set. Proof clad half dollar, silver dollar, and gold $5

6-coin set. One each of Proof and Uncirculated clad half dollar, silver dollar, and gold $5

"Young Collector" set. Clad half dollar

Victory Medal set. Uncirculated clad half dollar and reproduction medal

(1993) THOMAS JEFFERSON

3-piece set (issued in 1994). Silver dollar, Jefferson nickel, and $2 note

(1994) WORLD CUP SOCCER

2-coin set. Uncirculated clad half dollar and silver dollar

2-coin set. Proof clad half dollar and silver dollar

3-coin set. Uncirculated clad half dollar, silver dollar, and gold $5

3-coin set. Proof clad half dollar, silver dollar, and gold $5

6-coin set. One each of Proof and Uncirculated clad half dollar, silver dollar, and gold $5

"Young Collector" set. Uncirculated clad half dollar

"Special Edition" set. Proof clad half dollar and silver dollar

(1994) U.S. VETERANS

3-coin set. Uncirculated POW, Vietnam, and Women in Military Service silver dollars

3-coin set. Proof POW, Vietnam, and Women in Military Service silver dollars

(1995) SPECIAL OLYMPICS

2-coin set. Proof Special Olympics silver dollar, 1995S Kennedy half dollar

(1995) CIVIL WAR BATTLEFIELD PRESERVATION

2-coin set. Uncirculated clad half dollar and silver dollar

2-coin set. Proof clad half dollar and silver dollar

3-coin set. Uncirculated clad half dollar, silver dollar, and gold $5

3-coin set. Proof clad half dollar, silver dollar, and gold $5

6-coin set. One each of Proof and Uncirculated clad half dollar, silver dollar, and gold $5

"Young Collector" set. Uncirculated clad half dollar

2-coin "Union" set. Clad half dollar and silver dollar

3-coin "Union" set. Clad half dollar, silver dollar, and gold $5

(1995–1996) CENTENNIAL OLYMPIC GAMES

4-coin set #1. Uncirculated half dollar (Basketball), dollars (Gymnastics, Paralympics), gold $5 (Torch Bearer)

4-coin set #2. Proof half dollar (Basketball), dollars (Gymnastics, Paralympics), gold $5 (Torch Bearer)

2-coin set #1: Proof silver dollars (Gymnastics, Paralympics)

"Young Collector" set. Uncirculated Basketball half dollar

"Young Collector" set. Uncirculated Baseball half dollar

"Young Collector" set. Uncirculated Swimming half dollar

"Young Collector" set. Uncirculated Soccer half dollar

1995–1996 16-coin Uncirculated set. One each of all Uncirculated coins

1995–1996 16-coin Proof set. One each of all Proof coins

		Notes
1995–1996 8-coin Proof silver dollars set		
1995–1996 32-coin set. One each of all Uncirculated and Proof coins		
(1996) NATIONAL COMMUNITY SERVICE		
Proof silver dollar and Saint-Gaudens stamp		
(1996) SMITHSONIAN INSTITUTION 150TH ANNIVERSARY		
2-coin set. Proof silver dollar and gold $5		
4-coin set. One each of Proof and Uncirculated silver dollar and gold $5		
"Young Collector" set. Proof silver dollar		
(1997) U.S. BOTANIC GARDEN		
"Coinage and Currency" set. Uncirculated silver dollar, Jefferson nickel, and $1 note		
(1997) JACKIE ROBINSON		
2-coin set. Proof silver dollar and gold $5		
4-coin set. One each of Proof and Uncirculated silver dollar and gold $5		
3-piece "Legacy" set. Baseball card, pin, and gold $5		
(1997) FRANKLIN D. ROOSEVELT		
2-coin set. One each of Proof and Uncirculated gold $5		
(1997) NATIONAL LAW ENFORCEMENT OFFICERS MEMORIAL		
Insignia set. Silver dollar, lapel pin, and patch		
(1998) ROBERT F. KENNEDY		
2-coin set. RFK silver dollar and JFK silver half dollar		
2-coin set. Proof and Uncirculated RFK silver dollars		
(1998) BLACK REVOLUTIONARY WAR PATRIOTS		
2-coin set. Proof and Uncirculated silver dollars		
"Young Collector" set. Uncirculated silver dollar		
Black Revolutionary War Patriots set. Silver dollar and four stamps		
(1999) DOLLEY MADISON COMMEMORATIVE		
2-coin set. Proof and Uncirculated silver dollars		
(1999) GEORGE WASHINGTON DEATH		
2-coin set. One each of Proof and Uncirculated gold $5		
(1999) YELLOWSTONE NATIONAL PARK		
2-coin set. One each of Proof and Uncirculated silver dollars		
(2000) LEIF ERICSON MILLENNIUM		
2-coin set. Proof silver dollar and Icelandic 1,000 kronur		
(2000) MILLENNIUM COIN AND CURRENCY SET		
3-piece set. Uncirculated 2000 Sacagawea dollar; Uncirculated 2000 Silver Eagle; George Washington $1 note, series 1999		
(2001) AMERICAN BUFFALO		
2-coin set. One each of Proof and Uncirculated silver dollar		
"Coinage and Currency" set. Uncirculated American Buffalo silver dollar, face reprint of 1899 $5 Indian Chief Silver Certificate, 1987 Chief Red Cloud 10¢ stamp, 2001 Bison 21¢ stamp		
(2001) U.S. CAPITOL VISITOR CENTER		
3-coin set. Proof clad half dollar, silver dollar, and gold $5		
(2002) SALT LAKE CITY OLYMPIC GAMES		
2-coin set. Proof silver dollar and gold $5		
4-coin set. One each of Proof and Uncirculated silver dollar and gold $5		

	Notes

(2003) FIRST FLIGHT CENTENNIAL

3 coin set. Proof clad half dollar, silver dollar, and gold $10

(2003) LEGACIES OF FREEDOM™

Uncirculated 2003 $1 American Eagle silver bullion coin and an Uncirculated 2002 £2 Silver Brittania coin

(2004) THOMAS A. EDISON

Edison set. Uncirculated silver dollar and light bulb

(2004) LEWIS AND CLARK

Coin and Pouch set. Proof silver dollar and beaded pouch

"Coinage and Currency" set. Uncirculated silver dollar, Sacagawea golden dollar, two 2005 nickels, replica 1901 $10 Bison note, silver-plated Peace Medal replica, three stamps, two booklets

(2004) WESTWARD JOURNEY NICKEL SERIES™

Westward Journey Nickel Series™ Coin and Medal set. Proof Sacagawea golden dollar, two 2004 Proof nickels, silver-plated Peace Medal replica

(2005) WESTWARD JOURNEY NICKEL SERIES™

Westward Journey Nickel Series™ Coin and Medal set. Proof Sacagawea golden dollar, two 2005 Proof nickels, silver-plated Peace Medal replica

(2005) CHIEF JUSTICE JOHN MARSHALL

"Coin and Chronicles" set. Uncirculated silver dollar, booklet, BEP intaglio portrait

(2005) AMERICAN LEGACY

American Legacy Collection. Proof Marine Corps silver dollar, Proof John Marshall silver dollar, 11-piece Proof set

(2005) MARINE CORPS 230TH ANNIVERSARY

Marine Corps Uncirculated silver dollar and stamp set

(2006) BENJAMIN FRANKLIN

"Coin and Chronicles" set. Uncirculated "Scientist" silver dollar, four stamps, *Poor Richard's Almanack* replica, intaglio print

(2006) AMERICAN LEGACY

American Legacy Collection. Proof 2006P Benjamin Franklin, Founding Father silver dollar; Proof 2006S San Francisco Old Mint silver dollar; Proof cent, nickel, dime, quarter, half dollar, and dollar

(2007) AMERICAN LEGACY

American Legacy Collection. 16 Proof coins for 2007: five state quarters; four Presidential dollars; Jamestown and Little Rock Central High School Desegregation silver dollars; Proof cent, nickel, dime, half dollar, and dollar

(2007) LITTLE ROCK CENTRAL HIGH SCHOOL DESEGREGATION

Little Rock Coin and Medal set. Proof 2007S silver dollar, bronze medal

(2008) BALD EAGLE

3-piece set. Proof clad half dollar, silver dollar, and gold $5

Bald Eagle Coin and Medal set. Uncirculated silver dollar, bronze medal

"Young Collector" set. Uncirculated clad half dollar

(2008) AMERICAN LEGACY

American Legacy Collection. 15 Proof coins for 2008: cent, nickel, dime, half dollar, and dollar; five state quarters; four Presidential dollars; Bald Eagle silver dollar

		Notes
(2009) LOUIS BRAILLE		
Uncirculated silver dollar in tri-folded package		
(2009) ABRAHAM LINCOLN COIN AND CHRONICLES		
Four Proof 2009S cents and Abraham Lincoln Proof silver dollar		

PROOF AND MINT SETS

Proof Sets

Date	Quantity Minted		Notes
1936	(3,837)		
1937	(5,542)		
1938	(8,045)		
1939	(8,795)		
1940	(11,246)		
1941	(15,287)		
1942, Both nickels	(21,120)		
1942, One nickel			
1950	(51,386)		
1951	(57,500)		
1952	(81,980)		
1953	(128,800)		
1954	(233,300)		
1955, Box pack	(378,200)		
1955, Flat pack			
1956	(669,384)		
1957	(1,247,952)		
1958	(875,652)		
1959	(1,149,291)		
1960, With Large Date cent	(1,691,602)		
1960, With Small Date cent			
1961	(3,028,244)		
1962	(3,218,019)		
1963	(3,075,645)		
1964	(3,950,762)		
1968S	(3,041,506)		
1968S, With No S dime			
1969S	(2,934,631)		
1970S	(2,632,810)		

Date	Quantity Minted		Notes
1970S, With Small Date cent	Included above		
1970S, With No S dime *(estimated mintage: 2,200)*			
1971S	(3,220,733)		
1971S, With No S nickel *(estimated mintage: 1,655)*			
1972S	(3,260,996)		
1973S	(2,760,339)		
1974S	(2,612,568)		
1975S, With 1976 quarter, half, and dollar	(2,845,450)		
1975S, With No S dime			
1976S	(4,149,730)		
1976S, Silver-clad, 3-piece set	(3,998,621)		
1977S	(3,251,152)		
1978S	(3,127,781)		
1979S, Type 1	(3,677,175)		
1979S, Type 2			
1980S	(3,554,806)		
1981S, Type 1	(4,063,083)		
1981S, Type 2 (all six coins in set)			
1982S	(3,857,479)		
1983S	(3,138,765)		
1983S, With No S dime			
1983S, Prestige set (Olympic dollar)	(140,361)		
1984S	(2,748,430)		
1984S, Prestige set (Olympic dollar)	(316,680)		
1985S	(3,362,821)		
1986S	(2,411,180)		
1986S, Prestige set (Statue of Liberty half, dollar)	(599,317)		
1987S	(3,792,233)		
1987S, Prestige set (Constitution dollar)	(435,495)		
1988S	(3,031,287)		
1988S, Prestige set (Olympic dollar)	(231,661)		
1989S	(3,009,107)		
1989S, Prestige set (Congressional half, dollar)	(211,807)		
1990S	(2,793,433)		
1990S, With No S cent	(3,555)		
1990S, With No S cent (Prestige set)			
1990S, Prestige set (Eisenhower dollar)	(506,126)		
1991S	(2,610,833)		
1991S, Prestige set (Mt. Rushmore half, dollar)	(256,954)		
1992S	(2,675,618)		
1992S, Prestige set (Olympic half, dollar)	(183,293)		
1992S, Silver	(1,009,586)		
1992S, Silver Premier set	(308,055)		
1993S	(2,409,394)		
1993S, Prestige set (Bill of Rights half, dollar)	(224,045)		
1993S, Silver	(570,213)		

Date	Quantity Minted		Notes
1993S, Silver Premier set	(191,140)		
1994S	(2,308,701)		
1994S, Prestige set (World Cup half, dollar)	(175,893)		
1994S, Silver	(636,009)		
1994S Silver Premier set	(149,320)		
1995S	(2,010,384)		
1995S, Prestige set (Civil War half, dollar)	(107,112)		
1995S, Silver	(549,878)		
1995S, Silver Premier set	(130,107)		
1996S	(1,695,244)		
1996S, Prestige set (Olympic half, dollar)	(55,000)		
1996S, Silver	(623,655)		
1996S, Silver Premier set	(151,366)		
1997S	(1,975,000)		
1997S, Prestige set (Botanic dollar)	(80,000)		
1997S, Silver	(605,473)		
1997S, Silver Premier set	(136,205)		
1998S	(2,086,507)		
1998S, Silver	(638,134)		
1998S, Silver Premier set	(240,658)		
1999S, 9-piece set	(2,543,401)		
1999S, 5-piece quarter set	(1,169,958)		
1999S, Silver 9-piece set	(804,565)		
2000S, 10-piece set	(3,082,572)		
2000S, 5-piece quarter set	(937,600)		
2000S, Silver 10-piece set	(965,421)		
2001S, 10-piece set	(2,294,909)		
2001S, 5-piece quarter set	(799,231)		
2001S, Silver 10-piece set	(889,697)		
2002S, 10-piece set	(2,319,766)		
2002S, 5-piece quarter set	(764,479)		
2002S, Silver 10-piece set	(892,229)		
2003S, 10-piece set	(2,172,684)		
2003S, 5-piece quarter set	(1,235,832)		
2003S, Silver 10-piece set	(1,125,755)		
2004S, 11-piece set	(1,789,488)		
2004S, 5-piece quarter set	(951,196)		
2004S, Silver 11-piece set	(1,175,934)		
2004S, Silver 5-piece quarter set	(593,852)		
2005S, 11-piece set	(2,275,000)		
2005S, 5-piece quarter set	(987,960)		
2005S, Silver 11-piece set	(1,069,679)		
2005S, Silver 5-piece quarter set	(608,970)		
2006S, 10-piece set	(2,000,428)		
2006S, 5-piece quarter set	(882,000)		
2006S, Silver 10-piece set	(1,054,008)		

Date	Quantity Minted			Notes
2006S, Silver 5-piece quarter set	(531,000)			
2007S, 14-piece set	(1,702,116)			
2007S, 5-piece quarter set	(672,662)			
2007S, 4-piece Presidential set	(1,285,972)			
2007S, Silver 14-piece set	(875,050)			
2007S, Silver 5-piece quarter set	(672,662)			
2008S, 14-piece set	(1,405,674)			
2008S, 5-piece quarter set	(672,438)			
2008S, 4-piece Presidential set	(869,202)			
2008S, Silver 14-piece set	(763,887)			
2008S, Silver 5-piece quarter set	(429,021)			
2009S, 18-piece set	(1,482,502)			
2009S, 6-piece quarter set	(630,976)			
2009S, 4-piece Presidential set	(629,584)			
2009S, Silver 18-piece set	(697,365)			
2009S, Silver 6-piece quarter set	(299,183)			
2009S, 4-piece Lincoln Bicentennial set				
2010S, 14-piece set	(1,103,950)			
2010S, 5-piece quarter set	(272,721)			
2010S, 4-piece Presidential set	(535,463)			
2010S, Silver 14-piece set	(585,414)			
2010S, Silver 5-piece quarter set	(577,428)			
2011S, 14-piece set	(952,881)			
2011S, 5-piece quarter set	(124,570)			
2011S, 4-piece Presidential set	(256,640)			
2011S, Silver 14-piece set	(500,395)			
2011S, Silver 5-piece quarter set	(125,607)			

Uncirculated Mint Sets

Date	Quantity Minted			Notes
1947 P-D-S	5,000			
1948 P-D-S	6,000			
1949 P-D-S	5,000			
1951 P-D-S	8,654			
1952 P-D-S	11,499			
1953 P-D-S	15,538			
1954 P-D-S	25,599			
1955 P-D-S	49,656			
1956 P-D	45,475			
1957 P-D	34,324			
1958 P-D	50,314			
1959 P-D	187,000			

Date	Quantity Minted	Notes	Date	Quantity Minted	Notes
1960 P-D	260,485		2003 P-D (20 pieces)	1,001,532	
1961 P-D	223,704		2004 P-D (22 pieces)	842,507	
1962 P-D	385,285		2005 P-D (22 pieces)	1,160,000	
1963 P-D	606,612		2006 P-D (20 pieces)	847,361	
1964 P-D	1,008,108		2007 P-D (28 pieces)	895,628	
1968 P-D-S	2,105,128		2008 P-D (28 pieces)	745,464	
1969 P-D-S	1,817,392		2009 P-D (36 pieces)	784,614	
1970 P-D-S, With Large Date cent	2,038,134		2010 P-D (28 pieces)	583,912	
1970 P-D-S, With Small Date cent			2011 P-D (28 pieces)		
1971 P-D-S (no Eisenhower dollar)	2,193,396				
1972 P-D-S (no Eisenhower dollar)	2,750,000				
1973 P-D-S	1,767,691				
1974 P-D-S	1,975,981				
1975 P-D, With 1976 quarter, half, dollar	1,921,488				
1776–1976, Siver clad, 3-piece set	4,908,319				
1976 P-D	1,892,513				
1977 P-D	2,006,869				
1978 P-D	2,162,609				
1979 P-D	2,526,000				
1980 P-D-S	2,815,066				
1981 P-D-S	2,908,145				
1984 P-D	1,832,857				
1985 P-D	1,710,571				
1986 P-D	1,153,536				
1987 P-D	2,890,758				
1988 P-D	1,646,204				
1989 P-D	1,987,915				
1990 P-D	1,809,184				
1991 P-D	1,352,101				
1992 P-D	1,500,143				
1993 P-D	1,297,431				
1994 P-D	1,234,813				
1995 P-D	1,038,787				
1996 P-D, Plus 1996W dime	1,457,949				
1997 P-D	950,473				
1998 P-D	1,187,325				
1999 P-D (18 pieces)	1,243,867				
2000 P-D (20 pieces)	1,490,160				
2001 P-D (20 pieces)	1,116,915				
2002 P-D (20 pieces)	1,139,388				

Special Mint Sets

Date	Quantity Minted			Notes
1965	2,360,000			
1966	2,261,583			
1967	1,863,344			

Souvenir Sets

Date	Quantity Minted			Notes
1982P				
1982D				
1983P				
1983D				

SILVER BULLION

Actual size 3 inches.

America the Beautiful™ Silver Bullion

Date	Distribution	MS-67	PF-67		Notes
25¢, 2010(P), Hot Springs National Park (Arkansas)					
25¢, 2010P, Hot Springs National Park (Arkansas)					
25¢ 2010(P), Yellowstone National Park (Wyoming)					
25¢ 2010P, Yellowstone National Park (Wyoming)					
25¢ 2010(P), Yosemite National Park (California)					
25¢ 2010P, Yosemite National Park (California)					
25¢ 2010(P), Grand Canyon National Park (Arizona)					
25¢ 2010P, Grand Canyon National Park (Arizona)					
25¢ 2010(P), Mount Hood National Park (Oregon)					
25¢ 2010P, Mount Hood National Park (Oregon)					
25¢, 2011(P), Gettysburg National Military Park (Pennsylvania)					
25¢, 2011P, Gettysburg National Military Park (Pennsylvania)					
25¢, 2011(P), Glacier National Park (Montana)					
25¢, 2011P, Glacier National Park (Montana)					
25¢, 2011(P), Olympic National Park (Washington)					
25¢, 2011P, Olympic National Park (Washington)					

Date	Distribution	MS-67	PF-67			Notes
25¢, 2011(P), Vicksburg National Military Park (Mississippi)						
25¢, 2011P, Vicksburg National Military Park (Mississippi)						
25¢, 2011(P), Chickasaw National Recreation Area (Oklahoma)						
25¢, 2011P, Chickasaw National Recreation Area (Oklahoma)						

$1 Silver Eagles

Date	Distribution	MS-67	PF-67	Notes	Date	Distribution	MS-67	PF-67	Notes
$1 1986	5,393,005				$1 1995W	(30,125)			
$1 1986S	(1,446,778)				$1 1996	3,603,386			
$1 1987	11,442,335				$1 1996P	(500,000)			
$1 1987S	(904,732)				$1 1997	4,295,004			
$1 1988	5,004,646				$1 1997P	(435,368)			
$1 1988S	(557,370)				$1 1998	4,847,549			
$1 1989	5,203,327				$1 1998P	(450,000)			
$1 1989S	(617,694)				$1 1999	7,408,640			
$1 1990	5,840,210				$1 1999P	(549,769)			
$1 1990S	(695,510)				$1 2000(W)	9,239,132			
$1 1991	7,191,066				$1 2000P	(600,000)			
$1 1991S	(511,925)				$1 2001(W)	9,001,711			
$1 1992	5,540,068				$1 2001W	(746,398)			
$1 1992S	(498,654)				$1 2002(W)	10,539,026			
$1 1993	6,763,762				$1 2002W	(647,342)			
$1 1993P	(405,913)				$1 2003(W)	8,495,008			
$1 1994	4,227,319				$1 2003W	(747,831)			
$1 1994P	(372,168)				$1 2004(W)	8,882,754			
$1 1995	4,672,051				$1 2004W	(801,602)			
$1 1995P	(438,511)				$1 2005(W)	8,891,025			

Date	Distribution	MS-67	PF-67	Notes	Date	Distribution	MS-67	PF-67	Notes
$1 2005W	(816,663)								
$1 2006(W)	10,021,000								
$1 2006W, Burnished	468,020								
$1 2006W	(1,092,477)								
$1 2006P, Rev Proof	(248,875)								
$1 2007(W)	9,028,036								
$1 2007W, Burnished	621,333								
$1 2007W	(821,759)								
$1 2008(W)	20,583,000								
$1 2008W, Burnished	533,757								
$1 2008W, Burnished, Reverse of 2007	47,000								
$1 2008W	(700,979)								
$1 2009(W)	30,459,000								
$1 2010(W)	(273,312)								
$1 2010W	29,110,500								
$1 2011(W)(S)	39,768,000								
$1 2011W, Burnished									
$1 2011S	100,000								
$1 2011W	(849,861)								
$1 2011P, Rev Proof	(100,000)								

Silver Bullion Sets

		Notes			Notes
SILVER BULLION SETS			2011 25th Anniversary Five-Coin Set. 2011W Uncirculated, Proof; 2011P Reverse Proof; 2011S Uncirculated, 2011 Bullion (no mintmark)		
2006 20th Anniversary Silver Coin Set. Uncirculated, Proof, Reverse Proof					
2006W 20th Anniversary Set. 1-oz. Gold- and Silver-Dollar Set. Uncirculated					

GOLD BULLION

American Eagle $5 Tenth-Ounce Gold

Date	Distribution	MS-67	PF-67	Notes
$5 MCMLXXXVI (1986)	912,609			
$5 MCMLXXXVII (1987)	580,266			
$5 MCMLXXXVIII (1988)	159,500			
$5 MCMLXXXVIII (1988)P	(143,881)			
$5 MCMLXXXIX (1989)	264,790			
$5 MCMLXXXIX (1989)P	(84,647)			
$5 MCMXC (1990)	210,210			
$5 MCMXC (1990)P	(99,349)			
$5 MCMXCI (1991)	165,200			
$5 MCMXCI (1991)P	(70,334)			
$5 1992	209,300			
$5 1992P	(64,874)			
$5 1993	210,709			
$5 1993P	(58,649)			
$5 1994	206,380			
$5 1994W	(62,849)			
$5 1995	223,025			
$5 1995W	(62,667)			
$5 1996	401,964			
$5 1996W	(57,047)			
$5 1997	528,266			
$5 1997W	(34,977)			
$5 1998	1,344,520			
$5 1998W	(39,395)			
$5 1999	2,750,338			
$5 1999W	(48,428)			
$5 1999W, Unc made from unpolished PF dies	14,500			
$5 2000	569,153			
$5 2000W	(49,971)			
$5 2001	269,147			
$5 2001W	(37,530)			
$5 2002	230,027			
$5 2002W	(40,864)			
$5 2003	245,029			
$5 2003W	(40,027)			
$5 2004	250,016			
$5 2004W	(35,131)			
$5 2005	300,043			
$5 2005W	(49,265)			
$5 2006	285,006			
$5 2006W, Burnished	20,643			
$5 2006W	(47,277)			
$5 2007	190,010			
$5 2007W, Burnished	22,501			
$5 2007W	(58,553)			
$5 2008	305,000			
$5 2008W, Burnished	12,657			
$5 2008W	(28,116)			
$5 2009	270,000			
$5 2010	*380,000*			
$5 2010W	(19,704)			
$5 2011				
$5 2011W				

American Eagle $10 Quarter-Ounce Gold

Date	Distribution	MS-67	PF-67	Notes
$10 MCMLXXXVI (1986)	726,031			
$10 MCMLXXXVII (1987)	269,255			
$10 MCMLXXXVIII (1988)	49,000			
$10 MCMLXXXVIII (1988)P	(98,028)			
$10 MCMLXXXIX (1989)	81,789			
$10 MCMLXXXIX (1989)P	(54,170)			
$10 MCMXC (1990)	41,000			
$10 MCMXC (1990)P	(62,674)			
$10 MCMXCI (1991)	36,100			
$10 MCMXCI (1991)P	(50,839)			
$10 1992	59,546			
$10 1992P	(46,269)			
$10 1993	71,864			
$10 1993P	(46,464)			

Date	Distribution	MS-67	PF-67	Notes	Date	Distribution	MS-67	PF-67	Notes
$10 1994	72,650				$10 2003W	(30,292)			
$10 1994W	(48,172)				$10 2004	72,014			
$10 1995	83,752				$10 2004W	(28,839)			
$10 1995W	(47,526)				$10 2005	72,015			
$10 1996	60,318				$10 2005W	(37,207)			
$10 1996W	(38,219)				$10 2006	60,004			
$10 1997	108,805				$10 2006W, Burnished	15,188			
$10 1997W	(29,805)				$10 2006W	(36,127)			
$10 1998	309,829				$10 2007	34,004			
$10 1998W	(29,503)				$10 2007W, Burnished	12,766			
$10 1999	564,232				$10 2007W	(46,189)			
$10 1999W	(34,417)				$10 2008	70,000			
$10 1999W, Unc from unpolished Proof dies	10,000				$10 2008W, Burnished	8,883			
					$10 2008W	(18,877)			
$10 2000	128,964				$10 2009	110,000			
$10 2000W	(36,036)				$10 2010	58,000			
$10 2001	71,280				$10 2010W	(9,926)			
$10 2001W	(25,613)				$10 2011				
$10 2002	62,027				$10 2011W				
$10 2002W	(29,242)								
$10 2003	74,029								

American Eagle $25 Half-Ounce Gold

Date	Distribution	MS-67	PF-67	Notes	Date	Distribution	MS-67	PF-67	Notes
$25 MCMLXXXVI (1986)	599,566				$25 1994W	(44,584)			
$25 MCMLXXXVII (1987)	131,255				$25 1995	53,474			
$25 MCMLXXXVII (1987)P	(143,398)				$25 1995W	(45,388)			
					$25 1996	39,287			
$25 MCMLXXXVIII (1988)	45,000				$25 1996W	(35,058)			
$25 MCMLXXXVIII (1988)P	(76,528)				$25 1997	79,605			
					$25 1997W	(26,344)			
$25 MCMLXXXIX (1989)	44,829				$25 1998	169,029			
$25 MCMLXXXIX (1989)P	(44,798)				$25 1998W	(25,374)			
					$25 1999	263,013			
$25 MCMXC (1990)	31,000				$25 1999W	(30,427)			
$25 MCMXC (1990)P	(51,636)				$25 2000	79,287			
$25 MCMXCI (1991)	24,100				$25 2000W	(32,028)			
$25 MCMXCI (1991)P	(53,125)				$25 2001	48,047			
$25 1992	54,404				$25 2001W	(23,240)			
$25 1992P	(40,976)				$25 2002	70,027			
$25 1993	73,324				$25 2002W	(26,646)			
$25 1993P	(43,819)				$25 2003	79,029			
$25 1994	62,400				$25 2003W	(28,270)			

Date	Distribution	MS-67	PF-67	Notes	Date	Distribution	MS-67	PF-67	Notes
$25 2004	98,040				$25 2008W	(22,602)			
$25 2004W	(27,330)				$25 2009	110,000			
$25 2005	80,023				$25 2010	40,000			
$25 2005W	(34,311)				$25 2010W	(9,946)			
$25 2006	66,005				$25 2011				
$25 2006W, Burnished	15,164				$25 2011W				
$25 2006W	(34,322)								
$25 2007	47,002								
$25 2007W, Burnished	11,455								
$25 2007W	(44,025)								
$25 2008	61,000								
$25 2008W, Burnished	15,682								

American Eagle $50 One-Ounce Gold

Date	Distribution	MS-67	PF-67	Notes	Date	Distribution	MS-67	PF-67	Notes
$50 MCMLXXXVI (1986)	1,362,650				$50 1996	189,148			
					$50 1996W	(36,153)			
$50 MCMLXXXVI (1986)W	(446,290)				$50 1997	664,508			
					$50 1997W	(32,999)			
$50 MCMLXXXVII (1987)	1,045,500				$50 1998	1,468,530			
					$50 1998W	(25,886)			
$50 MCMLXXXVII (1987)W	(147,498)				$50 1999	1,505,026			
					$50 1999W	(31,427)			
$50 MCMLXXXVIII (1988)	465,000				$50 2000	433,319			
					$50 2000W	(33,007)			
$50 MCMLXXXVIII (1988)W	(87,133)				$50 2001	143,605			
					$50 2001W	(24,555)			
$50 MCMLXXXIX (1989)	415,790				$50 2002	222,029			
					$50 2002W	(27,499)			
$50 MCMLXXXIX (1989)W	(54,570)				$50 2003	416,032			
					$50 2003W	(28,344)			
$50 MCMXC (1990)	373,210				$50 2004	417,019			
$50 MCMXC (1990)W	(62,401)				$50 2004W	(28,215)			
$50 MCMXCI (1991)	243,100				$50 2005	356,555			
$50 MCMXCI (1991)W	(50,411)				$50 2005W	(35,246)			
$50 1992	275,000				$50 2006	237,510			
$50 1992W	(44,826)				$50 2006W, Burnished	45,053			
$50 1993	480,192				$50 2006W	(47,092)			
$50 1993W	(34,369)				$50 2006W, Rev Proof	(9,996)			
$50 1994	221,633				$50 2007	140,016			
$50 1994W	(46,674)				$50 2007W, Burnished	18,066			
$50 1995	200,636				$50 2007W	(51,810)			
$50 1995W	(46,368)				$50 2008	710,000			

Date	Distribution	MS-67	PF-67	Notes	Date	Distribution	MS-67	PF-67	Notes
$50 2008W, Burnished	11,908								
$50 2008W	(30,237)								
$50 2009	1,493,000								
$50 2010	988,500								
$50 2010W	(24,899)								
$50 2011									
$50 2011W, Burnished									
$50 2011W									

Gold Bullion Sets

	Notes			Notes
GOLD BULLION SETS		2002 Gold Set. $50, $25, $10, $5		
1987 Gold Set. $50, $25		2003 Gold Set. $50, $25, $10, $5		
1988 Gold Set. $50, $25, $10, $5		2004 Gold Set. $50, $25, $10, $5		
1989 Gold Set. $50, $25, $10, $5		2005 Gold Set. $50, $25, $10, $5		
1990 Gold Set. $50, $25, $10, $5		2006 Gold Set. $50, $25, $10, $5		
1991 Gold Set. $50, $25, $10, $5		2007 Gold Set. $50, $25, $10, $5		
1992 Gold Set. $50, $25, $10, $5		2008 Gold Set. $50, $25, $10, $5		
1993 Gold Set. $50, $25, $10, $5		2010 Gold Set. $50, $25, $10, $5		
1993 Bicentennial Gold Set. $25, $10,$5, $1 silver eagle, and medal		2011 Gold Set. $50, $25, $10, $5		
		2006 20TH ANNIVERSARY SETS		
1994 Gold Set. $50, $25, $10, $5		2006W $50 Gold Set. Uncirculated, Proof, Reverse Proof		
1995 Gold Set. $50, $25, $10, $5				
1995 Anniversary Gold Set. $50, $25, $10, $5, and $1 silver eagle		2006W 1-oz. Gold- and Silver-Dollar Set. Uncirculated		
1996 Gold Set. $50, $25, $10, $5		**GOLD BULLION BURNISHED SETS 2006–2008**		
1997 Gold Set. $50, $25, $10, $5				
1997 Impressions of Liberty Set. $100 platinum, $50 gold, $1 silver		2006W Burnished Gold Set. $50, $25, $10, $5		
1998 Gold Set. $50, $25, $10, $5		2007W Burnished Gold Set. $50, $25, $10, $5		
1999 Gold Set. $50, $25, $10, $5				
2000 Gold Set. $50, $25, $10, $5		2008W Burnished Gold Set. $50, $25, $10, $5		
2001 Gold Set. $50, $25, $10, $5				

American Buffalo .9999 Fine Bullion

Date	Distribution	MS-67	PF-67	Notes	Date	Distribution	MS-67	PF-67	Notes
$5 2008W, Burnished	17,429				$10 2008W	(13,125)			
$5 2008W	(18,884)				$25 2008W, Burnished	16,908			
$10 2008W, Burnished	9,949				$25 2008W	(12,169)			

Date	Distribution	MS-67	PF-67	Notes	Date	Distribution	MS-67	PF-67	Notes
$50 2006	337,012								
$50 2006W	(246,267)								
$50 2007	136,503								
$50 2007W	(58,998)								
$50 2008	189,500								
$50 2008W	(18,863)								
$50 2008W, Burnished	9,074								
$50 2009	200,000								
$50 2009W	(49,306)								
$50 2010	*209,000*								
$50 2010W	(49,263)								
$50 2011									
$50 2011W									

First Spouse $10 Bullion

Date	Distribution	MS-67	PF-67	Notes	Date	Distribution	MS-67	PF-67	Notes
$10 2007W, M. Washington	(19,169) 17,661				$10 2010W, Abigail Fillmore				
$10 2007W, Abigail Adams	(17,149) 17,142				$10 2010W, Jane Pierce				
$10 2007W, T. Jefferson's Lib	(19,815) 19,823				$10 2010W, James Buchanan's Liberty				
$10 2007W, Dolley Madison	(17,661) 11,813				$10 2010W, Mary Lincoln				
$10 2008W, Elizabeth Monroe	(7,933) 4,519				$10 2011W, Eliza Johnson				
$10 2008W, Louisa Adams	(7,454) 4,223				$10 2011W, Julia Grant				
$10 2008W, A. Jackson's Lib	(7,454) 4,281				$10 2011W, Lucy Hayes				
$10 2008W, M. Van Buren's Lib	(6,187) 3,443				$10 2011W, Lucretia Garfield				
$10 2009W, Anna Harrison	(5,801) 2,993				$10 2012W, Alice Paul				
$10 2009W, Letitia Tyler	(4,341) 2,381				$10 2012W, Frances Cleveland, Variety 1				
$10 2009W, Julia Tyler	(3,878) 2,188				$10 2012W, Caroline Harrison				
$10 2009W, Sarah Polk	(3,512) 1,893				$10 2012W, Frances Cleveland, Variety 2				
$10 2009W, Margaret Taylor									

Date	Distribution	MS-67	PF-67	Notes	Date	Distribution	MS-67	PF-67	Notes

MMIX Ultra High Relief

Date	Distribution	Unc.					Notes
MMIX Ultra High Relief $20 Gold Coin	114,427						

PLATINUM BULLION

American Eagle $10 Tenth-Ounce Platinum

Date	Distribution	MS-67	PF-67	Notes	Date	Distribution	MS-67	PF-67	Notes
$10 1997	70,250				$10 2004	15,010			
$10 1997W	(36,993)				$10 2004W	(7,161)			
$10 1998	39,525				$10 2005	14,013			
$10 1998W	(19,847)				$10 2005W	(8,104)			
$10 1999	55,955				$10 2006	11,001			
$10 1999W	(19,133)				$10 2006W, Burnished	3,544			
$10 2000	34,027				$10 2006W	(10,205)			
$10 2000W	(15,651)				$10 2007	13,003			
$10 2001	52,017				$10 2007W, Burnished	5,556			
$10 2001W	(12,174)				$10 2007W	(8,176)			
$10 2002	23,005				$10 2008	17,000			
$10 2002W	(12,365)				$10 2008W, Burnished	3,706			
$10 2003	22,007				$10 2008W	(5,138)			
$10 2003W	(9,534)								

American Eagle $25 Quarter-Ounce Platinum

Date	Distribution	MS-67	PF-67	Notes	Date	Distribution	MS-67	PF-67	Notes
$25 1997	27,100				$25 2006W, Burnished	2,676			
$25 1997W	(18,628)				$25 2006W	(7,813)			
$25 1998	38,887				$25 2007	8,402			
$25 1998W	(14,873)				$25 2007W, Burnished	3,690			
$25 1999	39,734				$25 2007W	(6,017)			
$25 1999W	(13,507)				$25 2007W, Frosted FREEDOM	(21)			
$25 2000	20,054								
$25 2000W	(11,995)				$25 2008	22,800			
$25 2001	21,815				$25 2008W, Burnished	2,481			
$25 2001W	(8,847)				$25 2008W	(4,153)			
$25 2002	27,405								
$25 2002W	(9,282)								
$25 2003	25,207								
$25 2003W	(7,044)								
$25 2004	18,010								
$25 2004W	(5,193)								
$25 2005	12,013								
$25 2005W	(6,592)								
$25 2006	12,001								

American Eagle $50 Half-Ounce Platinum

Date	Distribution	MS-67	PF-67	Notes	Date	Distribution	MS-67	PF-67	Notes
$50 1997	20,500				$50 2005W	(5,942)			
$50 1997W	(15,431)				$50 2006	9,602			
$50 1998	32,415				$50 2006W, Burnished	2,577			
$50 1998W	(13,836)				$50 2006W	(7,649)			
$50 1999	32,309				$50 2007	7,001			
$50 1999W	(11,103)				$50 2007W, Burnished	3,635			
$50 2000	18,892				$50 2007W	(25,519)			
$50 2000W	(11,049)				$50 2007W, Frosted FREEDOM	(21)			
$50 2001	12,815								
$50 2001W	(8,254)				$50 2008	14,000			
$50 2002	24,005				$50 2008W, Burnished	2,253			
$50 2002W	(8,772)				$50 2008W	(4,020)			
$50 2003	17,409								
$50 2003W	(7,131)								
$50 2004	13,236								
$50 2004W	(5,063)								
$50 2005	9,013								

American Eagle $100 One-Ounce Platinum

Date	Distribution	MS-67	PF-67	Notes	Date	Distribution	MS-67	PF-67	Notes
$100 1997	56,000				$100 2005	6,310			
$100 1997W	(20,851)				$100 2005W	(6,602)			
$100 1998	133,002				$100 2006	6,000			
$100 1998W	(14,912)				$100 2006W, Burnished	3,068			
$100 1999	56,707				$100 2006W	(9,152)			
$100 1999W	(12,363)				$100 2007	7,202			
$100 2000	10,003				$100 2007W, Burnished	4,177			
$100 2000W	(12,453)				$100 2007W	(8,363)			
$100 2001	14,070				$100 2007W, Frosted FREEDOM	(21)			
$100 2001W	(8,969)								
$100 2002	11,502				$100 2008	21,800			
$100 2002W	(9,834)				$100 2008W, Burnished	2,876			
$100 2003	8,007				$100 2008W	(4,769)			
$100 2003W	(8,246)				$100 2009W	(9,871)			
$100 2004	7,009				$100 2010W				
$100 2004W	(6,007)								

Platinum Bullion Sets

	Notes			Notes
PLATINUM BULLION SETS		2007W. $100, $50, $25, $10		
1997. $100, $50, $25, $10		2007W, Burnished Set. $100, $50, $25, $10		
1998. $100, $50, $25, $10				
1999. $100, $50, $25, $10		2008W. $100, $50, $25, $10		
2000. $100, $50, $25, $10		2008W, Burnished Set. $100, $50, $25, $10		
2001. $100, $50, $25, $10				
2002. $100, $50, $25, $10		**2007 10TH ANNIVERSARY SET**		
2003. $100, $50, $25, $10		Two-coin set containing one Proof platinum half-ounce and one Enhanced Reverse Proof half-ounce dated 2007W. Housed in hardwood box with mahogany finish		
2004. $100, $50, $25, $10				
2005. $100, $50, $25, $10				
2006W. $100, $50, $25, $10				
2006W, Burnished Set. $100, $50, $25, $10				

HARD TIMES TOKENS

						Notes

CIVIL WAR TOKENS

						Notes

OTHER TOKENS AND MEDALS

Notes

HAWAIIAN ISSUES

Kingdom of Hawaii

Date	Quantity Minted		VF-20	EF-40	AU-50	MS-60	MS-63	PF	Notes
1847 Cent		100,000							
1881 Five Cents									
1883 Ten Cents	(26)	249,974							
1883 Eighth Dollar	(20)								
1883 Quarter Dollar	(26)	499,974							
1883 Half Dollar	(26)	699,974							
1883 Dollar	(26)	499,974							

Plantation Tokens

Date	F-12	VF-20	EF-40	AU-50			Notes
Waterhouse / Kamehameha IV, ca. 1860							
Wailuku Plantation, 12-1/2 (cents), (1871), narrow starfish							
Similar, broad starfish							
Wailuku Plantation, VI (6-1/4 cents), (1871), narrow starfish							
Similar, broad starfish							
Wailuku Plantation, 1 Real, 1880							
Wailuku Plantation, Half Real, 1880							
Thomas H. Hobron, 12-1/2 (cents), 1879							
Similar, two stars on both sides							

Date	F-12	VF-20	EF-40	AU-50			Notes
Thomas H. Hobron, 25 (cents), 1879							
Haiku Plantation, 1 Real, 1882							
Grove Ranch Plantation, 12-1/2 (cents), 1886							
Grove Ranch Plantation, 12-1/2 (cents), 1887							
Kahului Railroad, 10 cents, 1891							
Kahului Railroad, 15 cents, 1891							
Kahului Railroad, 20 cents, 1891							
Kahului Railroad, 25 cents, 1891							
Kahului Railroad, 35 cents, 1891							
Kahului Railroad, 75 cents, 1891							

PUERTO RICAN ISSUES

Date	Quantity Minted	F	VF	EF	Unc.			Notes
1896 5 Centavos	600,000							
1896 10 Centavos	700,000							
1895 20 Centavos	3,350,000							
1896 40 Centavos	725,002							
1895 1 Peso	8,500,021							

THE PHILIPPINES (UNDER U.S. SOVEREIGNTY)

Half Centavo

Date	Quantity Minted		VF	EF	MS-60	MS-63	PF-63		Notes
1903	(2,558)	12,084,000							
1904	(1,355)	5,654,000							
1905, Proof only	(471)								
1906, Proof only	(500)								
1908, Proof only	(500)								

One Centavo

Date	Quantity Minted	VF	EF	MS-60	MS-63	PF-63			Notes
1903	(2,558) 10,790,000								
1904	(1,355) 17,040,400								
1905	(471) 10,000,000								
1906, Proof only	(500)								
1908, Proof only	(500)								
1908S	2,187,000								
1909S	1,737,612								
1910S	2,700,000								
1911S	4,803,000								
1912S	3,001,000								
1913S	5,000,000								
1914S	5,000,500								
1915S	2,500,000								
1916S	4,330,000								
1917S	7,070,000								
1918S	11,660,000								
1918S, Large S									
1919S	4,540,000								
1920S	2,500,000								
1920	3,552,259								
1921	7,282,673								
1922	3,519,100								
1925M	9,325,000								
1926M	9,000,000								
1927M	9,279,000								
1928M	9,150,000								
1929M	5,657,161								
1930M	5,577,000								
1931M	5,659,355								
1932M	4,000,000								
1933M	8,392,692								
1934M	3,179,000								
1936M	17,455,463								

Five Centavos, Large Size (1903–1928)

Date		Quantity Minted	VF	EF	MS-60	MS-63	PF-63			Notes
1903	(2,558)	8,910,000								
1904	(1,355)	1,075,000								
1905, Proof only	(471)									
1906, Proof only	(500)									
1908, Proof only	(500)									
1916S		300,000								
1917S		2,300,000								
1918S		2,780,000								
1918S, Mule, Small-Date Reverse of 20 centavos										
1919S		1,220,000								
1920		1,421,078								
1921		2,131,529								
1925M		1,000,000								
1926M		1,200,000								
1927M		1,000,000								
1928M		1,000,000								

Five Centavos, Reduced Size (1930–1935)

Date	Quantity Minted	VF	EF	MS-60	MS-63			Notes
1930M	2,905,182							
1931M	3,476,790							
1932M	3,955,861							
1934M	2,153,729							
1935M	2,754,000							

Ten Centavos, Large Size (1903–1906)

Date		Quantity Minted	VF	EF	MS-60	MS-63	PF-63			Notes
1903	(2,558)	5,102,658								

Date	Quantity Minted	VF	EF	MS-60	MS-63	PF-63		Notes
1903S	1,200,000							
1904	(1,355) 10,000							
1904S	5,040,000							
1905, Proof only	(471)							
1906, Proof only	(500)							

Ten Centavos, Reduced Size (1907–1935)

Date	Quantity Minted	VF	EF	MS-60	MS-63	PF-63		Notes
1907	1,500,781							
1907S	4,930,000							
1908, Proof only	(500)							
1908S	3,363,911							
1909S	312,199							
1911S	1,000,505							
1912S	1,010,000							
1913S	1,360,693							
1914S	1,180,000							
1915S	450,000							
1917S	5,991,148							
1918S	8,420,000							
1919S	1,630,000							
1920	520,000							
1921	3,863,038							
1929M	1,000,000							
1935M	1,280,000							

Twenty Centavos, Large Size (1903–1906)

Date	Quantity Minted	VF	EF	MS-60	MS-63	PF-63		Notes
1903	(2,558) 5,350,231							
1903S	150,080							
1904	(1,355) 10,000							
1904S	2,060,000							
1905, Proof only	(471) ·							

Date	Quantity Minted	VF	EF	MS-60	MS-63	PF-63			Notes
1905S	420,000								
1906, Proof only	(500)								

Twenty Centavos, Reduced Size (1907–1929)

Date	Quantity Minted	VF	EF	MS-60	MS-63	PF-63			Notes
1907	1,250,651								
1907S	3,165,000								
1908, Proof only	(500)								
1908S	1,535,000								
1909S	450,000								
1910S	500,259								
1911S	505,000								
1912S	750,000								
1913S	795,000								
1914S	795,000								
1915S	655,000								
1916S	1,435,000								
1917S	3,150,655								
1918S	5,560,000								
1919S	850,000								
1920	1,045,415								
1921	1,842,631								
1928M, Mule (reverse of 1903–1928 5 centavos)	100,000								
1929M	1,970,000								

Fifty Centavos, Large Size (1903–1906)

Date	Quantity Minted		VF	EF	MS-60	MS-63	PF-63			Notes
1903	(2,558)	3,099,061								
1903S *(2 known)*										

Date		Quantity Minted	VF	EF	MS-60	MS-63	PF-63	Notes
1904	(1,355)	10,000						
1904S		216,000						
1905, Proof only	(471)							
1905S		852,000						
1906, Proof only	(500)							

Fifty Centavos, Reduced Size (1907–1921)

Date	Quantity Minted	VF	EF	MS-60	MS-63	PF-63	Notes
1907	1,200,625						
1907S	2,112,000						
1908, Proof only	(500)						
1908S	1,601,000						
1909S	528,000						
1917S	674,369						
1918S	2,202,000						
1919S	1,200,000						
1920	420,000						
1921	2,316,763						

One Peso, Large Size (1903–1906)

Date		Quantity Minted	VF	EF	MS-60	MS-63	PF-63	Notes
1903	(2,558)	2,788,901						
1903S		11,361,000						
1904	(1,355)	11,355						
1904S		6,600,000						
1905, Proof only	(471)							
1905S, Curved Serif on "1"		6,056,000						
1905S, Straight Serif on "1"								

Date	Quantity Minted	VF	EF	MS-60	MS-63	PF-63		Notes
1906, Proof only	(500)							
1906S	201,000							

One Peso, Reduced Size (1907–1912)

Date	Quantity Minted	VF	EF	MS-60	MS-63	PF-63		Notes
1907S	10,278,000							
1908, Proof only	(500)							
1908S	20,954,944							
1909S	7,578,000							
1910S	3,153,559							
1911S	463,000							
1912S	680,000							

THE PHILIPPINES (COMMONWEALTH)

One Centavo

Date	Quantity Minted	VF	EF	MS-60	MS-63		Notes
1937M	15,790,492						
1938M	10,000,000						
1939M	6,500,000						
1940M	4,000,000						
1941M	5,000,000						
1944S	58,000,000						

Five Centavos, Copper-Nickel (1937–1941)

Date	Quantity Minted	VF	EF	MS-60	MS-63			Notes
1937M	2,493,872							
1938M	4,000,000							
1941M	2,750,000							

Five Centavos, Copper-Nickel-Zinc Alloy (1944–1945)

Date	Quantity Minted	VF	EF	MS-60	MS-63			Notes
1944	21,198,000							
1944S	14,040,000							
1945S	72,796,000							

Ten Centavos

Date	Quantity Minted	VF	EF	MS-60	MS-63			Notes
1937M	3,500,000							
1938M	3,750,000							
1941M	2,500,000							
1944D	31,592,000							
1945D	137,208,000							
1945D, D Over D								

Twenty Centavos

Date	Quantity Minted	VF	EF	MS-60	MS-63			Notes
1937M	2,665,000							
1938M	3,000,000							
1941M	1,500,000							

Date	Quantity Minted	VF	EF	MS-60	MS-63				Notes
1944D	28,596,000								
1944D, D Over S									
1945D	82,804,000								

Fifty Centavos

Date	Quantity Minted	VF	EF	MS-60	MS-63				Notes
1944S	19,187,000								
1945S	18,120,000								
1945S, S Over S									

Commemorative Coinage

Date	Quantity Minted	VF	EF	MS-60	MS-63				Notes
1936M, Silver, fifty centavos	20,000								
1936M, Silver, one peso, busts of Murphy and Quezon	10,000								
1936M, Silver, one peso, busts of Roosevelt and Quezon	10,000								

MISSTRIKES AND ERRORS

						Notes

AMERICAN ARTS MEDALS

Date	Quantity Minted	MS-63		Notes
1980, Marian Anderson half ounce	281,624			
1980, Grant Wood one ounce	312,709			

Date	Quantity Minted	MS-63		Notes
1981, Willa Cather half ounce	97,331			
1981, Mark Twain one ounce	116,371			

Date	Quantity Minted	MS-63		Notes
1981, Frank L. Wright half ounce	348,305			
1982, Louis Armstrong one ounce	409,098			

Date	Quantity Minted	MS-63		Notes
1983, Alexander Calder half ounce	74,571			
1983, Robert Frost one ounce	390,669			

Date	Quantity Minted	MS-63		Notes
1984, John Steinbeck half ounce	32,572			
1984, Helen Hayes one ounce	33,546			

CANADIAN COINS

Note: Collector coins from the Royal Canadian Mint come in a variety of finishes, not limited to Proof. In the charts that follow, all of these different finishes (which include Specimen, Brilliant Uncirculated, Prooflike, and Bullion) are represented by the PF (Proof) column. Additionally, Canada has treated "commemorative" coins differently. Sometimes the event was marked on both the obverse and reverse; sometimes only one side varied from the standard issue. Some took the place of the standard circulation coinage of that year, while others circulated alongside the regular issue. Some were released like standard "circulating" coins; others came in special packaging and/or in special finishes. Some were released by both methods.

For the purposes of this check list, commemoratives that (a) replaced the standard circulating design for a given year or (b) were only released through standard "circulating" methods will be found within the regular chronological charts for the appropriate denomination. Commemoratives that did not replace the standard design, or which were channeled directly to collectors, are at the end of the listings, in a special "Commemoratives" section.

Note as well that "commemorative"-type packaging was used to mark some recent design changes. These items, like First-Strike Folders for the introduction of the Royal Canadian Mint mark on Queen Elizabeth Uncrowned Portrait coins, appear within the regular flow of the denomination-by-denomination charts.

Large Cents

Queen Victoria (1876–1901)

Date	Quantity Minted	G	VG	F	VF	EF	Unc.	Notes
1876H (01)	4,000,000							
1881H (01, 1a), Normal Legend								
1881H (01, 1a), Mixed Fonts	2,000,000							
1881H (01, 1a), Large Over Small D								
1882H (01, 1a, 2)	4,000,000							
1884 (01)	2,500,000							
1884 (02)								
1886 (01a, 2)	1,500,000							
1887 (02)	1,500,000							
1888 (02)	4,000,000							
1890H (03)	1,000,000							
1891 (02, 3), Large Leaves, Large Date								
1891 (02, 3), Large Leaves, Small Date	1,452,000							
1891 (02, 3), Small Leaves, Small Date								
1892 (02)								
1892 (03)	1,200,000							
1892, (04)								

Date	Quantity Minted	G	VG	F	VF	EF	Unc.	Notes
1893 (O4)	2,000,000							
1894 (O4), Fine 4	1,000,000							
1894 (O4), Crude 4								
1895 (O4)	1,200,000							
1896 (O4)	2,000,000							
1897 (O4)	1,500,000							
1898H (O4)	1,000,000							
1899 (O4)	2,400,000							
1900 (O4)	1,000,000							
1900H (O4)	2,600,000							
1901 (O4)	4,100,000							

King Edward VII (1902–1910)

Date	Quantity Minted	G	VG	F	VF	EF	Unc.	Notes
1902	3,000,000							
1903	4,000,000							
1904	2,500,000							
1905	2,000,000							
1906	4,100,000							
1907	2,400,000							
1907H	800,000							
1908	2,401,506							
1909	3,973,339							
1910	5,146,487							

King George V (1911–1920)

Without DEI GRA:
(1911)

With DEI GRA:
(1912–1920)

Date	Quantity Minted	G	VG	F	VF	EF	Unc.	Notes
1911, Without DEI GRA:	4,663,486							
1912, With DEI GRA:	5,107,642							

Date	Quantity Minted	G	VG	F	VF	EF	Unc.	Notes
1913	5,735,405							
1914	3,405,958							
1915	4,932,134							
1916	11,022,367							
1917	11,899,254							
1918	12,970,798							
1919	11,279,634							
1920	6,762,247							

Small Cents

King George V (1920–1936)

Date	Quantity Minted	G	VG	F	VF	EF	Unc.	Notes
1920	15,483,923							
1921	7,601,627							
1922	1,243,635							
1923	1,019,002							
1924	1,593,195							
1925	1,000,652							
1926	2,143,372							
1927	3,553,928							
1928	9,144,860							
1929, Normal 9	12,159,840							
1929, High 9								
1930	2,538,613							
1931	3,842,776							
1932	21,316,190							
1933	12,079,310							
1934	7,042,358							
1935	7,526,400							
1936	8,768,769							
1936, Dot *(5 known)*	678,823							

King George VI (1937–1952)

With Et IND:IMP:
(1937–1947)

Without Et IND:IMP:
(1948–1952)

Date	Quantity Minted	G	VG	F	VF	EF	Unc.	Notes
1937								
1937, Matte Fields	10,040,231							
1937, Mirror Fields								
1938	18,365,608							
1939	21,600,319							
1940	85,740,532							
1941	56,336,011							
1942	76,113,708							
1943	89,111,969							
1944	44,131,216							
1945	77,268,591							
1946	56,662,071							
1947	31,093,901							
1947, Maple Leaf, Blunt 7	43,855,448							
1947, Maple Leaf, Pointed 7								
1948, "A" Points to Thin Denticle	25,767,779							
1948, "A" Points to Thick Denticle								
1948, "A" Points Between Denticles								
1949, "A" Points to Denticle	33,128,933							
1949, "A" Points Between Denticles								
1950	60,444,992							
1951	80,430,379							
1952	67,631,736							

Queen Elizabeth II, Laureate Portrait (1953–1964)

Date	Quantity Minted	VG	F	VF	EF	Unc.	PF	Notes
1953, No Shoulder Fold	67,806,016							
1953, With Shoulder Fold								
1954, With Shoulder Fold	22,181,760							
1954, No Fold (Prooflike only)								
1955, With Shoulder Fold	56,403,193							
1955, No Shoulder Fold								
1956	78,658,535							
1957	100,601,792							
1958	59,385,679							
1959	83,615,343							
1960	75,772,775							
1961	135,598,404							
1962	227,244,069							
1963	279,076,334							
1964	484,655,322							

Queen Elizabeth II, Tiara Portrait (1965–1989)
Round (1965–1981); 12-Sided (1982–1989)

Original Portrait (1965–1978) **Confederation Centennial (dated 1867–1967)** **Reduced Portrait (1979–1989)**

Date		Quantity Minted	VG	F	VF	EF	Unc.	PF	Notes
1965, Small Beads, Pointed 5									
1965, Small Beads, Blunt 5		304,441,082							
1965, Large Beads, Blunt 5									
1965, Large Beads, Pointed 5									
1966		184,151,087							
1967, Confederation Cent'l		345,140,645							
1968		329,695,772							
1969		335,240,929							
1970		311,145,010							
1971		298,228,936							
1972		451,304,591							
1973		457,059,852							
1974		692,058,489							
1975		642,318,000							
1976		701,122,890							
1977		453,762,670							
1978		911,170,647							
1979, Reduced Portrait		754,394,064							
1980		912,052,318							
1981	(199,000)	1,209,468,500							
1982, 12-Sided	(180,908)	911,001,000							
1983, Near Beads	(166,779)	975,510,000							
1983, Far Beads									
1984	(161,602)	838,225,000							
1985, Blunt 5	(153,950)	771,772,500							
1985, Pointed 5									
1986	(176,224)	740,335,000							
1987	(175,686)	774,549,000							
1988	(175,259)	482,676,752							
1989	(154,693)	1,077,347,200							

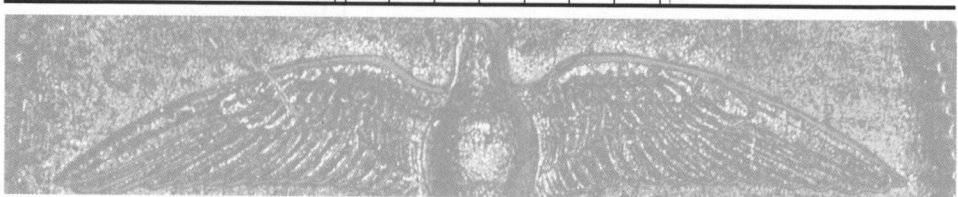

Queen Elizabeth II, Diadem Portrait (1990–2003)

**12-Sided
(1990–1996)**

**Round
(1997–2003)**

**125th Anniv. of
Confederation
(dated
1867–1992)**

**Golden Jubilee
(dated
1952–2002)**

Date		Quantity Minted	VG	F	VF	EF	Unc.	PF	Notes
1990	(158,068)	218,035,000							
1991	(131,888)	831,101,000							
1992, 125th Anniv of Confederation	(147,061)	673,512,000							
1993	(143,065)	752,034,000							
1994	(153,707)	639,516,000							
1995	(151,362)	624,983,000							
1996	(112,835)	445,746,000							
1997, Round		549,868,000							
1997, Bronze Proof	(113,647)								
1998		999,578,000							
1998W, Unc sets only	(—)								
1998, Bronze Proof	(93,362)								
1999		1,089,625,000							
1999, Bronze Proof	(95,113)								
1999P, Test only	(20,000+)								
2000		771,908,206							
2000W, Unc sets only	(—)								
2000, Bronze Proof	(90,921)								
2000P, Test only *(6 known)*									
2001		919,358,000							
2001, Bronze Proof	(74,194)								
2001P, BU, Specimen; Collector sets only	(—)								
2002, Golden Jubilee		716,367,000							
2002, Bronze Proof	(98,805)								
2002P		114,212,000							
2003, Diadem Portrait		92,219,775							
2003, Bronze Proof	(62,007)								
2003P		235,936,799							

Queen Elizabeth II, Uncrowned Portrait (2003 to Date)

Date	Quantity Minted	VG	F	VF	EF	Unc.	PF	Notes
2003, Uncrowned Portrait	56,877,144							
2003, Gold-Highlighted (from annual Mint report)	(10,000)							
2003P	354,994,666							
2003W, BU sets only	(71,142)							
2004	653,317,000							
2004P	134,906,000							
2004, Bronze Proof	(57,614)							
2005	759,658,000							
2005P	30,525,000							
2005P, First-Day Strike Folder	(1,919)							
2005, Bronze Proof	(62,286)							
2006, Zinc	886,275,000							
2006, Steel (error)								
2006P	233,000							
2006P/2006RCM, Last-Day/First-Day Strike Folder	(750)							
2006RCM, Zinc	176,000,000							
2006RCM, Steel	137,733,000							
2006, Bronze Proof	(57,885)							
2007, Zinc	9,625,999							
2007, Steel	938,270,000							
2007, Bronze Proof	(37,373)							
2008, Steel	820,350,000							
2008, Bronze Proof								
2009, Steel	419,105,000							
2009, Bronze Proof								
2010, Zinc								
2010, Steel								
2011, Zinc								
2011, Steel								
2012								

Five-Cent Pieces, Silver

Queen Victoria (1870–1901)

Date	Quantity Minted	G	VG	F	VF	EF	Unc.	Notes
1870, Wide Rim (O1)								
1870, Wide Rim, Plain Edge (Specimen only)	2,800,000							
1870, Narrow Rim (O2)								
1870, Narrow Rim, Plain Edge (Specimen only)								
1871 (O2)	1,400,000							
1872H (O2)	2,000,000							
1874H (O2), Plain 4	800,000							
1874H (O2), Crosslet 4								
1875H (O2), Small Date	1,000,000							
1875H (O2), Large Date								
1880H (O2, 3)	3,000,000							
1881H (O3)	1,500,000							
1882H (O4)	1,000,000							
1883H (O4) *(2 known)*	600,000							
1883H (O5)								
1884 (O5), Near 4	200,000							
1884 (O5), Far 4								
1885 (O5), Repunched Small 5								
1885 (O5), Small 5	1,000,000							
1885 (O5), Large 5								
1886 (O5), Small 6	1,700,000							
1886 (O5), Large 6								
1887 (O5)	500,000							
1888 (O5)	1,000,000							
1889 (O5)	1,200,000							
1890H (O5)	1,000,000							
1891 (O5, 2)	1,800,000							
1892 (O5, 2)	860,000							
1893 (O2)	1,700,000							
1894 (O2)	500,000							
1896 (O2)	1,500,000							
1897 (O2)	1,319,283							
1898 (O2)	580,717							
1899 (O2)	3,000,000							
1900 (O2), Round 0's (Large Date)	1,800,000							
1900 (O2), Oval 0's (Small Date)								
1901 (O2)	2,000,000							

King Edward VII (1902–1910)

Date	Quantity Minted	G	VG	F	VF	EF	Unc.	Notes
1902	2,120,000							
1902H, Large Broad H	2,200,000							
1902H, Small Narrow H								
1903H, Large H	2,640,000							
1903H, Small H								
1903	1,000,000							
1904	2,400,000							
1905	2,600,000							
1906	3,100,000							
1907	5,200,000							
1908, Small 8	1,220,524							
1908, Large 8								
1909, Round (Maple) Leaves	1,983,725							
1909, Pointed (Holly) Leaves								
1910, Round (Maple) Leaves	5,580,325							
1910, Pointed (Holly) Leaves								

King George V (1911–1921)

Without DEI GRA:
(1911)

With DEI GRA:
(1912–1921)

Date	Quantity Minted	G	VG	F	VF	EF	Unc.	Notes
1911, Without DEI GRA:	3,692,350							
1912, With DEI GRA:	5,863,170							
1913	5,488,048							
1914	4,202,179							
1915	1,172,258							
1916	2,481,675							
1917	5,521,373							
1918	6,052,298							
1919	7,835,400							
1920	10,649,851							
1921 *(400–450 known)*	2,582,495							

Five-Cent Pieces, Nickel

King George V (1922–1936)

Date	Quantity Minted	G	VG	F	VF	EF	Unc.	Notes
1922	4,794,119							
1923	2,502,279							
1924	3,105,839							
1925	201,921							
1926, Near 6	938,162							
1926, Far 6								
1927	5,285,627							
1928	4,577,712							
1929	5,611,911							
1930	3,704,673							
1931	5,100,830							
1932	3,198,566							
1933	2,597,867							
1934	3,827,304							
1935	3,900,000							
1936	4,400,450							

King George VI (1937–1952)

Round
(1937–1942)

12-Sided, ET IND:
IMP: on Obverse
(1942–1947)

12-Sided, Beaver Reverse
(1942; 1946–1950;
1951–1952)

12-Sided, DEI
GRATIA on Obverse
(1948–1952)

Victory Reverse
(1943–1945)

Isolation of Nickel Reverse
(dated 1751–1951)

Date	Quantity Minted	G	VG	F	VF	EF	Unc.	Notes
1937	4,593,263							
1937, Matte Fields	(1,295)							
1937, Mirror Fields								

Date	Quantity Minted	G	VG	F	VF	EF	Unc.	Notes
1937	4,593,263							
1938	3,898,974							
1939	5,661,123							
1940	13,920,197							
1941	8,681,785							
1942, Nickel	6,847,544							
1942, Tombac	3,396,234							
1943, Victory	24,760,256							
1944, Tombac *(1 known)*	—							
1944, Steel	11,532,784							
1944, No Chrome								
1945	18,893,216							
1945, No Chrome								
1946	6,952,684							
1947, Normal	7,603,724							
1947, Dot								
1947, Maple Leaf	9,595,124							
1948	1,810,789							
1949	13,037,090							
1950	11,970,521							
1951, Isolation of Nickel Reverse	8,329,321							
1951, High Relief (Second A in GRATIA Points to Denticle)	4,313,410							
1951, Low Relief (Second A in GRATIA Points Between Denticles)								
1952	10,891,148							

Queen Elizabeth, Laurate Portrait (1953–1964)

**12-Sided
(1953–1962)**

**Round
(1963–1964)**

Date	Quantity Minted	VG	F	VF	EF	Unc.	PF	Notes
1953, No Shoulder Fold, Far Leaf	16,635,552							
1953, No Shoulder Fold, Near Leaf (Mule)								
1953, With Shoulder Fold, Far Leaf (Mule)								
1953, With Shoulder Fold, Near Leaf								

Date	Quantity Minted	VG	F	VF	EF	Unc.	PF	Notes
1954								
1954, No Sholder Fold Mule *(2 known)*	6,998,662							
1955	5,355,028							
1956	9,399,854							
1957								
1957, Bugtail	7,387,703							
1958	7,607,521							
1959	11,552,523							
1960	37,157,433							
1961	47,889,051							
1962								
1962, Doubled Date	46,307,305							
1963, Round	43,970,320							
1964								
1964, Extra Water Line	78,075,068							

Queen Elizabeth, Tiara Portrait (1965–1989)

Original Portrait (1965–1978)   **Beaver Reverse (1965–1966; 1968–1989)**   **Confederation Centennial (dated 1867–1967)**   **Reduced Portrait (1979–1989)**

Date	Quantity Minted	VG	F	VF	EF	Unc.	PF	Notes
1965, Small Beads								
1965, Large Beads	84,876,018							
1966	27,976,648							
1967, Confederation Cent'l	36,876,574							
1968	99,253,330							
1969	27,830,229							
1970	5,726,010							
1971	27,312,609							
1972	62,417,387							
1973	53,507,435							
1974	94,704,645							
1975	138,882,000							
1976	55,140,213							
1977, High 7								
1977, Low 7	89,120,791							
1978	137,079,273							
1979, Reduced Portrait	186,295,825							
1980	134,878,000							

Date	Quantity Minted	VG	F	VF	EF	Unc.	PF	Notes
1981	(199,000) 99,107,900							
1982	(180,908) 64,924,400							
1983	(166,779) 72,596,000							
1984	(161,602) 84,088,000							
1985	(153,950) 126,618,000							
1986	(176,224) 156,104,000							
1987	(175,686) 106,299,000							
1988	(175,259) 75,025,000							
1989	(154,693) 141,570,538							

Queen Elizabeth II, Diadem Portrait (1990–2003)

Beaver Reverse (1990–1992; 1993–2001; 2003)   **125th Anniv. of Confederation (dated 1867–1992)**   **Golden Jubilee (dated 1952–2002)**

Date	Quantity Minted	VG	F	VF	EF	Unc.	PF	Notes
1990	(158,068) 42,537,000							
1991	(131,888) 10,931,000							
1992, 125th Anniv of Confederation	(147,061) 53,732,000							
1993	(143,065) 86,877,000							
1994	(153,707) 99,352,000							
1995	(151,362) 78,528,000							
1996, Far 6	36,686,000							
1996, Near 6								
1996, Near 6, Silver Proof	(112,835)							
1997	27,354,000							
1997, Silver Proof	(113,647)							
1998	156,873,000							
1998, Silver Proof	(93,632)							
1998W, Unc sets only	(—)							
1999	124,861,000							
1999, Silver Proof	(95,113)							
1999P, Test only	(20,000+)							
2000	105,868,000							
2000, Silver Proof	(90,921)							
2000W, Unc sets only	(—)							
2000P, Multi-Ply Steel	4,899,000							
2001	30,035,000							

Date	Quantity Minted	VG	F	VF	EF	Unc.	PF	Notes
2001P	136,656,000							
2001, Silver Proof	(74,194)							
2002P, Golden Jubilee	134,368,000							
2002, Silver Proof	(98,805)							
2003P, Diadem Portrait	31,388,921							

Queen Elizabeth II, Uncrowned Portrait (2003 to Date)

Date	Quantity Minted	VG	F	VF	EF	Unc.	PF	Notes
2003P, Uncrowned Portrait	61,392,180							
2003WP, BU sets only								
2003, Silver Proof	(62,007)							
2004P	132,097,000							
2004, Silver Proof	(57,614)							
2005P	89,664,000							
2005, Silver Proof	(62,286)							
2006P	96,286,000							
2006, No P / No RCM	43,008,000							
2006, Silver Proof	(57,885)							
2006RCM	43,022,000							
2007	221,472,000							
2007, Silver Proof	(37,373)							
2008	278,530,000							
2008, Silver Proof								
2009	121,632,000							
2009, Silver Proof								
2010	60,480,000							
2011								
2012								

Ten-Cent Pieces

Queen Victoria (1870–1901)

Date	Quantity Minted	VG	F	VF	EF	Unc.	PF	Notes
1870 (01), Narrow 0								
1870 (01), Plain Edge (Specimen only)	1,600,000							
1870 (01), Wide 0								
1871 (01)	800,000							
1871H (01)	1,870,000							
1872H (01)	1,000,000							
1874H (01)	1,600,000							
1875H (01)								
1880H (01, 2)	1,500,000							
1881H (01, 2)	950,000							
1882H (03)	1,000,000							
1883H (03)	300,000							
1884 (04)	150,000							
1885 (04)	400,000							
1885 (05)								
1886, Small 6 (04, 5)								
1886, Large Knobbed 6 (04, 5)	800,000							
1886, Large Pointed 6 (04, 5)								
1887 (05)	350,000							
1888 (05)	500,000							
1889 (05)	600,000							
1890H (05)	450,000							
1891 (05), 21 Leaves	800,000							
1891 (05), 22 Leaves								
1892 (05, 6), Large 9, 2 Over 1	520,000							
1892 (05, 6), Small 9								
1893 (05, 6), Flat-Top 3	500,000							
1893 (05, 6), Round-Top 3								
1894 (05, 6)	500,000							
1896 (05, 6)	650,000							
1898 (05, 6)	720,000							
1899 (06), Small 9's	1,200,000							
1899 (06), Large 9's								
1900 (06)	1,100,000							
1901 (06)	1,200,000							

King Edward VII (1902–1910)

Date	Quantity Minted	VG	F	VF	EF	Unc.	PF		Notes
1902	720,000								
1902H	1,100,000								
1903	500,000								
1903H	1,320,000								
1904	1,000,000								
1905	1,000,000								
1906	1,700,000								
1907	2,620,000								
1908	776,666								
1909, Victorian Leaves	1,697,000								
1909, Broad Leaves									
1910	4,468,331								

King George V (1911–1936)

Without DEI GRA: (1911)			**With DEI GRA:** (1912–1936)

Date	Quantity Minted	VG	F	VF	EF	Unc.	PF		Notes
1911, Without DEI GRA:	2,737,584								
1912, With DEI GRA:, .925 Silver	3,235,557								
1913, Broad Leaves	3,613,937								
1913, Small Leaves									
1914	2,549,811								
1915	688,057								
1916	4,218,114								
1917	5,011,988								
1918	5,133,602								
1919	7,877,722								
1920, .800 Silver	6,305,345								
1921	2,469,562								
1928	2,458,602								
1929	3,253,888								
1930	1,831,043								
1931	2,067,421								
1932	1,154,317								

Date	Quantity Minted	VG	F	VF	EF	Unc.	PF	Notes
1932	1,154,317							
1933	673,368							
1934	409,067							
1935	384,056							
1936	2,460,871							
1936, Dot (Specimen only) *(5 known)*	191,237							

King George VI (1937–1952)

With Et IND: IMP: (1937–1947)   **With DEI GRATIA** (1948–1952)

Date	Quantity Minted	VG	F	VF	EF	Unc.	PF	Notes
1937	2,500,095							
1937, Matte Fields	(1,295)							
1937, Mirror Fields								
1938	4,197,323							
1939	5,501,748							
1940	16,526,470							
1941	8,716,386							
1942	10,214,011							
1943	21,143,229							
1944	9,383,582							
1945	10,979,570							
1946	6,300,066							
1947	4,431,926							
1947, Maple Leaf	9,638,793							
1948	422,741							
1949	11,336,172							
1950	17,823,075							
1951	15,079,265							
1951, Doubled-Die Reverse								
1952	10,474,455							

Queen Elizabeth II, Laureate Portrait (1953–1964)

Date	Quantity Minted	VG	F	VF	EF	Unc.	PF	Notes
1953, No Shoulder Fold	17,706,395							
1953, With Shoulder Fold								
1954	4,493,150							
1955	12,237,294							
1956	16,732,844							
1956, Dot Below Date								
1957	16,110,229							
1958	10,621,236							
1959	19,691,433							
1960	45,446,835							
1961	26,850,859							
1962	41,864,335							
1963	41,916,208							
1964	49,518,549							

Queen Elizabeth, Tiara Portrait (1965–1989)

Original Portrait (1965–1978) **Large Schooner Reverse (1965–1966; 1968–1969)** **Confederation Centennial (dated 1867–1967)** **Small Schooner Reverse (1969–1989)** **Reduced Portrait (1979–1989)**

Date	Quantity Minted	VG	F	VF	EF	Unc.	PF	Notes
1965	56,965,392							
1966	34,567,898							
1967, Confederation Cent'l, .800 Silver	32,309,135							
1967, Confederation Cent'l, .500 Silver	.30,689,080							
1968, .500 Silver	70,460,000							
1968, Nickel, Ottawa Reeding	87,412,930							
1968, Nickel, Philadelphia Reeding	85,170,000							
1969, Large Schooner Reverse (15–20 known)	—							
1969, Small Schooner Reverse	55,833,929							
1970	5,249,296							
1971	41,016,968							
1972	60,169,387							
1973	167,715,435							
1974	201,566,565							
1975	207,680,000							

Date		Quantity Minted	VG	F	VF	EF	Unc.	PF	Notes
1976		95,018,533							
1977		128,452,206							
1978		170,366,431							
1979, Reduced Portrait		237,321,321							
1980		170,111,533							
1981	(199,000)	123,912,900							
1982	(180,908)	93,475,000							
1983	(166,779)	111,065,000							
1984	(161,602)	121,690,000							
1985	(153,950)	143,025,000							
1986	(176,224)	168,620,000							
1987	(175,686)	147,309,000							
1988	(175,259)	162,998,558							
1989	(154,693)	199,104,414							

Queen Elizabeth, Diadem Portrait (1990–2003)

Schooner, Denticles on Reverse (1990–1991)   **125th Anniversary of Confederation (dated 1867–1992)**   **Schooner, Beads on Reverse (1993–2003)**

International Year of the Volunteer (2001)   **Golden Jubilee (dated 1952–2002)**

Date		Quantity Minted	VG	F	VF	EF	Unc.	PF	Notes
1990	(158,068)	65,023,000							
1991	(131,888)	50,397,000							
1992, 125th Anniv of Confederation	(147,061)	174,476,000							
1993, Beads	(143,065)	135,569,000							
1994	(153,707)	145,800,000							
1995	(151,362)	128,875,000							
1996		51,814,000							
1996, Silver Proof	(112,835)								
1997		43,126,000							
1997, Silver Proof	(113,647)								
1998		203,514,000							
1998, Silver Proof	(93,632)								
1998W, Unc sets only	(—)								

Date	Quantity Minted	VG	F	VF	EF	Unc.	PF	Notes
1999	258,462,000							
1999, Silver Proof (95,113)								
1999P, Test only (20,000+)								
2000	159,125,000							
2000, Silver Proof (90,921)								
2000W, Unc sets only (—)								
2000P	200							
2001, Silver Proof (74,194)								
2001P	46,266,000							
2001P, International Year of the Volunteer	224,526,000							
2001P, International Year of the Volunteer, (37,029) Silver Proof								
2002P, Golden Jubilee (32,642)	251,278,000							
2002, Silver Proof (98,805)								
2003P, Diadem Portrait	162,398,000							
2003, Silver Proof (62,007)								

Queen Elizabeth II, Uncrowned Portrait (2003 to Date)

Date	Quantity Minted	VG	F	VF	EF	Unc.	PF	Notes
2003P, Uncrowned Portrait	104,137,595							
2003WP, BU sets only								
2004P	211,924,000							
2004, Silver Proof (57,614)								
2005P	212,175,000							
2005P, First-Day Strike Folder (1,961)								
2005, Silver Proof (62,286)								
2006P	312,122,000							
2006RCM								
2006P/2006RCM, Last-Day/First-Day Strike Folder (680)								
2006, Silver Proof (57,885)								
2007, Straight 7	304,110,000							
2007, Curved 7, BU Sets only								
2007, Silver Proof (37,373)								
2008	467,495,000							
2008, Silver Proof								

Date	Quantity Minted	VG	F	VF	EF	Unc.	PF	Notes
2009	209,550,000							
2009, Silver Proof								
2010	150,700,000							
2011								
2012								

Twenty-Five-Cent Pieces

Queen Victoria (1870–1901)

Date	Quantity Minted	VG	F	VF	EF	Unc.	PF	Notes
1870, Narrow 0 (O1)	900,000							
1870, Plain Edge (Specimen only)								
1870, Wide 0 (O2) *(4 known)*								
1871 (O1	400,000							
1871 (O2)								
1871H (O1	748,000							
1871H (O2)								
1872H (O2)	2,240,000							
1872H (O1) *(5 known)*								
1874H (O2)	2,600,000							
1875H (O2)								

Date	Quantity Minted	VG	F	VF	EF	Unc.	PF	Notes
1880H (O2), Wide 0								
1880H (O2), Narrow Over Wide 0	400,000							
1880H (O2), Narrow 0								
1881H (O2)	820,000							
1882H (O3)	600,000							
1883H (O4)	960,000							
1885 (O2)	192,000							
1886 (O2, 4, 5)								
1886, 6 Over 6 (O4, 5)	540,000							
1886, 6 Over 3 (O5)								
1887 (O5)	100,000							
1888 (O5), Narrow 8's								
1888 (O5), Broad 8's	400,000							
1889 (O5)	66,324							
1890H (O5)	200,000							
1891 (O5)	120,000							
1892 (O5)	510,000							
1893 (O5)	100,000							
1894 (O5)	220,000							
1899 (O5)	415,580							
1900 (O5)	1,320,000							
1901 (O5)	640,000							

King Edward VII (1902–1910)

Date	Quantity Minted	VG	F	VF	EF	Unc.	PF	Notes
1902	464,000							
1902H	800,000							
1903	846,150							
1904	400,000							
1905	800,000							
1906, Small Crown								
1906, Large Crown	1,237,843							
1907	2,088,000							
1908	495,016							
1909	1,335,929							
1910	3,577,569							

King George V (1911–1936)

Without DEI GRA: (1911)   **With DEI GRA:** (1912–1936)

Date	Quantity Minted	VG	F	VF	EF	Unc.	PF	Notes
1911, Without DEI GRA:	1,721,341							
1912, With DEI GRA:, .925 Silver	2,544,199							
1913	2,213,595							
1914	1,215,397							
1915	242,382							
1916	1,462,566							
1917	3,365,644							
1918	4,175,649							
1919	5,852,262							
1920, .800 Silver	1,975,278							
1921	597,337							
1927	468,096							
1928	2,114,178							
1929	2,690,562							
1930	968,748							
1931	537,815							
1932	537,994							
1933	421,282							
1934	384,350							
1935	537,772							
1936	972,094							
1936, Bar								
1936, Dot	153,322							

King George VI (1937–1952)

With Et IND: IMP: (1937–1947)   **With DEI GRATIA** (1948–1952)

Date	Quantity Minted	VG	F	VF	EF	Unc.	PF	Notes
1937	2,690,176							
1937, Doubled HP								

Date	Quantity Minted	VG	F	VF	EF	Unc.	PF	Notes
1937, Matte Fields	(1,295)							
1937, Mirror Fields								
1938	3,149,245							
1939	3,532,495							
1940	9,583,650							
1941	6,654,672							
1942	6,935,871							
1943	13,559,575							
1944	7,216,237							
1945	5,296,495							
1946	2,210,810							
1947	1,524,554							
1947, Dot								
1947, Maple Leaf	4,393,938							
1948	2,564,424							
1949	7,988,830							
1950	9,673,335							
1951, High Relief	8,290,719							
1951, Low Relief								
1952, Low Relief	8,859,642							
1952, High Relief								

Queen Elizabeth II, Laureate Portrait (1953–1964)

Date	Quantity Minted	VG	F	VF	EF	Unc.	PF	Notes
1953, No Shoulder Fold (Large Date)	10,546,769							
1953, With Shoulder Fold (Small Date)								
1954	2,318,891							
1955	9,552,505							
1956	11,269,353							
1957	12,770,190							
1958	9,336,910							
1959	13,503,461							
1960	22,835,327							
1961	18,164,368							
1962	29,559,266							
1963	21,180,652							
1964	36,479,343							

Queen Elizabeth, Tiara Portrait (1965–1989)

Original Portrait (1965–1978)	Caribou Reverse (1965–1966; 1968–1972; 1974–1989)	Confederation Centennial (dated 1867–1967)	RCMP Centennial Reverse (1973)	Reduced Portrait (1979–1989)

Date	Quantity Minted	VG	F	VF	EF	Unc.	PF	Notes
1965	44,708,869							
1966	25,626,315							
1967, Confederation Cent'l, .800 Silver	48,855,500							
1967, Confederation Cent'l, .500 Silver								
1968, .500 Silver	71,464,000							
1968, Nickel	88,686,931							
1969	133,037,929							
1970	10,302,010							
1971	48,170,428							
1972	43,743,387							
1973, RCMP, Small Bust, 120 Beads	134,958,587							
1973, RCMP, Large Bust, 132 Beads								
1974	192,360,598							
1975	141,148,000							
1976	86,898,261							
1977	99,634,555							
1978, Small Denticles	176,475,408							
1978, Large Denticles								
1979, Reduced Portrait	131,042,905							
1980	76,178,000							
1981	(199,000) 131,580,272							
1982	(180,908) 171,926,000							
1983	(166,779) 13,162,000							
1984	(161,602) 121,688,000							
1985	(153,950) 158,734,000							
1986	(176,224) 132,220,000							
1987	(175,686) 53,408,000							
1988	(175,259) 80,368,473							
1989	(154,693) 119,796,307							

Queen Elizabeth, Diadem Portrait (1990–2003)

| | **Caribou, Denticles
on Reverse
(1990–1991)** | **125th Anniversary
of Confederation
(dated 1867–1992)** | **Caribou,
Beads on Reverse
(1993–2003)** |

Date	Quantity Minted		VG	F	VF	EF	Unc.	PF		Notes
1990	(158,068)	31,258,000								
1991	(131,888)	459,000								
1992, 125th Anniv of Confederation, BU, Specimen sets only	(442,986)									
1992, 125th Anniv of Confederation, Proof	(147,061)									
1993, Beads	(143,065)	73,758,000								
1994	(153,707)	77,670,000								
1995	(151,362)	89,210,000								
1996		28,106,000								
1996, Silver Proof	(112,835)									
1997, BU, Specimen sets only	(314,015)									
1997, Silver Proof	(113,647)									
1998, BU, Specimen sets only	(234,288)									
1998, Silver Proof	(93,632)									
1998W, Unc sets only	—									
1999, BU, Specimen sets only	(342,587)									
1999, Silver Proof	(95,113)									
1999P, Test only		20,000+								
2000, BU, Specimen sets only	(377,833)									
2000, Silver Proof	(90,921)									
2000W, Unc sets only	—									
2000P, Test only (3–5 known)	—									
2001		8,409,000								
2001, Silver Proof	(74,194)									
2001P		52,153,000								
2002P	(32,642)	187,992,000								
2002, Silver Proof	(98,805)									
2003P, Diadem Portrait		15,905,090								
2003, Silver Proof	(62,007)									

Queen Elizabeth, Uncrowned Portrait (2003 to Date)

Date	Quantity Minted	VG	F	VF	EF	Unc.	PF	Notes
2003P, Uncrowned Portrait	66,861,633							
2003WP, BU sets only	71,142							
2004P	177,466,000							
2004, Silver Proof	(57,614)							
2005P	206,346,000							
2005RCM, First-Day Strike Folder	(1,911)							
2005, Silver Proof	(62,286)							
2006P	423,189,000							
2006RCM								
2006P/2006RCM, Last-Day/ First-Day Strike Folder	(742)							
2006, Silver Proof	(57,885)							
2007	274,763,000							
2007, Silver Proof	(40,218)							
2008	286,322,000							
2008, Silver Proof	(40,306)							
2009	20,446,000							
2009, Silver Proof	(27,549)							
2010								
2010, Silver Proof								
2011								
2011, Silver Proof								
2012								

Fifty-Cent Pieces

Queen Victoria (1870–1901)

Date	Quantity Minted	VG	F	VF	EF	Unc.	PF	Notes
1870, No LCW (O1)								
1870 (O1), No LCW, Plain Edge (Specimen only)	450,000							
1870, LCW (O2)								
1870, LCW (O2), Plain Edge (Specimen only)								
1871 (O2)	200,000							
1871H (O2)	45,000							
1872H (O2)	80,000							
1872H (O2), Inverted A Over V								
1881H (O3)	150,000							
1888 (O2, 3)	60,000							
1890H (O4)	20,000							
1892 (O3, 4)	151,000							
1894 (O4)	29,036							
1898 (O4)	100,000							
1899 (O4)	50,000							
1900 (O4)	118,000							
1901 (O4)	80,000							

King Edward VII (1902–1910)

Date	Quantity Minted	VG	F	VF	EF	Unc.	PF	Notes
1902	120,000							
1903H	140,000							
1904	60,000							
1905	40,000							

Date	Quantity Minted	VG	F	VF	EF	Unc.	PF	Notes
1906	350,000							
1907	300,000							
1908	128,119							
1909	302,118							
1910, Victorian Leaves	649,521							
1910, Edwardian Leaves								

King George V (1911–1936)

Without DEI GRA:
(1911)

With DEI GRA:
(1912–1936)

Date	Quantity Minted	VG	F	VF	EF	Unc.	PF	Notes
1911, Without DEI GRA:	209,972							
1912, With DEI GRA:	285,867							
1913	265,889							
1914	160,128							
1916	459,070							
1917	752,213							
1918	754,989							
1919	1,113,429							
1920, Narrow 0	584,691							
1920, Wide 0								
1921 *(fewer than 100 known)*	206,328							
1929	228,328							
1931	57,581							
1932	19,213							
1934	39,539							
1936	38,550							

King George VI (1937–1952)

With Et IND: IMP:
(1937–1947)

With DEI GRATIA
(1948–1952)

Date	Quantity Minted		VG	F	VF	EF	Unc.	PF	Notes
1937	192,016								
1937, Matte Fields	(1,295)								
1937, Mirror Fields									
1938	192,018								
1939	287,976								
1940	1,996,566								
1941	1,714,874								
1942	1,974,164								
1943	3,109,583								
1944	2,460,205								
1945	1,959,528								
1946	950,235								
1946, Design in 6									
1947, Straight or Curved Left 7	424,885								
1947, Curved Right 7									
1947, Maple Leaf, Straight or Curved Left 7	38,433								
1947, Maple Leaf, Curved Right 7									
1948	37,784								
1949	858,991								
1949, Hoof Over 9									
1950, Lines in 0	2,384,179								
1950, No Lines									
1951	2,421,730								
1952	2,596,465								

Queen Elizabeth II, Laureate Portrait (1953–1964)

Coat of Arms Reverse (1953–1954)   **Smaller Coat of Arms Reverse (1955–1958)**   **Modified Coat of Arms Reverse (1959–1964)**

Date	Quantity Minted		VG	F	VF	EF	Unc.	PF	Notes
1953, Small Date, No Shoulder Fold	1,630,429								
1953, Large Date, No Shoulder Fold									
1953, Large Date, With Shoulder Fold									

Date	Quantity Minted	VG	F	VF	EF	Unc.	PF	Notes
1954	506,305							
1955, Smaller Coat of Arms	753,511							
1956	1,379,499							
1957	2,171,689							
1958	2,957,266							
1958, Dot								
1959, Modified Coat of Arms	3,095,535							
1960	3,488,897							
1961	3,584,417							
1962	5,208,030							
1963	8,348,871							
1964	9,377,676							

Queen Elizabeth II, Tiara Portrait (1965–1989)

Original Portrait (1965–1967)

Coat of Arms Reverse (1965–1966)

Confederation Centennial (dated 1867–1967)

Reduced Diameter (1968–1976; 1978–1989 [with modifications])

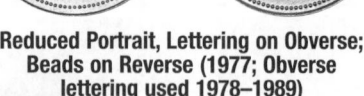

Reduced Portrait, Lettering on Obverse; Beads on Reverse (1977; Obverse lettering used 1978–1989)

Date	Quantity Minted	VG	F	VF	EF	Unc.	PF	Notes
1965	12,629,974							
1966	7,920,496							
1967, Confederation Cent'l	4,211,392							
1967, Double Strike								
1967, Triple Strike								
1967, Flip Strike								
1968, Reduced Diameter	3,966,932							
1969	7,113,929							
1970	2,429,526							
1971	2,166,444							
1972	2,515,632							
1973	2,546,096							

Date		Quantity Minted	VG	F	VF	EF	Unc.	PF	Notes
1974		3,436,650							
1975		3,710,000							
1976		2,940,719							
1977		709,839							
1978, Square Jewels		3,341,892							
1978, Round Jewels									
1979		3,425,000							
1980		1,574,000							
1981	(199,000)	2,690,272							
1982, Large Beads, High Relief	(180,908)	2,236,674							
1982, Small Beads, Low Relief									
1983	(166,779)	1,177,000							
1984	(161,602)	1,502,989							
1985	(153,950)	2,188,374							
1986	(176,224)	781,400							
1987	(175,686)	373,000							
1988	(175,259)	220,000							
1989	(154,693)	266,419							

Queen Elizabeth, Diadem Portrait (1990–2003)

Coat of Arms, Denticles on Reverse (1990–1991)

125th Anniversary of Confederation (dated 1867–1992)

Coat of Arms, Beads on Reverse (1993–1996)

Redesigned Coat of Arms, (1997–2003)

Date		Quantity Minted	VG	F	VF	EF	Unc.	PF	Notes
1990	(158,068)	207,000							
1991	(131,888)	490,000							
1992, 125th Anniv of Confederation	(147,061)	445,000							
1993, Beads	(143,065)	393,000							

Date		Quantity Minted	VG	F	VF	EF	Unc.	PF		Notes
1994	(153,707)	987,000								
1995	(151,362)	626,000								
1996		458,000								
1996, Silver Proof	(112,835)									
1997, Redesigned Coat of Arms		387,000								
1997, Silver Proof	(113,647)									
1998		308,000								
1998, Silver Proof	(93,632)									
1998W, Unc sets only	(—)									
1999		496,000								
1999, Silver Proof	(95,113)									
1999P, Test only		20,000+								
2000		559,000								
2000, Silver Proof	(90,921)									
2000W, Unc sets only	(—)									
2000P, BU, in RCM Presentation Clocks only	50									
2001P		389,000								
2001P, Silver Proof	(86,194)									
2002, Silver Proof	(65,315)									
2002P, Unc, Specimen sets only	(67,672)									
2003P, Unc, Specimen sets only	(—)									
2003, Silver Proof	(62,007)									

Queen Elizabeth II, Uncrowned Portrait (2003 to Date)

Date	Quantity Minted	VG	F	VF	EF	Unc.	PF		Notes
2003WP, BU sets only	(71,142)								
2004P, Unc, Specimen sets only	(—)								
2004, Silver Proof	(57,614)								
2005P	200,000								
2005P, First-Day Strike Folder	(2,445)								
2005, Silver Proof	(62,286)								

Date	Quantity Minted	VG	F	VF	EF	Unc.	PF	Notes
2006P	98,000							
2006RCM, BU sets only								
2006P/2006RCM, Last-Day/ First-Day Strike Folder	(933)							
2006, Silver Proof	(57,885)							
2006 Gold-Plated Silver Proof (from annual Mint Report)	(4,162)							
2007	250,000							
2007, Silver Proof	(40,218)							
2008, Unc, Specimen sets only	(—)							
2008, Silver Proof	(40,306)							
2009, Unc, Specimen sets only	(—)							
2009, Silver Proof	(27,549)							
2010, Silver Proof								
2011								
2012								

One-Dollar Pieces

King George V (1935–1936)

Silver Jubilee Obverse (1935)

Standard Obverse (1936)

Date	Quantity Minted	VG	F	VF	EF	Unc.	PF	Notes
1935, Silver Jubilee	428,707							
1935, Matte Specimen								
1936	306,100							
1936, Matte Specimen								

King George VI (1937–1952)

With Et IND: IMP:
(1937–1939;
1945–1947)

Voyageur Reverse
(1937–1938; 1945–1948;
1950–1952)

With DEI GRATIA
(1948–1952)

Royal Visit
Reverse (1939)

Newfoundland
Reverse (1949)

Date	Quantity Minted	VG	F	VF	EF	Unc.	PF	Notes
1937	241,002							
1937, Matte Fields	(1,295)							
1937, Mirror Fields								
1938	90,304							
1939, Royal Visit	1,363,816							
1945	38,391							
1946	93,055							
1947, Pointed 7	65,595							
1947, Pointed 7, Dot								
1947, Pointed 7, Doubled HP								
1947, Pointed 7, Doubled HP, Dot								
1947, Pointed 7, Tripled HP								
1947, Pointed 7, Tripled HP, Dot								
1947, Pointed 7, Quadrupled HP								
1947, Pointed 7, Quadrupled HP, Dot								
1947, Blunt 7								
1947, Matte Specimen								
1947, Matte Specimen, Doubled HP								
1947, Maple Leaf	21,135							
1947, Maple Leaf, Doubled HP								
1948	18,780							
1949, Newfoundland	672,218							

Date	Quantity Minted	VG	F	VF	EF	Unc.	PF	Notes
1950, Full Water Lines								
1950, Matte Specimen								
1950, 3–4 Short Water Lines	261,002							
1950, "Arnprior," 2-1/2 Water Lines								
1951, Full Water Lines								
1951, 3–4 Short Water Lines	416,395							
1951, "Arnprior," 2-1/2 Water Lines								
1952, Full Water Lines								
1952, 3–4 Short Water Lines	406,148							
1952, "Arnprior," 1-1/2 Short Water Lines								
1952, No Water Lines								

Queen Elizabeth II, Laureate Portrait (1953–1964)

Voyageur Reverse (1953–1957; 1959–1963)

British Columbia Reverse (1958)

Confederation Meetings Reverse (1964)

Date	Quantity Minted	VG	F	VF	EF	Unc.	PF	Notes
1953, No Shoulder Fold, Narrow Rim								
1953, No Shoulder Fold, Narrow Rim, Short Water Lines	1,074,578							
1953, Shoulder Fold, Wide Rim								
1953, Shoulder Fold, Wide Rim, Short Water Lines								
1954, Full Water Lines	246,606							
1954, Short Water Lines								
1955, Full Water Lines								
1955, "Arnprior," 1-1/2 Water Lines	268,105							
1955, "Arnprior," Obv Die Breaks								
1956	209,092							

Date	Quantity Minted	VG	F	VF	EF	Unc.	PF	Notes
1957, Full Water Lines	496,389							
1957, One Water Line								
1958, British Columbia	3,039,630							
1959	1,443,502							
1960	1,420,486							
1961	1,262,231							
1962	1,884,789							
1963	4,179,981							
1964, Confederation Meetings	7,296,832							

Queen Elizabeth II, Tiara Portrait (1965–1989)

**Round, Original Diameter
(1965–1967)**

**Voyaguer Reverse
(1965–1966)**

**Confederation Centennial
(dated 1867–1967)**

Date	Quantity Minted	VG	F	VF	EF	Unc.	PF	Notes
1965, Sm Beads, Pointed 5, Type 1	10,768,569							
1965, Sm Beads, Blunt 5, Type 2								
1965, Lg Beads, Blunt 5, Type 3								
1965, Lg Beads, Pointed 5, Type 4								
1965, Med Beads, Ptd 5, Type 5								
1966, Large Beads	9,912,178							
1966, Small Beads								
1967, Confederation Cent'l, Large Beads Reverse, Flat Fields	6,767,496							
1967, Small Beads Reverse, Concave Fields								
1967, Diving Goose, 45 Degrees								

**Reduced Diameter;
Original Portrait
(1968–1972)**

**Reduced Diameter,
Reduced Portrait
(1973–1977)**

**Reduced Diameter, Pre-
1973 Portrait, Beaded
(1978–1987)**

**Reduced Diameter;
Voyageur Reverse
(1968–1969; 1972;
1975–1976)**

**Reduced Diameter;
Voyageur Reverse,
First Modified (1977)**

**Reduced Diameter;
Voyageur Reverse,
Second Modified
(1978–1987)**

**Manitoba
(1970)**

**British Columbia
(1971)**

**Prince Edward Island
(1973)**

**Winnipeg
(1974)**

Date	Quantity Minted	VG	F	VF	EF	Unc.	PF	Notes
1968, Island								
1968, Small Island								
1968, No Island	5,579,714							
1968, Extra Water Lines								
1968, Doubled Horizon Lines								
1968, Doubled Top Horizon Line								
1969	4,809,313							
1970, Manitoba	4,140,058							
1970, Manitoba, Prooflike (cased)	(349,120)							
1970, Manitoba, Specimen	(1,000)							
1971, British Columbia	4,260,781							
1971, British Columbia, Prooflike (cased)	(181,091)							
1971, British Columbia, Silver	(585,217)							
1972	2,193,000							
1972, Silver	(341,581)							
1973, Prince Edward Island	3,196,452							
1973, Prince Edward Island, Prooflike (cased)	(466,881)							
1974, Winnipeg Centennial	2,799,363							
1974, Winnipeg Centennial, Doubled Yoke, any variety								

Date	Quantity Minted	VG	F	VF	EF	Unc.	PF	Notes
1974, Winnipeg Cent'l, Prooflike (cased)								
1974, Winnipeg Cent'l, Prooflike (cased), Doubled Yoke	(363,786)							
1974, Winnipeg Centennial, Silver	(713,485)							
1975	3,256,000							
1976	2,101,000							
1977	1,393,745							
1977, Short Water Lines								
1978	2,948,488							
1979	2,954,842							
1980	3,291,221							
1981	(199,000) 2,788,900							
1982	(180,908) 1,098,500							
1983	(166,779) 2,267,525							
1984	(161,602) 1,223,486							
1985	(153,950) 3,104,092							
Mule, 1985 New Zealand 50¢ Obverse, 1985 Canada Voyageur $1 Reverse	—							
1986	(176,224) 3,089,225							
1987, Voyaguer	(175,686)							

11-sided, Aureate Bronze Plated (1987–1989)   **Loon Reverse (1987–1989)**

Date	Quantity Minted	VG	F	VF	EF	Unc.	PF	Notes
1987, Loon	(178,120) 205,405,000							
1988	(175,259) 138,893,539							
1989	(154,693) 184,773,902							

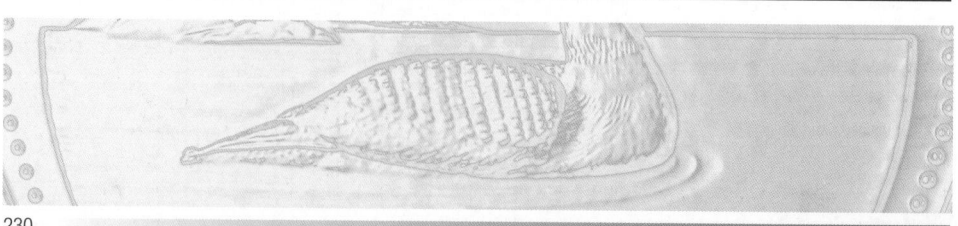

Queen Elizabeth II, Diadem Portrait (1990–2003)

**Loon Reverse
(1990–1991;
1993–2003)**

**125th Anniversary
of Confederation
(dated 1867–1992)**

**Golden Jubilee
(dated 1952–2002;
no date on reverse)**

Date	Quantity Minted		VG	F	VF	EF	Unc.	PF	Notes
1990	(158,068)	68,402,000							
1991	(131,888)	23,156,000							
1992, 125th Anniv of Confederation	(147,061)	4,242,085							
1993	(143,065)	33,662,000							
1994	(104,485)	16,232,530							
1995	(101,560)	27,492,630							
1996	(112,835)	17,101,000							
1997	(113,647)								
1998	(93,632)								
1998W	(—)								
1999	(95,113)								
2000	(90,921)								
2000W									
2001	(86,194)								
2002, Golden Jubilee	(98,805)	2,302,000							
2003, Diadem Portrait	(62,007)	5,101,000							

Queen Elizabeth II, Uncrowned Portrait (2003 to Date)

Date	Quantity Minted		VG	F	VF	EF	Unc.	PF	Notes
2003, Uncrowned Portrait	Incl. in 2003, Diadem								
2003W, BU and Proof sets only									
2004	(57,614)	3,408,000							
2005	(63,562)	32,336,000							
2005, First-Day Strike Folder	(2,048)								

Date	Quantity Minted	VG	F	VF	EF	Unc.	PF	Notes
2006 (54,022)	37,085,000							
2006RCM								
2006P/2006RCM Last-Day/ First-Day Strike Folder (901)								
2007 (37,413)	38,045,000							
2008 (38,630)	18,710,000							
2009 (27,549)	29,351,000							
2010								
2011								
2012								

Two-Dollar Pieces

Queen Elizabeth II, Diadem Portrait (1996–2003)

**Golden Jubilee
(dated 1952–2002)**

Date		Quantity Minted	VG	F	VF	EF	Unc.	PF	Notes
1996		375,483,000							
1996, Specimen (cased) (66,843)									
1996, Proof (foldered)									
1996, Proof (cased)									
1996, Silver Ring, Gold-Plated Core Proof									
1996, White Gold Ring, Gold Core Proof	(5,000)								
1996, Silver Proof Piedfort	(11,526)								
1997	(113,647)	16,942,00							
1998									
1998W, Unc Collector sets only	(93,632)	5,309,000							
1999, Collector sets only	(95,113)								
2000, Collector sets only	(90,921)								
2000W, Unc Collector sets only									
2001	(74,194)	11,910,000							
2002, Golden Jubilee	(98,805)	27,008,000							
2003, Diadem Portrait	(62,007)	7,123,697							

Queen Elizabeth II, Uncrowned Portrait (2003 to Date)

Date	Quantity Minted	VG	F	VF	EF	Unc.	PF	Notes
2003, Uncrowned Portrait	4,120,104							
2003W, BU sets only	71,142							
2004	12,907,000							
2005	38,318,000							
2005, First-Day Strike Folder	2,501							

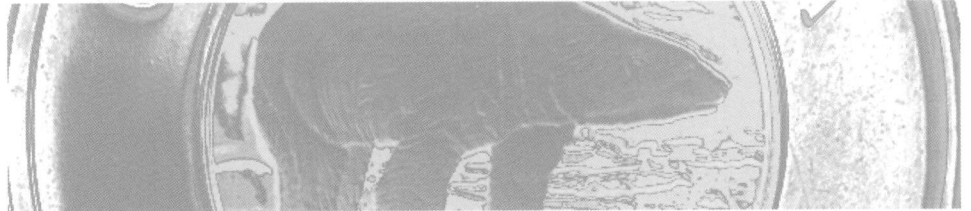

Date	Quantity Minted	VG	F	VF	EF	Unc.	PF	Notes
2006	25,274,000							
2006RCM								
2006/2006RCM, Last-Day/First-Day Strike Folder (1,971)								
2007 (37,373)	38,957,000							
2008	12,390,000							
2009	38,430,000							
2010	8,220,000							
2011								
2012								

CANADIAN COMMEMORATIVE ISSUES

Date	Distribution	Unc.	PF	Notes
ONE-CENT PIECES				
1998, Mint Anniversary, Matte Proof	(18,376)			
1998, Mint Anniversary, Mirror Proof	(24,893)			
2003, Queen Elizabeth II 50th Anniversary	(21,537)			
2003, RCM Annual Report	(7,746)			
THREE-CENT PIECES				
2001 First Canadian Postage Stamp Coin/Medal/Stamp Set	(59,573)			
FIVE-CENT PIECES				
1998, Mint Anniversary, Matte Proof	(18,376)			
1998, Mint Anniversary, Mirror Proof	(24,893)			
2000, Les Voltigeurs de Québec	(34,024)			
2001, Royal Military College	(25,834)			
2002, Vimy Ridge	(22,646)			
2003, Coronation Aniversary, Silver Proof	(21,537)			
2004, 60th Anniversary D-Day	(20,019)			
2005, 60th Anniv VE Day	59,258,000			
TEN-CENT PIECES				
1997, J. Cabot Silv Pf	(49,848)			

Date	Distribution	Unc.	PF	Notes
1998, Mint Anniversary Matte Proof	(18,376)			
1998, Mint Anniversary, Mirror Proof	(24,893)			
2000, Credit Union, Silver Proof	(69,791)			
2003, Coronation Aniversary, Silver Proof	(21,537)			
2004P, Canadian Open Golf	39,486			
2004,P Canadian Open Golf Set: 10¢ (2), stamps, divot tool	20,736			
TWENTY-FIVE-CENT PIECES				
1992, New Brunswick* (149,387)	2,174,000			
1992, New Brunswick, 180° Rotated Rev Die	Incl. above			
1992, New Brunswick, 90° Rotated Rev Die	Incl. above			
1992, N'west Terr.* (149,387)	12,580,000			
1992, N'west Terr., 90° Rotated Rev Die	Incl. above			
1992, Newfoundland* (149,387)	11,405,000			
1992, Manitoba* (149,387)	11,349,000			
1992, Yukon Territory* (149,387)	10,388,000			

*Proof coins are silver.

Date	Distribution	Unc.	PF	Notes	Date	Distribution	Unc.	PF	Notes
TWENTY-FIVE-CENT PIECES					1999, Millennium, August*	(113,645) 18,153,700			
1992, Alberta*	(149,387) 12,133,300				1999, Millennium, September(	(113,645) 31,539,350			
1992, PE Island*	(149,387) 13,001,000				Mule, 1999 Non-Denom Obv, Sept Millennium Rev	—			
1992, Ontario*	(149,387) 14,263,000				1999, Millennium, October*	(113,645) 32,136,650			
1992, Nova Scotia*	(149,387) 13,600,000				1999, Millennium, November*	(113,645) 27,162,800			
1992, Quebec*	(149,387) 13,607,000				Mule, 1999 Non-Denominated Obverse, November Millennium Reverse	—			
1992, Saskatchewan*	(149,387) 14,165,000				1999, Millennium, December*	(113,645) 43,339,200			
1992, Saskatch., 180° Rotated Reverse Die	Incl. above				2000, Canada Day	26,106			
1992, British Columbia*	(149,387) 14,001,000				2000, Unc RCM Nickel Set (12)	876,041			
1992/1993 Mule, 1867– 1992 Obverse, 1993 Caribou Rev (1 known)	—				2000, Unc Nickel, RCM Medallion Set				
1998, Mint Anniversary, Matte Proof	(18,376)				2000, Unc Nickel, Nestlé Medallion Set				
1998, Mint Anniversary, Mirror Proof	(24,893)				2000, Unc Nickel Deluxe Set				
1999, Unc RCM Nickel Set (12)	1,499,973				2000, Proof Silver Set (12)	(37,940)			
1999, Unc Nickel, RCM Medallion Set	Incl. above				1999–2000, Proof Silver (24) Chinese Set				
1999, Unc Nickel, Nestlé Medallion Set	Incl. above				2000, Millennium, Pride (January)*	(76,956) 50,666,800			
1999, Proof Silver Set	(60,245)				2000, Millen., Pride (Jan) 90° Rotated Rev Die	Incl. above			
1999, Millennium, January*	(113,645) 12,181,200				2000, Millennium, Pride (January) (Enameled)	49,399			
1999, Millennium, February*	(113,645) 14,469,250				2000, Millennium, Ingenuity (February)*	(76,956) 36,078,360			
1999, Millennium, March*	(113,645) 15,033,500				Mule, Feb 25¢ Obverse, RCM Medallion Obverse	—			
1999, Millennium, April*	(113,645) 15,446,000				2000, Millenium, Achievm't (March)*	(76,956) 35,312,750			
1999, Millennium, May*	(113,645) 15,566,100				2000, Millennium, Health (April)*	(76,956) 35,470,900			
1999, Millennium, June*	(113,645) 20,432,750				2000, Millenium, Natural Legacy (May)*	(76,956) 36,236,900			
1999, Millennium, July*	(113,645) 17,321,000								

*Proof coins are silver.

Date	Distribution	Unc.	PF	Notes
TWENTY-FIVE-CENT PIECES				
2000, Millenium, Harmony (June)*	(76,956) 35,184,200			
2000, Millen., Harmony (June) 90° Rotated Reverse Die	Incl. above			
2000, Millenium, Celebration (July)*	(76,956) 35,144,100			
2000, Millenium, Family (August)*	(76,956) 35,107,700			
2000, Millenium, Wisdom (Sept)*	(76,956) 35,123,950			
2000, Millenium, Creativity (October)*	(76,956) 35,316,770			
2000, Millenium, Freedom (Nov)*	(76,956) 35,188,900			
2000, Millenium, Community (Dec)*	(76,956) 35,155,400			
2001P, Canada Day	96,352			
2002P, Canada Day (Enameled)	49,901			
2002P, Canada Day (Non-enameled)	30,627,000			
2003P, Canada Day	63,511			
2003, Coronation Anniv, Silver Proof	(21,537)			
2004P, Canada Day, Maple Leaves	44,752			
2004P, Canada Day, Moose	16,028			
2004P, Poppy (Enameled)	28,972,000			
2004, Poppy (Gold-Highlighted Silver, from annual Mint Report)	(12,677)			
2004, Poppy, First-Day Strike	9,824			
2004P, Île St. Croix	15,400,000			
2004P, Santa Claus	62,777			
2005P, Canada Day	58,370			
2005P, Alberta Cent'l	20,640,000			
2005P, Alberta Cent'l, First-Day Strike	9,108			
2005P, Saskatch. Centennial	19,290,000			

Date	Distribution	Unc.	PF	Notes
2005P, Saskatch. Cent'l, First-Day Strike	6,980			
2005P, Year of Vet	29,390,000			
2005P, Year of Vet, First-Day Strike	8,361			
2005P, Netherlands Liberation*	(3,500) 17,500			
2005P, Stocking	72,831			
2006P, Canada Day	30,328			
2006P, Breast Cancer	29,798,000			
2006P, Breast Cancer, First-Day Strike	7,348			
2006P, Mont. Canadiens				
2006P, Ottawa Senators	11,765			
2006P, Tor. Maple Leafs				
2006P, Quebec Winter Carnival	8,200			
2006, QEII's 80th Birthday	24,977			
2006, Medal of Bravery	20,040,000			
2006, Medal of Bravery, First-Day Strike	4,906			
2006P, Santa/Rudolph	99,258			
2007RCM, Canada Day	27,743			
2007, Maple Leaf (Enameled; Oh! Canada! sets only	23,582			
2007, Hummingbird	25,000			
2007, Nuthatch	25,000			
2007, Baby Rattle	29,964			
2007, Balloons	24,531			
2007, Fireworks	8,910			
2007, Bouquet	10,318			
2007, Calgary Flames	832			
2007, Edmonton Oilers	2,2123			
2007, Montreal Canadiens	2,952			
2007, Ottawa Senators	1,634			
2007, Toronto Maple Leafs	3,527			
2007, Vancouver Canucks	1,264			
2007, Curling	22,400,000			
2007, Curling, First-Day Strike Folder	10,000			
2007, Ice Hockey	22,400,000			
2007, Ice Hockey, First-Day Strike Folder	10,000			

*Proof coins are silver.

Date	Distribution	Unc.	PF	Notes
TWENTY-FIVE-CENT PIECES				
2007, Wheelchair Curling	22,400,000			
2007, Wheelchair Curling, First-Day Strike Folder	10,000			
2007, Biathlon	22,400,000			
2007, Biathlon, First-Day Strike Folder	10,000			
2007, Alpine Skiing	22,400,000			
2007, Alpine Skiing, First-Day Strike Folder	10,000			
2007, Christmas Tree	8,910			
2008, Canada Day				
2008, Snowboarding	22,400,000			
2008, Snowboarding, First-Day Strike Folder	10,000			
2008, Freestyle Skiing	22,400,000			
2008, Freestyle Skiing, First-Day Strike Folder	10,000			
2008, Figure Skating	22,400,000			
2008, Figure Skating, First-Day Strike Folder	10,000			
2008, Bobsleigh	22,400,000			
2008, Bobsleigh, First-Day Strike Folder	10,000			
2008, Woodpecker	25,000			
2008, Cardinal	25,000			
2008, Teddy Bear				
2008, Party Hat				
2008, Trophy				
2008, Flag				
2008, Wedding Cake				
2008, Miga				
2008, Quatchi				
2008, Sumi				
2008, Santa				
2009, Oh! Canada				
2009, Balloons				
2009, Baby				
2009, Fireworks				
2009, Flower				
2009, Wedding Doves				

Date	Distribution	Unc.	PF	Notes
2009, Men's Ice Hockey (Non-enameled)	19,000,000			
2009, Men's Ice Hockey (Enameled)				
2009, Women's Ice Hockey (Non-enameled)	19,000,000			
2009, Women's Ice Hockey (Enameled)				
2009, Cindy Klassen (Non-enameled)	19,000,000			
2009, Cindy Klassen (Enameled)				
2009, Notre-Dame-du-Saguenay				
2009, Speed Skating	22,400,000			
2009, Speed Skating, First-Day Strike Folder	10,000			
2009, Cross-Country Skiing	22,400,000			
2009, Cross-Country Skiing, First-Day Strike Folder	10,000			
2009, Ice Sledge Hockey	22,400,000			
2009, Ice Sledge Hockey, First-Day Strike Folder	10,000			
2009, Santa/Maple Leaves				
2010, Goldfinch	14,000			
FIFTY-CENT PIECES				
1995, Silver Proof, Atlantic Puffins				
1995, Silver Proof, Whooping Crane				
1995, Silver Proof, Gray Jays	(172,377)			
1995, Silver Proof, Ptarmigans				
1995, Puffins-Crane 2-Coin Set				
1995, Jays-Ptarmigan 2-Coin Set				

Date	Distribution	Unc.	PF	Notes	Date	Distribution	Unc.	PF	Notes
FIFTY-CENT PIECES					1998, Firsts in Sports Silver Proof Set				
1996, Little Wild Ones Silver Proof Set					1998, Silver Proof, 1888 Figure Skating				
1996, Silver Proof, Moose Calf					1998, Silver Proof, 1898 Ski Racing	(56,428)			
1996, Silver Proof, Wood Ducklings	(206,552)				1998, Silver Proof, 1888 Soccer Tour				
1996, Silver Proof, Cougar Kittens					1998, Silver Proof, 1978 Grand Prix				
1996, Silver Proof, Black Bear Cubs					1999, Cats of Canada Silver Proof Set				
1996, Moose– Ducklings 2-Coin Set					1999, Silver Proof, Tonkinese	(83,423)			
1996, Cougars–Bears 2-Coin Set					1999, Silv Pf, Lynx				
1997, Best Friends Silver Proof Set					1999, Silv Pf, Cymric				
1997, Silver Proof, Newfoundland					1999, Silv Pf, Cougar				
1997, Silver Proof, Duck Tolling Retriever	(184,536)				1999, Firsts in Sports Silver Proof Set				
1997, Silver Proof, Labrador Retriever					1999, Silver Proof, 1904 Canadian Open				
1997, Silver Proof, Eskimo Dog					1999, Silver Proof, 1874 Int'l Yacht Race	(52,115)			
1997, Newfoundland– Duck Tolling 2-Coin Set					1999, Silver Proof, 1909 Grey Cup				
1997, Labrador– Eskimo Dog 2-Coin Set					1999, Silver Proof, 1939 Basketball				
1998, Ocean Giants Silver Proof Set					2000, Birds of Prey Silver Proof Set				
1998, Silver Proof, Killer Whales					2000, Silver Proof, Bald Eagle				
1998, Silver Proof, Humpback Whale	(133,310)				2000, Silv Pf, Osprey	(123,628)			
1998, Silver Proof, Beluga Whales					2000, Silv Pf, Great Horned Owl				
1998, Silver Proof, Blue Whale					2000, Silver Proof Red-Tailed Hawk				
1998, Mint Anniversary, Matte Proof	(18,376)				2000, Firsts in Sports Silver Proof Set				
1998, Mint Anniversary, Mirror Proof	(24,893)				2000, Silver Proof, 1875 Hockey				
					2000, Silver Proof, 1760 Curling	(50,091)			
					2000, Silver Proof, 1840 Steeplechase				
					2000, Silver Proof, 1910 5-Pin Bowling				

Date	Distribution	Unc.	PF	Notes	Date	Distribution	Unc.	PF	Notes
FIFTY-CENT PIECES					2002, Tulips (Gold-Highlighted)	(19,986)			
2001, Canadian Festivals Silver Proof Set					2003, Canadian Festivals Silver Proof Set				
2001, Silv Pf, Quebec									
2001, Silver Proof, Nunavut	(58,123)				2003, Silver Proof, Yukon				
2001, Silver Proof, Newfoundland					2003, Silver Proof, Saskatchewan	(26,451)			
2001, Silver Proof, Prince Edward Island					2003, Silver Proof, Northwest Territories				
2001, Folklore/Legends Silver Proof Set					2003, Silver Proof, New Brunswick				
2001, Silver Proof, The Sled	(28,979)				2003, Daffodils (Gold-Highlighted)	(36,293)			
2001, Silver Proof, The Maiden's Cave					2003, Coronation Anniversary, Silv Pf	(21,537)			
2001, Silver Proof, Les Petits Sauteux					2004, Easter Lily (Gold-Highlighted)	(24,495)			
2002, Golden Jubilee					2004, QEII 4-Effigies Silver Proof Set	(12,230)			
2002, Golden Jubilee 5-Piece Gift Set	14,440,000				2004, Silv Pf, Laureate	(12,230)			
2002, Golden Jubilee 10-Piece Gift Set					2004, Silv Pf, Diademed	(12,230)			
					2004, Silv Pf, Crowned	(12,230)			
2002, Golden Jubilee, Gold Plated, Accession set only	(33,490)				2004, Silver Proof, Uncrowned	(12,230)			
2002, Canadian Fests Silver Proof Set					2004, Tiger Swallowtail (Hologram)	(20,462)			
2002, Silver Proof, Nova Scotia					2004, Clouded Sulphur (Gold-Highlighted)	(15,281)			
2002, Silver Proof, Ontario	(61,900)				2005, Spangled Fritillary (Hologram)	(35,950)			
2002, Silver Proof, Manitoba					2005, Monarch (Enameled)				
2002, Silver Proof, Alberta					2005, Battles of WWII Specimen Set	20,000			
2002, Silver Proof, British Columbia					2005, Battle of Britain	20,000			
2002, Folklore/Legends Silver Proof Set					2005, Liberation of the Netherlands	20,000			
2002, Silver Pf, The Pig					2005, Conquest of Sicily	20,000			
2002, Silver Proof, The Shoemaker	(19,789)				2005, Battle of the Scheldt	20,000			
					2005, Raid on Dieppe	20,000			
2002, Silver Proof, Le Vaisseau Fantome					2005, Battle of the Atlantic	20,000			

Date	Distribution	Unc.	PF	Notes
FIFTY-CENT PIECES				
2005, Montreal Canadiens Legends Set				
2005, Jean Beliveau	25,000			
2005, Guy LaFleur				
2005, Jacques Plante				
2005, Maurice Richard				
2005, Toronto Maple Leafs Legends Set				
2005, Johnny Bower	25,000			
2005, Tim Horton				
2005, Dave Keon				
2005, Daryl Sittler				
2005, Rose (Gold-Highlighted)	(17,418)			
2006, Daisies (Gold-Highlighted)	(18,190)			
2006, Silvery Blue (Hologram)	(24,016)			
2006, Short-Tailed Swallowtail (Enameled)				
2006, RCM Annual Report	(4,162)			
2007, Forget-Me-Not (Gold-Highlighted)	(22,882)			
2007, Holiday Ornaments	(16,989)			
2008, Holiday Snowman				
2008, Mint Anniversary	(16,000)			
2008, Milk Delivery	(25,000)			
2009, Six-String Nation Guitar	30,000			
2009, Holiday Toy Train				
2009, Calgary Flames				
2009, Edmonton Oilers				
2009, Montreal Canadiens				
2009, Ottawa Senators				
2009, Toronto Maple Leafs				
2009, Vancouver Canucks				
2009–2010, Calgary Flames				
2009–2010, Edmonton Oilers				

Date	Distribution	Unc.	PF	Notes
2009–2010, Montreal Canadiens				
2009–2010, Ottawa Senators				
2009–2010, Toronto Maple Leafs				
2009–2010, Vancouver Canucks				
2010, Miga Ice Hockey				
2010, Quatchi Ice Hockey				
2010, Sumi Ice Sledge Hockey				
2010, Quatchi Miga Skating				
2010, Quatchi Miga Bobsleigh				
2010, Miga Ariels				
2010, Miga Skeleton				
2010, Quatchi Snowboard				
2010, Miga Alpine Skiing				
2010, Sumi Paralympic Skiing				
2010, Quatchi Slalom				
2010, Miga Speed Skating				
2010, Vancouver and Inukshuk (Lenticular)				
ONE-DOLLAR PIECES				
1973, RCMP	1,031,271			
1975, Calgary	833,095			
1976, Library of Parliament	483,722			
1977, Silver Jubilee	744,848			
1978, Commonwealth Games	640,000			
1979, Griffon Tercentennial	688,671			
1980, Arctic Territories	389,564			
1981, Trans-Canada Railway	(353,742) 148,647			

Date	Distribution	Unc.	PF	Notes
ONE-DOLLAR PIECES				
1982, Regina Centennial	(577,959) 144,989			
1982, Constitution	(107,353) 11,812,000			
1982, Constitution, Coin Alignment	Incl. above			
1982, Constitution, Thin Planchet (3 known)	Incl. above			
1983, University Games	(340,068) 159,450			
1984, Toronto Sesquicentennial	(571,563) 133,563			
1984, Jacques Cartier	(87,776) 7,009,323			
1985, National Parks	(537,297) 162,813			
1986, Vancouver	(496,418) 127,574			
1987, John Davis Expeditions	(405,688) 118,722			
1988, Saint-Maurice Ironworks	(259,230) 106,702			
1989, MacKenzie River	(272,319) 110,650			
1990, Henry Kelsey	(222,983) 85,763			
1991, SS *Frontenac*	(222,892) 82,642			
1992, Kingston-York Stage	(187,612) 78,160			
1992, Confederation 125th Anniversary	(108,614) 23,915,000			
1993, Stanley Cup	(294,314) 88,150			
1994, RCMP Dog Sled	(178,485) 62,295			
1994, War Memorial	(103,746) 20,004,830			
1995, Peacekeeping Monument	(93,095) 18,502,750			
1995, Hudson's Bay Co.	(166,259) 61,819			
1996, McIntosh Apple	(133,779) 58,834			

Date	Distribution	Unc.	PF	Notes
1997, Flying Loon 10th Anniversary, Specimen and BU sets only	97,595			
1997, Flying Loon 10th Anniversary, Silver Proof	(24,995)			
1997, Canada-USSR Hockey	(184,965) 155,252			
1998, RCMP 125th Anniversary	(130,795) 81,376			
1999, Juan Perez Voyage	(126,435) 67,655			
1999, International Year of Older Persons	(24,976)			
2000, Voyage of Discovery	(121,575) 62,975			
2001, National Ballet	(89,390) 53,668			
2001, Pattern Dollar of 1911	(24,996)			
2002, Accession Golden Jubilee, Silver	(29,688) 65,410			
2002, Accession Golden Jubilee (Gold-Highlighted)	(65,315)			
2002, Queen Mother Elizabeth	(9,994)			
2002, Family of Loons (150th Anniversary), Specimen sets only	67,672			
2002, Centre Ice Loon (Gold-Plated), Souvenir Album only	(25,000)			
2003, Cobalt Silver Discovery	(88,536) 51,130			
2003, Coronation Golden Jubilee	(21,537)			
Accession / Coronation Golden Jubilee	(unique)			
2004, Olympic Lucky Loonie	6,526,000			
2004, Olympic Lucky Loonie, First Strike	34,488			
2004, Lucky Loonie (Enameled Silver)	(19,994)			

Date	Distribution	Unc.	PF	Notes	Date	Distribution	Unc.	PF	Notes
ONE-DOLLAR PIECES					2007, Trumpeter Swans, Specimen sets only	40,000			
2004, Jack Miner Sanctuary / Goose, Specimen sets only	46,493				2007, Thayendanegea	(32,224) 16,378			
2004, Elusive Loon, Coin/Stamps sets only	(25,105)				2007, Thayendanegea (Gold-Highlighted)	(60,000)			
2004, Île Sainte-Croix	(106,974) 42,582				2007, Thayendanegea (Enameled)	(4,760)			
2004, Île Sainte-Croix, Fleur-de-lis Privy Mark	8,315				2007, Rattle				
2004, The Poppy	(24,547)				2007, Rattle (Gold-Highlighted), Baby Gift Proof sets only				
2005, Terry Fox	12,909,000								
2005, Terry Fox, First-Day Strike	19,933				2007, Child's Blocks, Baby Keepsake Tins sets only				
2005, National Flag	(95,431) 50,948				2007, Celebration of Arts	(6,466)			
2005, National Flag (Gold-Highlighted)	(62,483)				2007, .9999 Gold Louis d'Or	(3,457)			
2005, National Flag (Enameled)	(4,898)				2008, Luckie Loonie (first issued in 2007 Collection)				
2005, Tufted Puffin, Specimen sets only	40,000				2008, Lucky Loonie	(30,000)			
2006, Olympic Lucky Loonie	10,495,000				2008, Quebec City	(65,000) 35,000			
2006RCM, Olympic Lucky Loonie					2008, Quebec City (Gold-Highlighted)	(60,000)			
2006RCM, Olympic Lucky Loonie, First-Day Strike	20,010				2008, RCM Centennial	(25,000)			
2006RCM, Olym Lucky Loonie, Pf (Bookmark)	(104,432)				2008, "The Poppy" Armistice	(5,000)			
2006, Lucky Loonie (Enameled Silver)	(19,973)				2008, Olympic Lucky Loon	10,851,000			
2006, Lullaby Loonie, Baby Gift sets only	(18,225)				2008, Olympic Lucky Loon, First-Day Strike	4,297			
2006, Snowy Owl, Specimen sets only	40,000				2008, Olympic Lucky Loon, Key Chain	591			
2006, Victoria Cross	(59,599) 27,254				2008, Olympic Lucky Loon (Enameled Silver)	(30,000)			
2006, Victoria Cross (Gold-Highlighted)	Incl. above				2008, Common Eider	40,000		·	
2006, Medal of Bravery	(8,343)				2008, .9999 Louis d'Or	(10,000)			
2006, Medal of Bravery (Enameled)	(4,999)				2008, Calgary Flames, Road Jersey				
2006, .9999 Gold Louis d'Or	(5,648)				2008, Calgary Flames, Home Jersey				
					2008, Edmonton Oilers, Road Jersey				
					2008, Edmonton Oilers, Home Jersey				

Date	Distribution	Unc.	PF	Notes
ONE-DOLLAR PIECES				
2008, Montreal Canadiens, Road Jersey				
2008, Montreal Canadiens, Home Jersey				
2008, Ottawa Senators, Road Jersey				
2008, Ottawa Senators, Home Jersey				
2008, Toronto Maple Leafs, Road Jersey				
2008, Toronto Maple Leafs, Home Jersey				
2008, Vancouver Canucks, Road Jersey				
2008, Vancouver Canucks, Home Jersey				
2009, Great Blue Heron	40,000			
2009, Montreal Canadiens Centennial	9,500			
2009, Montreal Canadiens Cent'l (Gold-Highlighted)	9,500			
2009, Centennial of Flight	(50,000) 30,000			
2009, Centennial of Flight (Gold-Highlighted)	(50,000)			
2009, Calgary Flames, Road Jersey				
2009, Edmonton Oilers, Road Jersey				
2009, Montreal Canadiens, Road Jersey				
2009, Ottawa Senators, Road Jersey				
2009, Toronto Maple Leafs, Road Jersey				
2009, Vancouver Canucks, Road Jersey				
2009, Calgary Flames				
2009, Edmonton Oilers				
2009, Montreal Canadiens				
2009, Ottawa Senators				
2009, Toronto Maple Leafs				
2009, Vancouver Canucks				
2010, The Sun	(5,000)			

Date	Distribution	Unc.	PF	Notes
2010, Vancouver Lucky Loonie	10,250,000			
2010, Vancouver Lucky Loonie (First-Day Folder)	12,000			
2010, Vancouver Lucky Loonie (Enameled; With Puck)				
2010, Vancouver Lucky Loonie (Enameled; With Bag)	2,140			
2010, Vancouver Lucky Loonie (Enameled; With lanyard)	7,062			
2010, Vancouver Lucky Loonie (Enameled Silver)	(40,000)			
2010, Navy Centennial	7,000,000			
2010, Saskatchewan Roughriders	3,100,000			
2010, Anticipating the Games	40,000			
2010, Ilanaaq (first issued in 2007 Collection)				
TWO-DOLLAR PIECES				
1999, Nunavut	375,483,000			
1999, Nunavut, Specimen	20,000			
1999, Nunavut, Silver/Gilt	(39,873)			
1999, Nunavut, White Gold / Gold	(4,298)			
1999, Nunavut, Mule				
2000, Path of Knowledge	29,880,000			
2000, Path of Knowledge, Nickel/Bronze	1,500			
2000, Path of Knowledge, Silver/Gilt	(39,768)			
2000, Path of Knowledge, White Gold / Gold	(5,881)			
2002, Golden Jubilee	(98,805) 27,008,000			
2006, Churchill	25,274,000			
2006, Churchill, Brilliant Uncirculated Strike	25,208			

Date	Distribution	Unc.	PF	Notes
TWO-DOLLAR PIECES				
2006, 10th Anniversary (57,885) Polar Bear 5,005,000				
2006, 10th Anniversary Polar Bear, First-Day Strike 4,991				
2006, 10th Anniversary Polar Bear, Gold Proof (2,068)				
2008, Quebec 400th Anniversary 6,010,000				
THREE-DOLLAR PIECES				
2006, The Beaver	20,000			
2010, Return of the Tyee	(15,000)			
FOUR-DOLLAR PIECES				
2007, Parasaurolophus	(13,010)			
2008, Triceratops	(20,000)			
2009, T. Rex	(20,000)			
2009, Hanging Stockings	(15,000)			
2010, Dromaeosaurus	(20,000)			
FIVE-DOLLAR PIECES				
1973, Map of North America	537,898			
1973, Kingston and Sailboats				
1974, Athlete w. Torch	1,990,570			
1974, Olympic Rings and Wreath				
1974, Canoeing	1,990,570			
1974, Rowing				
1975, Marathon	1,985,000			
1975, Women's Javelin				
1975, Diving	1,985,000			
1975, Swimming				
1976, Fencing	1,887,630			
1976, Boxing				
1976, Olympic Village	1,887,629			
1976, Olympic Flame				
1998, Norman Bethune	(65,831)			
1999, Viking Settlement	(28,450)			
2001, Wireless Transmission (in Set With British £2 Coin)	(15,011)			
2003, FIFA World Cup	(21,542)			
2004, Canadian Open	(18,750)			
2004, Majestic Moose	(12,822)			
2005, White-Tailed Deer	(6,439)			

Date	Distribution	Unc.	PF	Notes
2005, Atlantic Walrus	(5,519)			
2005, Peregrine Falcon	(7,226)			
2005, 60th Anniversary of WWII	(10,000) 25,000			
2005, Alberta Centennial	(20,000)			
2005, Saskatchewan Centennial	(20,000)			
2006, Sable Island Horse	(10,108)			
2006, Breast Cancer Awareness	(11,048)			
2006, Snowbirds	(10,034)			
2009, Canada in Japan, Silver	(40,000)			
EIGHT-DOLLAR PIECES				
2004, Great Grizzly	(12,942)			
2005, Railway Bridge	(9,892)			
2005, Chinese Memorial (Packaged With Above)	(9,892)			
2007, Ancient China	(19,954)			
2007, Maple of Long Life	(11,624)			
2009, Maple of Wisdom	(14,888)			
TEN-DOLLAR PIECES				
1973, Map of World	543,098			
1973, Montreal Skyline				
1974, Head of Zeus	1,974,939			
1974, Temple of Zeus				
1974, Lacrosse	1,974,939			
1974, Cycling				
1975, Men's Hurdles	2,476,217			
1975, Women's Shot Put				
1975, Paddling	2,476,216			
1975, Sailing				
1976, Field Hockey	1,985,257			
1976, Soccer				
1976, Olym Stadium	1,985,257			
1976, Olym Velodrome				
2005, Year of the Veteran	(6,549)			
2005, Pope John Paul II	(24,716)			
2006, Fortress of Louisbourg	(5,544)			

Date	Distribution	Unc.	PF	Notes
FIFTEEN-DOLLAR PIECES				
1992, Speed Skater				
1992, Speed Skater, No Edge Lettering				
1992, Spirit of the Generations	(105,645)			
1992, Spirit of the Generations, No Edge Lettering				
1998, Year of the Tiger	(68,888)			
1999, Year of the Rabbit	(77,791)			
2000, Year of the Dragon	(88,634)			
2001, Year of the Snake	(60,754)			
2002, Year of the Horse	(59,395)			
2003, Year of the Ram	(53,714)			
2004, Year of the Monkey	(46,175)			
2005, Year of the Rooster	(44,690)			
2006, Year of the Dog	(41,617)			
2007, Year of the Pig	(48,888)			
2008, Year of the Rat	(48,888)			
2009, Year of the Ox	(48,888)			
2008, Victoria	10,000			
2008, Edward VII	10,000			
2008, George V	10,000			
2008, George VI	10,000			
2008, Elizabeth II	10,000			
2008, Jack of Hearts	(25,000)			
2008, Queen of Spades	(25,000)			
2009, King of Hearts	(25,000)			
2009, Ten of Spades	(25,000)			
2010, Year of the Tiger, Scalloped	(19,888)			
2010, Year of the Tiger, Round	(9,999)			
TWENTY-DOLLAR PIECES				
1967, Centennial of Confederation, Gold	334,288			
1985, Downhill Skiing	(406,360)			
1985, Speed Skating				
1985, Speed Skating, No Edge Lettering	(354,222)			
1986, Hockey				
1986, Hockey, No Edge Lettering	(396,602)			

Date	Distribution	Unc.	PF	Notes
1986, Biathlon				
1986, Biathlon, No Edge Lettering	(308,086)			
1986, Cross-Country Skiing	(303,199)			
1986, Free-Style Skiing				
1986, Free-Style Skiing No Edge Lettering	(294,322)			
1987, Figure Skating	(334,875)			
1987, Curling	(286,457)			
1987, Ski-Jumping	(290,954)			
1987, Bobsleigh	(274,326)			
1990, Avro Anson / N.A. Harvard	(41,844)			
1990, Avro Lancasater	(43,596)			
1991, A.E.A. Silver Dart	(35,202)			
1991, de Havilland Beaver	(36,197)			
1992, Curtiss JN-4	(33,105)			
1992, de Havilland Gipsy Moth	(32,537)			
1993, Fairchild 71c	(32,199)			
1993, Lockheed 14 Super Electra	(32,550)			
1994, Curtiss HS-2L	(31,242)			
1994, Canadian Vickers Vedette	(30,880)			
1995, Fleet 80 Canuck	(17,438)			
1995, DHC-1 Chipmunk	(17,722)			
1996, CF-100 Canuck	(18,508)			
1996, CF-105 Arrow	(27,163)			
1997, F86 Sabre	(16,440)			
1997, Tutor Jet	(18,414)			
1998, Argus	(14,711)			
1998, Waterbomber	(15,237)			
1999, Twin Otter	(14,173)			
1999, Dash 8	(14,138)			
2000, Taylor Steam Buggy				
2000, The Bluenose	(44,367)			
2000, The Toronto				
2001, The Russell "Light Four"				
2001, The Marco Polo	(41,828)			
2001, The Scotia				

Date	Distribution	Unc.	PF	Notes	Date	Distribution	Unc.	PF	Notes
TWENTY-DOLLAR PIECES					2008, Holiday Carols	(10,000)			
2002, The Gray-Dort					2008, Crystal Raindrop (Enameled, With Crystal)	(15,000)			
2002, The William Lawrence	(35,944)								
2002, D-10 Locomotive					2008, The Royal Hudson	(10,000)			
2003, HMCS Bras d'Or					2008, Agriculture	(10,000)			
2003, C.N.R. FA-1 Diesel Electric Locomotive	(31,997)				2009, Coal Mining	(10,000)			
					2009, The Jubilee	(10,000)			
2003, Bricklin SV-1					2009, Autumn Showers Raindrop (Enameled, With Crystal)	(10,000)			
2003, Niagara Falls	(29,967)								
2003, Rocky Mountains	(28,793)								
2004, Icebergs, Holog	(24,879)				2009, Crystal Snowflake (Blue)	(15,000)			
2004, Northern Lights, Hologram	(34,135)								
					2009, Crystal Snowflake (Pink)	(15,000)			
2004, Hopewell Rocks	(16,918)								
2005, Diamonds	(35,000)				2009, Calgary Flames	(10,000)			
2005, Three-Masted Ship	(18,276)				2009, Edmonton Oilers	(10,000)			
2005, North Pacific Rim	(21,695)				2009, Montreal Canadiens	(10,000)			
2005, Mingan Archip									
2006, Ketch	(10,299)				2009, Ottawa Senators	(10,000)			
2006, Georgian Bay Islands	(20,218)				2009, Toronto Maple Leafs	(10,000)			
2006, Nahanni National Park					2009, Vancouver Canucks	(10,000)			
2006, Jasper National Park					2009, Summer Moon Mask	(10,000)			
2006, Notre Dame Basilica					2009, Jacques Cartier at Gaspé	(1,534)			
2006, CN Tower	(30,353)				**TWENTY-FIVE-DOLLAR PIECES**				
2006, Pengrowth Saddledome					2007, Curling	(45,000)			
					2007, Ice Hockey	(45,000)			
2007, Brigantine	(7,490)				2007, Athletes' Pride	(45,000)			
2007, First International Polar Year, Silver	(8,352)				2007, Biathlon	(45,000)			
					2007, Alpine Skiing	(45,000)			
2007, First International Polar Year (Blue Plasma)	(3,005)				2008, Snowboarding	(45,000)			
					2008, Freestyle Skiing	(45,000)			
2007, Crystal Snowflake (Aquamarine)	(1,433)				2008, Home of Winter Games	(45,000)			
2007, Crystal Snowflake (Iridescent)	(1,404)				2008, Figure Skating	(45,000)			
					2008, Bobsleigh	(45,000)			
2007, Holiday Sleigh Ride	(6,041)				2009, Speed Skating	(45,000)			
2008, Crystal Snowflake (Amethyst)	(15,000)				2009, Cross Country Skiing	(45,000)			
2008, Crystal Snowflake (Sapphire)	(15,000)				2009, Olympic Spirit	(45,000)			
					2009, Skeleton	(45,000)			

Date	Distribution	Unc.	PF	Notes
TWENTY-FIVE-DOLLAR PIECES				
2009, Ski Jumping	(45,000)			
THIRTY-DOLLAR PIECES				
2005, Welcome Figure Totem Pole	(9,904)			
2006, Dog Sled Team	(7,384)			
2006, National War Memorial	(8,876)			
2006, Beaumont-Hamel Memorial	(15,325)			
2006, 5th Anniversary of Canadarm	(9,357)			
2007, Vimy Memorial	(5,190)			
2007, Panoramic Niagara Falls	(5,181)			
2008, IMAX	(15,000)			
2009, International Year of Astronomy	(10,000)			
FIFTY-DOLLAR PIECES				
2005, 60th Anniversary End of WWII	4,000			
2006, The Four Seasons	(1,999)			
2006, Spring	300			
2006, Summer	300			
2006, Autumn	300			
2006, Winter	300			
2007, 60th Wedding Anniversary Queen Elizabeth and Prince Philip	(1,945)			
2008, 100th Anniv RCM	(4,000)			
2009, 150th Anniversary Parliament	(2,000)			
SEVENTY-FIVE-DOLLAR PIECES				
2005, Pope John Paul II	(1,870)			
2007, RCMP	(8,000)			
2007, Athletes' Pride	(8,000)			
2007, Canada Geese	(8,000)			
2008, Four Host First Nations	(8,000)			
2008, Home of the Winter Games	(8,000)			
2008, Inukshuk	(8,000)			
2009, Wolf	(8,000)			
2009, Olympic Spirit	(8,000)			
2009, Moose	(8,000)			

Date	Distribution	Unc.	PF	Notes
$100 PIECES				
1976, 14-kt Montreal Olympics	650,000			
1976, 22-kt Montreal Olympics	(337,342)			
1977, Silver Jubilee	(180,396)			
1978, Canadian Unity	(200,000)			
1979, Year of the Child	(250,000)			
1980, Arctic Territories	(130,000)			
1981, "O Canada"	(100,950)			
1982, Constitution	(121,708)			
1983, St. John's Newfoundland	(83,128)			
1984, Jacques Cartier	(67,662)			
1985, National Parks	(61,332)			
1986, Year of Peace	(76,409)			
1987, XV Winter Olym, Lettered Edge	(142,750)			
1987, XV Winter Olym, Plain Edge				
1988, Bowhead Whale	(52,594)			
1989, Sainte-Marie	(59,657)			
1990, International Literacy Year	(49,940)			
1991, Empress of India	(33,966)			
1992, Montreal	(28,162)			
1993, Featherstonhaugh	(25,971)			
1994, The Home Front	(16,201)			
1995, Louisbourg	(16,916)			
1996, Klondike	(17,973)			
1997, Alexander Graham Bell	(14,775)			
1998, Insulin	(11,220)			
1999, Newfoundland	(10,242)			
2000, Northwest Passage	(9,767)			
2001, Library of Parliament	(8,080)			
2002, Oil Industry (Enameled)	(9,994)			
2003, Marquis Wheat	(9,993)			
2004, St. Lawrence Seaway	(7,454)			
2005, Supreme Court	(5,092)			
2006, Military Academy Hockey Series	(5,402)			

Date	Distribution	Unc.	PF	Notes
$100 PIECES				
2007, Dominion 140th Anniversary	(5,000)			
2008, Fleuve Fraser River	(5,000)			
2009, 10th Anniversary of Nunavut	(5,000)			
$150 PIECES				
1995, Canada Lynx	(908)			
1996, Peregrine Falcon	(871)			
1997, Wood Bison	(529)			
1998, Grey Wolf	(855)			
2000, Year of the Dragon	(8,874)			
2001, Year of the Snake	(6,571)			
2002, Year of the Horse	(6,843)			
2003, Year of the Sheep	(3,927)			
2004, Year of the Monkey	(3,392)			
2005, Year of the Rooster	(3,731)			
2006, Year of the Dog	(2,604)			
2007, Year of the Pig	(4,888)			
2008, Year of the Rat	(4,888)			
2009, Year of the Ox	(4,888)			
2009, Blessings of Wealth	(5,000)			
2010, Year of the Tiger	(4,888)			
2010, Year of the Tiger, Round	(2,500)			
2011, Year of the Rabbit	(4,888)			
$175 PIECES				
1992, Olympics Cent'l	(22,092)			
$200 PIECES				
1992, Olympics Cent'l	(22,092)			
1990, Flag's Silver Jubilee	(20,980)			
1991, Hockey	(10,215)			
1992, Niagara Falls	(9,465)			
1993, RCMP	(10,807)			
1994, Anne of Green Gables	(10,655)			
1995, The Sugar Bush	(9,579)			
1996, Canadian Pacific Railway	(8,047)			
1997, Haida Raven Legend	(11,610)			
1998, Legend of the White Buffalo	(7,149)			
1999, Mi'kmaq Butterfly	(6,510)			

Date	Distribution	Unc.	PF	Notes
2000, Inuit Mother and Child	(6,284)			
2001, Cornelius Krieghoff	(5,406)			
2002, Tom Thompson	(5,264)			
2003, Lionel LeMoine FitzGerald	(4,118)			
2004, Alfred Pellan	(3,917)			
2005, Fur Traders	(3,699)			
2006, Lumbering	(3,185)			
2007, Cod Fishing	(4,000)			
2008, Agriculture	(4,000)			
2009, Coal Mining	(4,000)			
2010, First Canadian Olympic Gold	(2,010)			
$250 PIECES				
2006, Dog Sled Team	(953)			
2007, Early Canada	(2,500)			
$300 PIECES				
2002, Queen Elizabeth II Triple Cameos	(999)			
2003, Great Seal of Canada	(998)			
2004, QEII Quadruple Cameos	(998)			
2005, Britannia 1870 25¢ Note	(994)			
2005, Pacific Time 4:00				
2005, Mountain Time 5:00				
2005, Central Time 6:00				
2005, Eastern Time 7:00	(1,199)			
2005, Atlantic Time 8:00				
2005, Newfoundland Time 8:30				
2005, "Welcome" Totem Pole	(948)			
2006, Britannia 1900 25¢ Note	(940)			
2006, Canadarm2	(565)			
2006, Crystal Snowflake (Embedments)	(861)			
2006, Queen's 80th Birthday (Enameled)	(996)			
2007, Britannia 1923 25¢ Note	(1,250)			
2007, Olympic Ideals	2,500			

Date	Distribution	Unc.	PF	Notes
$300 PIECES				
2007, Panoramic Camera, Rockies	(1,000)			
2007, Woolly Mammoth	(400)			
2008, Scimitar Cat	(200)			
2008, Competition	(2,500)			
2008, Newfoundland and Labrador	(1,000)			
2008, Alberta	(1,000)			
2008, Four Seasons Moon Mask	(1,200)			
2008, IMAX	(1,000)			
2009, Steppe Bison	(200)			
2009, Yukon Territory	(1,000)			
2009, PE Island	(1,000)			
2009, Summer Moon Mask	(1,200)			
2009, Friendship	(2,500)			
$350 PIECES				
1998, Flowers of the Coat of Arms (Canada)	(1,999)			
1999, Golden Slipper (Prince Edward Island)	(1,990)			
2000, Pacific Dogwood (British Columbia)	(1,971)			
2001, Mayflower (Nova Scotia)	(1,988)			
2002, Wild Rose (Alberta)	(2,001)			
2003, White Trillium (Ontario)	(1,865)			
2004, Fireweed (Yukon Territory)	(1,836)			
2005, Western Red Lilly (Saskatchewan)	(1,845)			
2006, Iris Versicolor (Quebec)	(1,624)			
2007, Purple Violet (New Brunswick)	(1,400)			
2008, Purple Saxifrage (Nunavut)	(1,400)			
2009, Pitcher Plant, Newfoundland/Labrador	(1,400)			
$500 PIECES				
2007, Queen's 60th Wedding Anniversary	(200)			

Date	Distribution	Unc.	PF	Notes
2008, 100th Anniversary RCM	(250)			
2009, 150th Anniversary Parliament	(200)			
$2,500 PIECES				
2007, Early Canada	(20)			
2009, Canada of Today	(50)			
2009, Surviving the Flood	(40)			
2010, The Eagle	(20)			
2010, The Eagle (Enameled)	(20)			
2010, The Eagle (Antique)	(20)			

Notes